Intelligent Guides to Wines

G000016648

Burgundy

2020 Edition

Benjamin Lewin MW

Copyright © 2018, 2019, 2020 Benjamin Lewin

ISBN: 9781674279510

Vendange Press

www.vendangepress.com

Preface

This Guide is devoted to Burgundy, specifically the Côte d'Or, consisting of the Côte de Beaune and Côte de Nuits. (Two other guides cover the rest of Burgundy, the Guide to Chablis and the Guide to Southern Burgundy, which focuses on the Côte Chalonnaise and Mâcon, as well as Beaujolais and Jura-Savoie.)

The first part of the guide discusses the regions, and explains the character and range of the wines. The second part profiles the producers. There are detailed profiles of the leading producers, showing how each winemaker interprets the local character, and mini-profiles of other important estates.

In the first part, I address the nature of the wines made today and ask how this has changed, how it's driven by tradition or competition, and how styles may evolve in the future. I show how the wines are related to the terroir and to the types of grape varieties that are grown, and I explain the classification system. For each region, I suggest reference wines that illustrate the character and variety of the area.

In the second part, there's no single definition for what constitutes a top producer. Leading producers range from those who are so prominent as to represent the common public face of an appellation to those who demonstrate an unexpected potential on a tiny scale. The producers profiled in the guide represent the best of both tradition and innovation in wine in the region. In each profile, I have tried to give a sense of the producer's aims for his wines, of the personality and philosophy behind them—to meet the person who makes the wine, as it were, as much as to review the wines themselves.

Each profile shows a sample label, a picture of the winery, and details of production, followed by a description of the producer and winemaker. Each producer is rated (from one to four stars). For each producer I suggest reference wines that are a good starting point for understanding the style. Most of the producers welcome visits, although some require appointments: details are in the profiles. Profiles are organized geographically, and each group of profiles is preceded by maps showing the locations of producers to help plan itineraries.

The guide is based on many visits to France over recent years. I owe an enormous debt to the hundreds of producers who cooperated in this venture by engaging in discussion and opening innumerable bottles for tasting. This guide would not have been possible without them.

Benjamin Lewin

Contents

Tables

Appellation Maps

Producer Maps

Overview of Burgundy

They leave kisses in the wine, I found one inside of mine
When the rhythm's really fine, rare and sweet as vintage wine
(Grateful Dead)

I'm not sure anyone's actually described Burgundy in terms of kisses in the wine, but if there's any wine for which this is appropriate, it's red Burgundy. At its peak, the Pinot Noir of Burgundy has a sublime, sensuous quality that no other wine in the world can match. Of course, while Burgundy remains unchallenged as the pinnacle for Pinot Noir, the greatest Chardonnays in the world also come from here.

No one knows exactly when wine production started in Burgundy, but there was a vineyard in Gevrey Chambertin by the first century. Vines were well distributed in Burgundy by 312, when Emperor Constantin visited Autun and discussed the economic difficulties of producing wine in the region. Burgundy originated as a distinct region in the fifth century.

With Dijon as their capital from the ninth to fifteenth centuries, the Dukes of Burgundy ruled from the eastern end of the Loire (around Sancerre) to Auxerre in the north (the present area of Chablis), across to the Dijon-Mâcon axis. Aside from Sancerre, which was split off in the fifteenth century, the old Duchy more or less coincides with the limits of Burgundy today.

During the thousand years following the fall of the Roman Empire, the Church became the driving force for viticulture. Many of today's top vineyards were established in the first millennium. Founded near Mâcon in 910, the Benedictine abbey of Cluny was a major influence, until it declined and was replaced by the Cistercian abbey of Cîteaux. The monks kept busy, and the region from Auxerre to Beaune was described as "a sea of vines."

The notion that Burgundy should be devoted to producing wine of high quality goes back at least to the end of the fourteenth century, when Philip the Bold issued his famous edict requiring "bad and disloyal" Gamay grapes to be uprooted, and to be replaced by Pinot. (The basic objection to Gamay was that it was too productive).

Burgundy's focus on Pinot Noir and Chardonnay dates from the replanting that was forced by the phylloxera epidemic at the end of the nineteenth century. Today Burgundy produces 65% white wine and 26% red wine: another 9% is Crémant (sparkling wine). The heart of Burgundy, where the greatest wines are produced, is the Côte d'Or, a narrow strip of vineyards running south from Dijon through Beaune to Chagny. It is divided into two parts: in the north, the Côte de Nuits produces almost

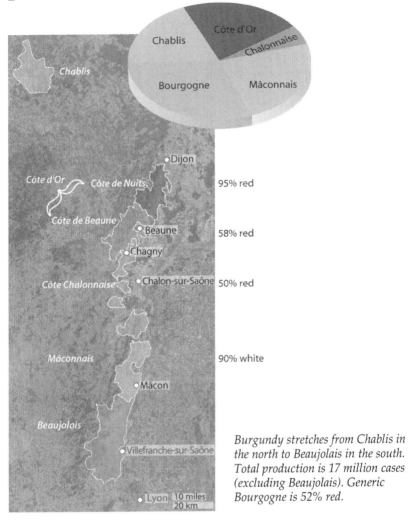

95% red

58% red

50% red

90% white

Burgundy stretches from Chablis in the north to Beaujolais in the south. Total production is 17 million cases (excluding Beaujolais). Generic Bourgogne is 52% red.

exclusively red wine; in the south, the Côte de Beaune is split between red and white. There's a trend to move from black to white grapes when vineyards are replanted.

Chablis is an outpost well to the north and west, where the cooler climate supports only white wine. To the south, the Côte Chalonnaise follows the Côte d'Or in style, but with less concentration and complexity. Then farther south the Mâconnais is devoted almost exclusively to Chardonnay. Over the border from the Mâconnais lies Beaujolais, almost entirely producing red wine, but with a switch to Gamay as the sole black grape (see *Guide to Southern Burgundy and Beaujolais*).

The Grape Varieties

Chardonnay is the only variety for almost all white wines. It can make good wine at all levels, with its style greatly influenced by winemaking, and in particular the extent of exposure to new oak. It can be soft, nutty, and opulent (the old stereotype of Meursault) or more linear and mineral, even with a whiff of gunflint, as in Puligny Montrachet.

Aligoté is an old variety that is now mostly restricted to two AOPs: Bourgogne Aligoté (a regional AOP) and Bouzeron (on Côte Chalonnaise). Its major characteristic is very high acidity. There is one high-end Aligoté: Domaine Ponsot's Clos des Monts Luisants from Morey St. Denis. It's allowed to be a premier cru because the vines were planted in 1911, before the AOC was created. However, there may be other odd patches of old vines. "You'd be surprised how much old Aligoté there is in Corton Charlemagne," one producer says darkly.

There are vanishingly small amounts of Pinot Blanc and Pinot Gris. The best known example of *Pinot Blanc* is the spontaneous mutant of Pinot Noir that appeared Henri Gouge's vineyards; having lost its color, it is used to make a white wine. *Pinot Gris* (known locally as Pinot Beurot) is now illegal in Burgundy, but there is the occasional producer who still has some.

Pinot Noir is the only black variety for village wines and crus, but Gamay can be included in a blend with Pinot Noir in Bourgogne Passe-Tout-Grains. Pinot Noir can be bright and cherry-like from regional AOPs, but is not really a variety for entry-level wines; it becomes interesting at village level, where it can be precise from Volnay, broader from Pommard, softer from Beaune, generous from Clos Vougeot, powerful from Vosne Romanée, elegant from Chambolle Musigny, or forceful from Gevrey Chambertin.

The Hierarchy of Appellations

The view that every vineyard has a different potential is the basis for Burgundy's highly hierarchical appellation system. The classification system is organized into a relatively steep pyramid, steadily narrowing from the base of two thirds of regional AOPs, to a quarter in village appellations, with 11% of premier crus and 1.4% of grand crus at the peak.

At the base of the pyramid, generic Bourgogne AOPs can come from anywhere in the entire region of Burgundy. This includes a very wide range of wines, extending from those including Gamay and Aligoté to those coming from Pinot Noir or Chardonnay from just outside the borders of famous villages. It's now allowed to put the name of the grape variety on the label. The name of the producer is the only guide to the potential quality of Bourgogne AOP.

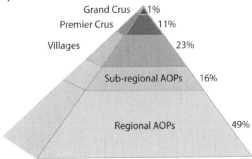

Grand crus and premier crus (in the Côte d'Or and Chablis) are only a small part of production.

The next level up is sub-regional, indicated by Bourgogne followed by the name of a region. such as Bourgogne Côte Chalonnaise or Bourgogne Hautes Côtes de Nuits. (Officially they are described as regional appellations with a geographical denomination.)

Smaller areas identified simply by their name, such as Chablis or Mâcon or Côtes de Nuits, are higher in the hierarchy. Within these areas, the next level consists of individual villages. The communes of the Côte d'Or and Côte Chalonnaise, and also some of the Mâconnais, are the most important village AOPs. Of course, there is significant variation in quality among them. Within each area there's a more or less continuous gradation of quality from the lesser to the best regarded villages. A village wine is identified by the name of the village followed by AOP. But the villages are only the start of detailed classification in Burgundy: within each village, the best plots are assigned to premier or grand crus. The definition of Crus is at its most detailed in the Côte d'Or, where it originated.

The Scale of Burgundy

"I have 10 ha and I make 10 different wines," really tells the story of Burgundy: when you ask a producer how many hectares he has and how many different appellation wines he makes, the answers are often pretty much the same. So the typical wine is made in quite small quantities— around 15-20 barrels or 5,000 bottles. Sometimes amounts of premier crus are so small that it's not worth maturing them separately, in which case a label may simply say premier cru, without an individual name, meaning that the wine comes from a blend of from premier crus within a village.

Usually a producer's range starts with Bourgogne, continues with a village wine, and then has several individual premier or sometimes grand crus. Bourgogne from a small producer usually comes from vines just outside his village, and may therefore be at a completely different level from Bourgogne sourced from lesser areas of Burgundy. A new sub-regional AOP was introduced for the Côte d'Or in 2017, and may now be used for vineyards outside the famous communes that previously were only Bourgogne. It has not had much impact on the market yet, because, at least for small growers, their name has more significance. "Bourgogne Côte d'Or doesn't mean much for us. Our clients know where our wines come from, it may have more significance for larger negociants," says winemaker Thomas Pascal at Domaine François Carillon.

Before the French Revolution in 1789, most vineyards were owned by the Church or large landowners. Afterwards they were confiscated as "biens nationaux" and subdivided. Now most premier and grand crus are divided between multiple owners, and the situation is exacerbated by the requirement of French inheritance law that an estate must be split equally between all the heirs. Once a single vineyard, today Clos Vougeot's 50 hectares are distributed among 80 growers; the largest has only 5.5 ha, and the smallest has only a few rows of vines. In Chambertin, the largest proprietors have a couple of hectares, producing less than 10,000 bottles per year, and the holdings of the smallest proprietors are measured in ares (a hundredth of a hectare or 100 square meters), producing at most a few hundred bottles.

The price of land has become a major issue. The sea change is indicated by Marie-Andrée Mugneret's recollection that, "A Clos Vougeot was the first parcel my father (Georges Mugneret) bought in 1953 when he was a medical student. But I doubt that a medical student could afford to buy in Clos Vougeot now!" A single hectare in Vosne Romanée now runs for more than $2 million, premier crus achieve a multiple of that, and the peak, at Le Montrachet, commands around $20 million. This is a driving force for family estates to sell out to larger organizations. "Burgundy is the most authentic region. This is a family domain, I work with my brother, my parents live here—but we may be the last generation," says Fabrice Amiot at Domaine Guy Amiot in Chassagne Montrachet.

Concern that Burgundy may be on a spiral in which only the ultra-rich can afford vineyards was enhanced by successive sales of adjacent properties in Morey St. Denis. The 11 ha of Clos de Lambrays was bought in 2014 by Bernaud Arnault of LVMH for €101 million; the 7 ha of Clos de Tart was purchased in 2017 for more than €210 million by François Pinault, who owns Château Latour in Bordeaux and Domaine d'Eugénie in Vosne Romanée. Following the sale in 2014 of Bonneau du Martray in Corton, which had remained in the same family for two centuries, to Stanley Kroenke, owner of Screaming Eagle in Napa Valley, it seems that none of the old domains can afford to remain in Burgundian hands. "This isn't over yet," says Dominique Lafon of Comtes Lafon.

Growers and Negociants

The major part of production in Burgundy as a whole comes from negociants, followed by cooperatives, with independent growers as the smallest category. On the Côte d'Or, the cooperatives are much less important, and the proportion of independent producers is higher. The boundaries between growers and negociants are less fixed than the numbers might suggest. Negociants in Burgundy are not usually mere traders in finished wine: as *negociant-éleveurs*, they buy grapes, juice, or wine, and are responsible for the major production decisions.

There's a split between the fragmented nature of the holdings of small growers and the increasing holdings of the large negociants. Today the major negociants usually also own vineyards and produce wines from their own estate as well as from grapes bought from outside growers. And at the other end of the scale, many growers who formerly produced only estate wine have small negociant businesses in which they extend their range by buying grapes. But even this is becoming more difficult. "The négoce has been a bit challenging in recent years," says Jean-Nicolas Méo of Méo-Camuzet. "Prices in the bulk market have increased and make it more difficult for people like us to purchase grapes."

The latest trend in Burgundy is the micro-negociant, so named not just because of their small size, but because they tend to make many different cuvées in very small amounts. One factor is that grapes from top appellations may be scarce. "Many (of my wines) are made in small quantities, sometimes only 1-3 barrels. If we were anywhere else it would be a total nonsense, but that's how it is in Burgundy," says Pascal Marchand in Nuits St. Georges. In some ways, because they are not committed to estate vineyards, micro-negociants have a freer hand.

Even if you don't have the capital to buy land, you can buy grapes. New negociants come from a variety of sources: winemakers at established estates who strike out on their own; people from winemaking families who left the family firm; and outsiders whose passion is to make wine in Burgundy. Some of the new negociants really don't like the term. "We are at the border of the domain and the micro-negociants. I don't like the word negociant, because we are doing the same work as the domain," says Olivier Bernstein, a micro-negociant in Beaune.

"I make the wine, from the beginning of vinification to bottling, I view myself as a winemaker, even though there's no word for it in French, not as a negociant," says Olivier Leflaive. Alex Gambal, who started as a negociant but now owns vineyards that provide a third of his supply, says that, "The lines between the traditional domains and the *négoce* have become blurred."

The label may indicate whether a wine comes from a domain or negociant, as the word "Domaine" can be used only for estate-grown grapes, whereas "Maison" indicates that they come from a negociant activity. Some producers who undertake both activities distinguish between them by different labels; others don't use either Domaine or Maison, and make no distinction. The blurring of the boundaries means you can no longer make the traditional assumption that estate-bottled wines will be superior.

One of the common criticisms of the large negociants is that house style may be more evident than nuances of place. But Olivier Masmondet of Maison Jadot explains, "The style of the house does show beyond ter-

Red Winemaking

There's a consensus on winemaking on some issues, and differences on others. The biggest differences come before and after fermentation.

Grapes are harvested as bunches in the vineyard. Until the modern era, the whole bunches were used for fermentation. Including the stems increases the extraction of tannins (and also reduces alcohol slightly as the stems have water but no sugar). Destemming the crop before fermentation, so that only grapes go into the vat, became fashionable due to the influence of Henri Jayer in the 1970s-1980s. This makes for softer, richer wines. While some producers today are committed either to using whole bunches or to destemming completely, many use a combination, with more whole bunches for stronger wines or more powerful vintages.

Some producers use cold maceration, in which grapes are kept at low temperature for a few days before fermentation is allowed to start, to increase extraction of softer tannins. During fermentation, pigeage (punch-down) is usually used to immerse the cap of skins in the wine, as pump-over is considered too strong for Pinot Noir. Maceration after fermentation, when the wine is kept in contact with the skins, extracts more powerful tannins than cold maceration, due to the presence of alcohol.

Virtually all Burgundy above the generic level is aged in oak barriques (see p. 11) with a capacity of 228 liters, about 300 bottles. Barriques can be used for several years, and the main determinant of the effect of oak is what proportion is new and how the long wine stays in the barriques. The tendency in recent years has been to reduce the proportion of new oak.

roir, but this is just as true of small producers as the large negociants." It's just that when a producer only has a few wines, the differences between them may be more evident than the similarities.

Indeed, you could find half a dozen "minimalist" producers in, say, Chambolle Musigny, all claiming to allow the grapes to speak clearly in the wine, and yet every one of their village wines will be different. The key thing is not so much whether styles are distinct from producer to producer as whether any one producer's wines show relative differences reflecting each individual terroir.

The Côte d'Or

The Côte d'Or is the heart of Burgundy. Its spine consists of 5,000 hectares (12,000 acres), divided into 27 communes, mostly between 100 and 300 ha each. It accounts for 10% of the production of all Burgundy.

The villages include 470 premier crus and 32 grand crus, mostly less than 10 ha. The Crus give Burgundy its great complexity. Almost all the villages have premier crus, but of course their significance is relative to the village. A premier cru in the Côte Chalonnaise will not be as interesting as (say) a village Vosne Romanée.

An extract from the map of the Côte d'Or prepared in 1860 could be used as a guide to the appellations today.

Wide variation in quality among premier crus is due partly to the intrinsic difficulties in classification on such a scale, and partly to political compromises. The definition of the crus goes back to the nineteenth century, when an official map of 1860 coded the vineyards with pink for first class vineyards, yellow for second class, and green for third. Only minor changes have occurred in the classification since then, although price differences have widened enormously.

When the AOCs were defined in 1935, the grand crus became appellations in their own right. Standing at the very top of the hierarchy, they are considered so grand that they do not need to include the village name: I suppose this is a way of saying that each is unique. In fact, there is a reversal here. The greatest grand cru of Gevrey Chambertin, Le Chambertin, had its name when the village was simply called Gevrey. Later the village became Gevrey Chambertin to reflect the glory of the grand cru.

Premier crus were created later, when Burgundy was part of occupied France during the second world war. Classification as premier crus allowed wines to be protected from requisition by the occupying forces. Introduced rather hastily, the system basically followed the old map. Premier crus were regarded as part of each village, so the system requires

The Gevrey Chambertin village wine (left) has the name of the village; the premier cru Cazetiers has the name of the Cru in smaller letters than the village name, and states Appellation Gevrey Chambertin Premier Cru (center); and the grand cru (right) just has the name of the Cru without any village name.

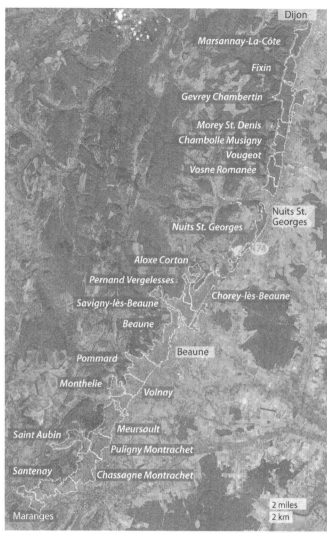

The Côte d'Or consists of the Côte de Nuits (running north from Nuits St. Georges) and the Côte de Beaune (running south from Aloxe Corton). The great communes in the Côte de Nuits all produce red wine. In the Côte de Beaune, Aloxe Corton and Beaune produce more red than white, Pommard and Volnay are exclusively red, while Meursault, Puligny Montrachet, and Chassagne Montrachet are white. The AOPs of the Hautes Côtes and Côtes de Beaune and Nuits lie on either side of the narrow line of communes.

both the village name and the premier cru to be stated on the label.

The names of *lieu-dits* (individually named vineyards) may be used on the label when the wine comes from the specific vineyard, even if it is only classified at village level. (But it must appear in smaller type than the

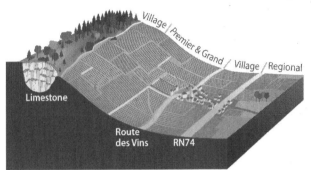

The best terrior lies in the middle of the slope along the Côte d'Or. The grand crus have an elevation of 250-300m. Courtesy Ecole des Vins de Bourgogne, L. Groffier.

name of the AOP.) Some lieu-dits are well respected and considered to be better than a communal AOP as such. But beware: casual brand descriptions for cuvées are also used, and no distinction is made between them and the authentic lieu-dits. So when you see a name on the label under the communal AOP, you have no means of knowing whether it really represents wine from a special vineyard or is merely a fantasy name.

Sometimes individual sites are identified within a premier or grand cru. Burgundy has always had a focus on identifying particular sites—the word *climat* has become very fashionable—but has the trend gone too far? "The press is forcing us to identify every *climat*, and it's very difficult to work with such small quantities," says Fabrice Latour at Maison Louis Latour. "When I hear people are making one barrel of Montrachet—how can you do that? We've gone too far into the terroir concept, there is too small as well as too big."

Appellations are an accurate guide insofar as a producer's premier cru will be better than his village wine, and any grand crus will be better than premier crus. The hierarchy is only a relative guide, however, as it's certainly true that a top producer's village wine may be better than another producer's premier cru. We had better not get into the issue of whether one producer's generic Bourgogne can be better than another producer's village wine...

The principle is that the appellation system identifies the *potential* of the land. As Beaune negociant Alex Gambal says: "It's a totally confusing system. You automatically think just because you've got a grand cru or a premier cru you've got a good wine—but it is just a ranking of the potential of the land. The quality of wine produced from a similar piece of land will vary greatly according to who has made it."

The areas for red and white wines are more or less segregated. Most villages of the Côte de Nuits are basically red, with only occasional plots of white grapevines. The most northern parts of the Côte de Beaune, Aloxe Corton and Beaune, produce both red and white wines. South of Beaune, Pommard and Volnay turn back to red, but when you reach the Montra-

Oak

Barriques are characterized by the age of the barrel, as new (never used for aging wine previously), to 1-year (used in one previous year) 2-year (used in two previous years), and so on. New barriques will convey the strongest impression of oak to the wine, and the effect of the oak then diminishes with the age of the barrel, until after about 4 years, the barrique is basically a neutral container. Oak offers more exposure to oxygen than vats of concrete or stainless steel, and this does not depend on the age of the oak.

Except for wines that are aged in 100% new oak, a mix of barriques of different ages is often used. Oak exposure is often characterized simply in terms of the per cent of new barriques, but this can be a bit misleading as large proportions of 1-year or 2-year barriques still have a strong effect.

The most common approach in Burgundy is to assume that the stronger the wine, the more it benefits from oak exposure, and to increase the proportion of new oak going from regional to communal wine to premier crus and then to grand crus, and also to increase the length of time in aging (élevage). At the extremes, a communal wine might spend 12 months in older barriques, while a grand cru might spend 24 months all in new barriques. There's a minority view that it's more interesting to compare different terroirs when the oak regime is the same for all cuvées.

Barriques are not used in the form of raw oak, but are "toasted" first. In some regions, the extent of toasting (light, medium, or strong) is an issue, but in Burgundy there's more a less a consensus on a medium level.

Oak can be an obvious presence in a young wine, but should integrate and become imperceptible with time. One of the arguments for using more new oak with stronger wines is that they are expected to age longer.

chets and Meursault, there is very little red wine (although some parts of Chassagne Montrachet might be more suited to growing black grapes).

Within the appellation hierarchy, differences between village, premier cru, and grand cru wines are intricately connected with yields. The principle is that vineyards classified at higher levels are restricted to lower yields. In Burgundy, the nominal limits for red wines are 55 hl/ha for generic or regional Bourgogne, 40 hl/ha for village wines and premier crus, and 35-37 hl/ha for grand crus. (Values are slightly higher for white wines.) Curiously, village wines have the same yield limits as premier crus. Yet for my money, the sharpest increase in quality level when I taste Burgundy is going from village wine to premier cru.

The key to Burgundy is understanding that apparently imperceptible differences in vineyards consistently produce significant differences in the wines. How differences in soils and micro-climates determine the characters of the wines is not at all obvious, but over and over again there are

The Côte de Nuits is a narrow band of vineyards stretching up the slope from the N74 to the woods at the top.

examples of adjacent vineyards seeming all but identical, but producing consistently different wines. This is the mystery of terroir.

Each village has its own character. Of course, this is only an approximation, as each producer also has his own style, and the relative characters of villages, or premier or grand crus within them, are interpreted through the prism of the producers' styles.

Côte de Nuits

Côte d'Or might perfectly well mean "hillside of gold" judging from the price of Burgundy today, but for all its fame, the exact derivation is unknown. The name originated after the Revolution, but it is unclear whether it was an abbreviation for Côte d'Orient, meaning a slope facing east, or was a reference to the fame of the vineyards. The Côte is an escarpment running roughly south to north, with hills sharply defining its western boundary, and a plain opening out to the east.

The Côte de Nuits is quite narrow, at some points only a couple of hundred meters deep; even at its widest it is not much more than a kilometer. The common features giving the region its general character are the gentle slope and southeast exposure. A myriad of small faults cause the underlying structure to change rapidly, but the major defining feature is the Saône fault, a large break running along the side of the Côte d'Or. The N74 (Route Nationale 74) is the dividing line. To the north of Nuits St. Georges, the Saône fault is just to the east of the road, and to the south it is just to the west. (Farther south, the road crosses back over the fault around Beaune.)

To the west of the fault, the terroir has variations of limestone, ranging from white limestone at the top of the slope to ochre-colored limestone at the bottom. There is also some marl (a mixture of clay and shale). Chardonnay tends to be planted on the soils that are richer in marl, Pinot Noir on the most active limestone. To the east of the fault, the soils are deeper and richer, having filled in when the fault collapsed, and the water table is higher (increasing fertility of the vines).

Two geographical axes impact the wine. Going up the N74 from the Côte de Beaune to the Côte de Nuits, the wines become firmer, less earthy, perhaps even a touch more austere, although each commune is different. And going up the slope from the N74 at the bottom to the woods at the top, the highest quality is found in the middle. Position on the slope is the main determinant of level in the classification hierarchy, with premier and grand crus occupying the center of the slope. Vineyards at the top and bottom are classified for village wines (those across the fault on the other side of the N74 are classified as regional).

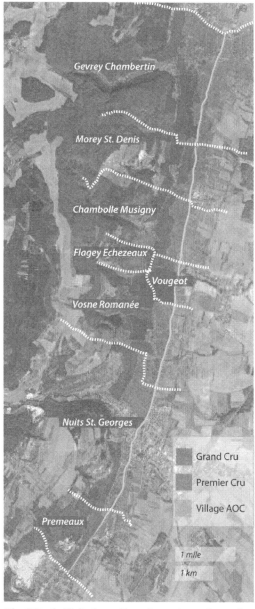

The Côte de Nuits has a line of premier and grand crus along the middle of the slope. Village AOPs are on either side.

The slope gives good drainage and the best exposure to the sun. The climate in Burgundy historically has been marginal for ripening Pinot Noir. The key to quality in a marginal climate is always which sites ripen best. When the relationships between the village vineyards, premier crus, and grand crus were defined, those in mid-slope had an advantage and became the premier and grand crus. Will this remain true if global warming continues? So far, the rising tide has lifted all boats, but there may come a point when the relationship changes.

Almost all the wines from the Côte de Nuits are red, although in the early nineteenth century, white wines from Clos Vougeot and Le Chambertin were regarded on a par with Le Montrachet. There are only a few whites now. De Vogüé makes a famous Musigny Blanc, and Domaine de la Vougeraie make a white premier cru from the Clos Blanc de Vougeot. There is also a little white Morey St. Denis. Moving away from Chardonnay, Ponsot's Mont St. Luisants stands out as an Aligoté of unusual quality; and Gouges makes a Pinot Blanc from Nuits St. Georges Les Perrières (from a mutant of Pinot Noir that occurred spontaneously in the vineyard).

The emphasis on nuances of terroir sharpens on the Côte de Nuits, where there are 135 premier crus and 24 grand crus. The grand crus start with La Tâche in Vosne Romanée and extend in a line all the way up to Chambertin and Clos de Bèze. (Corton is the only grand cru for red wine south of Vosne Romanée.) This is where you will find the ultimate expression of Pinot Noir in Burgundy; and this is the place to try to define the quality that lifts a wine from premier to grand cru.

Nuits St. Georges

Nuits St. Georges
297 ha
  97% red
41 premier crus
  136 ha
Top Crus
Les St. Georges
Les Boudots
126 producers

Nuits St. Georges is the largest town between Beaune and Dijon and is in the center of the appellation.

At the southern end of the Côte de Nuits, size and variability make it difficult to draw a clear bead on Nuits St. Georges. It used to be said that

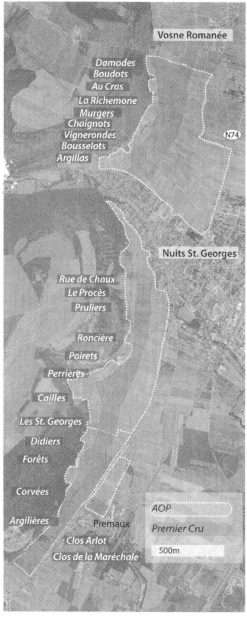

Nuits St. Georges AOP is divided into two parts by the town. The 37 premier crus form a band along the middle of the slope, except at the very narrow southern end where they fill the whole width. Premeaux is the start of the Côte de Nuits.

Nuits St. Georges had a certain four-square quality, a lack of the refinement that you see farther north. The two major parts of the commune are separated by the town, which is now quite gentrified. The appellation has something of a split personality between heavier wines north of the town and lighter wines to its south.

The best premier cru in the northern part, Les Boudots, is adjacent to Vosne Romanée. The main sweep of premier crus in the southern half runs down to Les St. Georges, widely recognized as the best premier cru in Nuits St. Georges, and often mentioned as a possible candidate for promotion. (When the grand crus were defined, Pierre Gouges refused to have Les St. Georges considered, on the grounds that this would "create inequalities.") The mixture of clay and limestone along this stretch makes this the best part of Nuits St. Georges. The wines can be rich and structured, but even here they rarely achieve the finesse and silkiness of Vosne Romanée. Perhaps there is too much clay in the soil. At the very southern end in Premeaux, the wines are lighter. Two monopoles, Clos de la Maréchale and Clos de l'Arlot, stand out as the most elegant.

A new generation of winemakers is steadily changing the view of Nuits St. Georges. "The reputation of Nuits St. Georges for rusticity is largely undeserved," says Jean-Nicolas Méo of Méo-Camuzet, although he admits that perhaps the classification is a little too generous with some of the premier crus that still show traditional robustness. A revealing comment about traditional attitudes comes from Domaine Arnoux-Lachaux, where Pascal Lachaux comments on his premier cru Clos des Corvées Pagets, "This is not typical Nuits St. Georges, it is too elegant." The old generalizations of village character don't always apply any more.

Vosne Romanée

Vosne Romanée
152 ha
  100% red
  6 grand crus
  14 premier crus
  85 ha
Top Premier Crus
Les Suchots
Beaux Monts
87 producers

The premier and grand crus of Vosne Romanée are directly above the village.

Immediately to the north of Nuits St. Georges, Vosne Romanée is by general acclamation the best village on the Côte de Nuits. It's usually considered together with Flagey-Echézeaux, because, with the exception of the grand crus Echézeaux and Grands Echézeaux, the wines of Flagey-Echézeaux are labeled as Vosne Romanée premier crus. (There is no separate appellation for Flagey-Echézeaux.) The quality of Vosne Romanée is indicated by the fact that grand and premier crus account for more than half of the appellation.

Vosne Romanée is the epitome of refinement. "There are no ordinary wines in Vosne," said a French historian dryly in the eighteenth century. Four of the grand crus are monopoles, most famously Romanée Conti and La Tâche, owned by the Domaine de la Romanée Conti; the others are La Romanée (owned by Liger-Belair) and La Grande Rue (owned by François Lamarche, and unusually having been promoted from premier to grand cru in 1992). The other grand crus are divided among many producers.

Richebourg and Romanée St. Vivant are widely acknowledged to be the best crus after the monopoles. Their reputations are not hurt by the fact that their largest proprietors are the Domaine de la Romanée Conti and

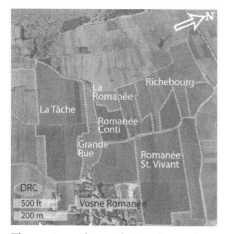

The great grand crus of Vosne Romanée are immediately outside the village. La Tâche and Romanée Conti are monopoles of DRC, which also owns about half of Richebourg and Romanée St. Vivant.

Domaine Leroy (generally acknowledged as the best producers in Burgundy). Richebourg is more powerful, Romanée St. Vivant is more elegant. Grands Echézeaux is in third place.

The most fabled wine of all, Romanée Conti comes from the middle of the slope, and has the most homogeneous terroir. The measure of greatness is not power, but subtlety and variety, with endless, seamless, layers of flavor. Second by reputation, and somewhat larger, with more variation going up the slope, La Tâche has more body. To the north is Richebourg, with its relatively full style, and below comes the delicate Romanée St. Vivant. From the hill above the town, you see a panorama of grand crus, but their differences are not at all obvious to the eye.

At the north of Vosne Romanée, Echézeaux and Clos Vougeot are the two largest, and most dubious, grand crus. Echézeaux is rather variable, and many people believe that much of it does not live up to grand cru status. (Echézeaux should not be confused with Grands Echézeaux, a much smaller area of 9 ha, which lies between Echézeaux and Clos Vougeot, and is undoubtedly grand cru.)

Clos Vougeot

Vougeot
65 ha
95% red
5% white
1 grand cru
50 ha
4 premier crus
11 ha
70 producers

The walled clos surrounding Clos is now broken up into many holdings. The château belongs to the Confrérie du Tastevin.

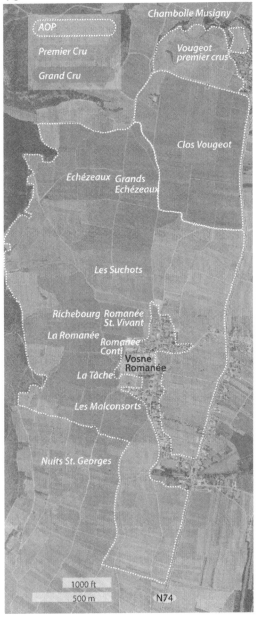

Clos Vougeot symbolizes the monastic history of Burgundy and was at the center of winemaking in Burgundy until it was confiscated during the French Revolution. It is a single grand cru only because it was physically enclosed by a wall when the monks created the vineyard. In fact, the monks were well aware of differences within the clos, and a sixteenth century map identifies 16 individual *climats* within it. The monks were said to make three cuvées: the best came from the top of the slope and was kept for crowned heads and princes. The second, from the middle, was almost as good and was sold at high price. The third, from the bottom, was somewhat cheaper.

Clos Vougeot extends across the Saône fault, so only the upper half has the characteristic limestone base of the Côte d'Or; the lower part is more like the land that usually lies on the other side of the N74. Attempts to distinguish parts of the Clos during classification were beaten off, so in due course it became the biggest discrepancy in the AOC. At its best, Clos

Romanée Conti, La Tâche, Richebourg, and Romanée St. Vivant are the top grand crus, but Clos Vougeot and Echézeaux are questionable.

Vougeot makes the most overtly generous and fleshy wine of the Côte de Nuits, rich and round. Yet while the quality is certainly variable, it is not always easy to distinguish wines by their position on the slope in blind tasting.

Clos Vougeot and Echézeaux together total 86 ha, almost a fifth of the 471 total hectares of grand crus on the Côte d'Or. Couple this with the 160 ha of Corton (on the Côte de Beaune), a rather sprawling grand cru with a variety of *climats* of varying quality, and this is not a very impressive start to viewing classification as a guide to the quality of terroir. But it's fair to say that the rest of the grand crus, ranging in size from under 1 ha to almost 20 ha, consistently produce the very finest Burgundy (with the addition of a couple of under-classified premier crus).

Chambolle Musigny and Morey St. Denis

Chambolle Musigny
153 ha
100% red
2 grand crus
24 premier crus
55 ha
Top Crus
Bonnes Mares
Le Musigny
Les Amoureuses
98 producers

Chambolle Musigny is a tiny village on the Côte de Nuits. Le Musigny is immediately to the south, Bonnes Mares is immediately to the north, and leads directly into the line of grand crus in Morey. St. Denis.

To the north of Clos Vougeot come Chambolle Musigny and Morey St. Denis, the lightest wines of the Côte de Nuits. Chambolle Musigny produces the most elegant wines, with a delicate floral edge, sometimes described as feminine. The pebbly soils are marked by a high proportion of active limestone (which decreases acidity) and a low proportion of clay, making for lightness in the wine.

At the south end of Chambolle Musigny, the grand cru Le Musigny is just west of Clos Vougeot. At the north end, Bonnes Mares is adjacent to the grand crus in Morey St. Denis, where Clos de la Roche usually has the edge over Clos St. Denis. Les Amoureuses, the best premier cru in Chambolle, is often judged to be of grand cru quality; often more expensive than most grand crus, it would very likely be promoted in the unlikely event of a reclassification. All these crus show silky elegance with a sense of precision more than power.

Gevrey Chambertin

	Gevrey Chambertin
	495 ha
	100% red
	9 grand crus
	86 ha
	29 premier crus
	80 ha
	Top Premier Crus
	Clos St. Jacques
	Les Cazetiers
	140 producers

Gevrey Chambertin's most important grand crus and premier crus are just under the woods at the top of the slope. Clos St. Jacques (in photo) is a premier cru, but is often considered equivalent to the grand crus.

With vineyards extending from village level to premier and grand crus, Gevrey Chambertin is the largest commune on the Côte d'Or. As a rarity, it includes some vineyards on the "wrong" side of the N74, among which Clos de la Justice is an exception that can offer wines above the village level.

Premier and grand crus fall into two stretches. The lineup of grand crus runs almost uninterrupted from the town south to the boundary with Morey St. Denis. At the center, Chambertin and Clos de Bèze occupy the upper edge of the slope. They are flanked by other grand crus both to north and south, and just below on the slope. Some premier crus are adjacent. Then beyond the town itself, running around the edge of the hill to the west, is a sweep of premier crus, including Lavaux St. Jacques, Estournelles St. Jacques, and Clos St. Jacques, with Les Cazetiers and Combe aux Moines to their north.

Differences in exposure may be more important than soils here. A comparison between Combe aux Moines and Les Cazetiers is compelling because the plots are contiguous. "The tractor doesn't stop," says Jérôme Flous of Maison Faiveley. Combe aux Moines has a cooler exposure because it angles more to the north than Cazetiers, which extends farther down the slope and so has slightly lower average elevation. Ripening is slightly slower in Combe aux Moines, which harvests two days later than

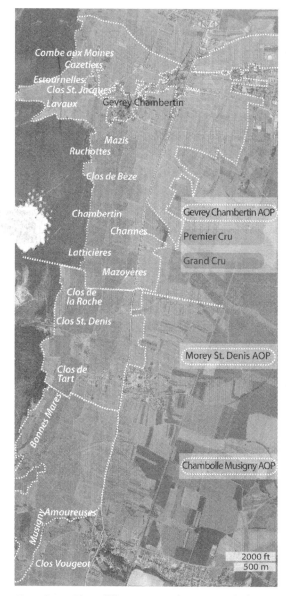

The northernmost part of the Côte de Nuits stretches from Chambolle Musigny to Gevrey Chambertin.

Cazetiers. The difference is due to sunlight exposure; phenolic ripeness doesn't quite catch up in Combe aux Moines. Yet the impression is not simply that Cazetiers is riper than Combe aux Moines; Cazetiers always has a finer impression, Combe aux Moines seems more four-square.

Clos St. Jacques, the top premier cru of Gevrey Chambertin, provides an unusually clear demonstration of the impact of producers. Often considered to be at the level of the grand crus, it was a rated as a premier cru

Chambertin and Clos de Bèze are intimately connected. Wine made in Clos de Bèze can also be labeled as Chambertin, which has been known by its present name since 1276, deriving from Champs de Bertin (the fields of Bertin, an early proprietor). Clos de Bèze takes its name from the Abbaye de Bèze, which was given the vineyard by the Duke of Burgundy in 630.

because its owner at the time refused to comply with the classification procedure. It has a good slope with perfect southeast exposure, and was a monopole until 1956, when the present five owners purchased it. Unusually for Burgundy, instead of being subdivided higgledy-piggledy, each owner has a strip running from top to bottom of the Clos.

There's quite a bit of variation in soil from top to bottom, but not much from side to side, so each owner has the same diversity of soils. Since their plots are exactly parallel, it's reasonable to associate differences in the wines with differences in viticulture or vinification. The wines range from Fourrier's characteristic elegance, Rousseau's earthiness, Jadot's roundness, Bruno Clair's sturdiness, to Esmonin's sometimes stern representation. Differences result from factors such as harvest dates to the amount of destemming. Here is a powerful demonstration of the effect of the producer on style.

At the very top of the hierarchy, only the grand crus of Gevrey Chambertin, notably Le Chambertin itself and Clos de Bèze, challenge those of Vosne Romanée for leadership. Until the start of the twentieth century, the reputation of Le Chambertin was more or less level pegging with Romanée Conti. One reason why Romanée Conti and La Tâche are now far ahead may be their status as monopoles; under the aegis of Domaine de la Romanée Conti, their quality has been consistently at the top. Divided among many growers, by contrast, Chambertin's quality is far more variable.

Chambertin and Clos de Bèze have historically been set apart from all the other crus of Gevrey Chambertin, but the distinction between them has not always been clear. Clos de Bèze can be sold under its own name, as Chambertin, or as Chambertin-Clos de Bèze. The name of Chambertin became better known to the point at which few wines were labeled as Clos de Bèze during the eighteenth or nineteenth centuries; almost all were simply described as Chambertin. (Chambertin is supposed to have been Napoleon's favorite wine.)

In terms of climate, there's a slight difference between Chambertin and Clos de Bèze, because Chambertin is more exposed to the small valley that divides Gevrey Chambertin from Chambolle Musigny. Cold winds that slide across the upper part may make Le Chambertin cooler than Clos de Bèze, which is more protected. No one has actually measured any physical difference, but a telling measure is that Eric Rousseau says that Domaine Rousseau always harvests Clos de Bèze earlier than Chambertin.

Comparing vintages, my impression is that Chambertin has the advantage in warmer vintages, when its fruits take on a delicious ripeness, but in cooler vintages the best balance is obtained by Clos de Bèze. I am inclined to the view that there is a continuum of differences all along the length of the two appellations, and that differences in the wines depend on the individual microplots. Terroir and climate are crucial determinants, but they are not defined by an arbitrary line between the two appellations.

Marsannay

This is not the end of the Côte de Nuits: beyond Gevrey Chambertin come Fixin and Marsannay, running into the outskirts of Dijon. Marsannay has the only appellation in Burgundy for rosé. "Back in the fifties and sixties, people knew Marsannay for the rosé, and although the image of rosé was poor at the time, people thought of Marsannay rosé as being made more like a red wine. In the last 25 years, Marsannay has gone from rosé into making good red wines. When you taste blind, Marsannay is better than Fixin," says Bruno Clair, whose grandfather was instrumental in creating the AOC for rosé.

Marsannay became a village AOC in 1987; previously the wines were Bourgogne. Vineyards are classified according to color. Those to the west are mostly able to produce all colors; those on the east are mostly classified for rosé, and if they produce red it is labeled as simple Bourgogne. "The problem with Marsannay is that Dijon is expanding. We are resisting as best we can, the best way is to make top wines," Bruno declares.

There are no premier crus. Marsannay has had a dossier at INAO since 2002 requesting the definition of premier crus, and producers are hopeful of some action in the near future. Anticipating approval, they already distinguish between village wines and the lieu-dits, much as though they were premier crus. The best are Clos du Roy (well regarded in the nineteenth century) and Longeroies.

Marsannay is allowed to include Pinot Gris in its rosé, and the law of unintended consequences means that in fact there is sometimes Pinot Gris in the white wines. The style of Marsannay, both red and white, has a relatively light sense of extraction for the Côte de Nuits, tending to freshness rather than power, but similar in flavor to the great communes to its south.

Côte de Nuits versus Côte de Beaune

The classification of grand and premier crus does not completely correspond with current reputation. The Côte de Nuit's dominance of red wines is shown by ranking appellations on the basis of price. The grand crus of Vosne Romanée and Gevrey Chambertin fill most of the top twenty places, rounded out by entries from Chambolle Musigny and Morey St. Denis. Two premier crus, Les Amoureuses (Chambolle Musigny) and Clos St. Jacques (Gevrey Chambertin) place among the grand crus. The next group is dominated by premier crus of Vosne Romanée. The top entries from the Côte de Beaune are the best *climats* of Corton, whose varying reputations intersperse them among the premier crus. Several premier crus make Volnay the only other village to be well represented in the top hundred.

The distinction between the Côte de Nuits and Côte de Beaune is not completely consistent, but as a general rule the Côte de Nuits provides sterner red wines, as much inclined to black fruits as to red fruits, somewhat more generous and rounded, often forceful at premier and grand cru level. Gevrey Chambertin is perhaps the sternest, sometimes with a hard edge when young. Nuits St. Georges ranges from sturdy, almost rustic wines to elegance. Clos Vougeot at its best can be the most generous. There is absolutely no gainsaying Vosne Romanée's unique combination of power and smoothness, whereas Chambolle Musigny and Morey St. Denis can verge on delicate.

This compares with the soft roundness of Corton at its best, the sheen of Aloxe-Corton, the very varied range of Beaune from soft fruits to relatively thin wines, the rustic sturdiness of Pommard, and the crystalline purity of Volnay. With the exception of that taut precision in Volnay, the Côte de Beaune is more likely to offer earthy strawberries than black fruits.

Reference Wines for Côte de Nuits	
Nuits St. Georges	Henri Gouges
Vosne Romanée	Arnoux-Lachaux
Chambolle Musigny	Jean-Marie Fourrier
Morey St. Denis	Domaine Ponsot
Gevrey Chambertin	Armand Rousseau
Fixin	Méo-Camuzet
Marsannay	Bruno Clair

Reference Wines for Côte de Nuits Grand Cru	
Chambertin	Armand Rousseau
Clos de Bèze	Bruno Clair
Chapelle Chambertin	Domaine Trapet Père
Charmes Chambertin	Louis Jadot
Griotte Chambertin	Joseph Drouhin
Mazis Chambertin	Maison Faiveley
Ruchottes Chambertin	Georges Roumier
Clos St. Denis	Domaine Dujac
Clos de la Roche	Domaine Ponsot
Bonnes Mares	Jacques Frédéric Mugnier
Le Musigny	Comte de Vogüé
Echézeaux	Mongeard-Mugneret
Clos Vougeot	Lucien Le Moine

Côte de Beaune

Beaune is the center of the wine trade. Most of the old negociants have their headquarters here, although they have been moving steadily out of the old town to more practical, purpose built, locations on the outskirts. In the center of the old town is the Hospice de Dieu, established as a hospital in the Middle Ages, and funded by wine produced from its own vineyards.

One of the highlights of the year in Beaune is an auction at which the latest vintage from the Hospice is sold to local negociants, who then mature the barrels in their own particular styles. At one time these wines were well regarded for their quality, but today the auction is more an occasion to kick off sales of the current vintage than a supply of top-flight wine.

To the west, the city of Beaune is surrounded by the semicircle of the appellation of Beaune. To the south, a continuum of vineyards extends to the Côte Chalonnaise.

Corton and Corton Charlemagne

The hill of Corton dominates Aloxe Corton.

Aloxe Corton
242 ha
98% red
Grand crus
Corton (95% red)
95 ha
Corton Charlemagne (white)
48 ha
14 premier crus

Vineyards wind around the hill of Corton. Corton Charlemagne is on the southwest slopes. Corton runs down the eastern flank; the most important climats are indicated. Aloxe-Corton premier crus are below, and village wines are at the bottom.

To the north of Beaune, Corton is the largest grand cru in Burgundy. "Everything seems so easy to understand in Burgundy. There are village wines, premier crus, and grand crus. But in Corton you have all the different *climats* inside the grand cru," says Philippe Prost at Bouchard Père.

Occupying 160 ha, Corton is somewhat of an anomaly: nominally a single grand cru, occupying the upper slopes going up the hill of Corton to the forest at the top, it is divided into many separate *climats,* and it's really their individual names that carry weight. The best, at the top, are worthy of grand cru status: the rest are more doubtful. Clos du Roi is the best.

Below Corton, the premier crus of Aloxe-Corton are on the lower slopes of the hill, and the village appellation is just below. The best reds of Aloxe-Corton have a glossy sheen, with more body than, say, Beaune, but not approaching the structure of the Côte de Nuits.

Corton is famous for the white wine of Corton Charlemagne, from southwest end of the hill. Its name reflects Emperor Charlemagne's ownership of vineyards on the hill; the story goes that the wine originated when he demanded white wine to avoid staining his beard with red.

The proportions of red and white wine from Corton have changed dramatically with time. At the start of the nineteenth century, most Corton was red. The focus changed to white during the twentieth century, and today 72 ha are classified for the white Corton Charlemagne. Some of this area can also be used for red; for example, the *climat* of Corton-Pougets is contained entirely within Corton Charlemagne. Corton Blanc describes white wine produced elsewhere in the grand cru.

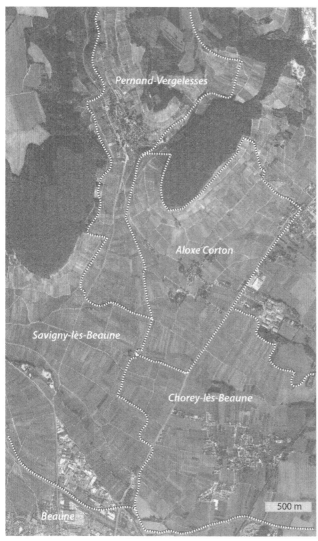

Pernand-Vergelesses

Aloxe Corton

Savigny-lès-Beaune

Chorey-lès-Beaune

500 m

Beaune

Aloxe Corton has the best exposure, with Pernand-Vergelesses facing more to the west, and Savigny-lès-Beaune and Chorey-lès-Beaune at lower elevations.

The hill is based on a substratum of limestone, but there is a difference in the topsoil going up the slope, from more iron and pebbles lower down (thought to be better suited to Pinot Noir) to higher clay content at the top. But here as elsewhere, market forces push growers to replant with Chardonnay when vineyards come up for renewal. Going round the hill from Aloxe-Corton towards Pernand Vergelesses, there is more flint in the soil, giving more austerity to the white wine (and creating difficulties for black grapes in ripening.) So the terroir is far from homogeneous.

The two poles of Corton Charlemagne are expressed by the largest two owners, with full force opulence from Louis Latour, and restrained minerality from Bonneau du Martray. At its best, Corton Charlemagne has a wonderful rich generosity, with a touch of citrus cutting the stone fruits, and sometimes a sense of austerity that recalls the white wines of the Côte de Nuits. But given the variety of terroirs, there is no single character. Bonneau du Martray's block extends from Pernand Vergelesses to Aloxe Corton. "The styles provided by each block are quite distinct," said former owner Jean-Charles le Bault de la Morinière, and of course you see that variety in the wines expressed by other producers from smaller holdings.

The Environs of Beaune

Around Corton are satellite appellations—Pernand-Vergelesses to the north, Savigny-lès-Beaune to the south, and Chorey-lès-Beaune to the east. They produce both red and white wines, with the best vineyards marked out as premier crus. Less well known than the major appellations along the core of the Côte d'Or, the wines are more straightforward, and can offer good value.

Île-des-Vergelesses, at the border with Savigny-lès-Beaune, is generally considered the best of the premier crus of Pernand-Vergelesses. Adjacent to it, Les Vergelesses is one of the best premier crus of Savigny-lès-Beaune, so this is a favored patch, extending in fact to Les Lavières just beyond.

Immediately to the east, most of the vineyards of Chorey-lès-Beaune are on the relatively flat land on the other side of the N74; the greater content of clay means that the wines here are not so fine, and there are no premier crus. Before Chorey was granted its appellation in 1970, the wines were sold as Côte de Beaune Villages, and some still are.

Beaune

Beaune
410 ha
  90% red
  10% white
42 premier crus
  317 ha
Top Crus
Clos des Mouches
Les Grèves
Les Bressandes
177 producers

Vineyards extend from the town of Beaune, but reflecting the large size of the appellation, are the most variable on the Côte de Beaune. Clos des Mouches is one of the premier crus in Beaune that has both red and white plantings.

The largest appellation on the Côte d'Or, Beaune is hard to pin down. Vineyards stretch from Savigny-lès-Beaune to Pommard. The large size, high number of premier crus, and the fact that they represent three quarters of the appellation, makes for what might kindly be described as variability in quality. (Personally I would demote several of the premier crus, and judging from the low prices they fetch, the market agrees with me.) There is more Pinot Noir than Chardonnay in Beaune, but the whites can be finely structured, sometimes a little tight.

The effects of terroir are shown by the different characters of two of the top premier crus. At the southern boundary of Beaune with Pommard, Clos des Mouches is calcareous. Terraces face from east to southeast and are relatively breezy. Two kilometers to the north, the steep slope of Grèves angles more east; the soil is clay and limestone, shallow with lots of stones and there is often a water deficit. (Grèves is local dialect for stony.) There is a lot of iron in the soil. Clos des Mouches is lighter with more aromatics and finesse, Grèves is sturdier with firmer tannins and structure.

Volnay and Pommard

Volnay
220 ha
 100% red
29 premier crus
 135 ha
Top Crus
Caillerets
Taillepieds
Clos des 60 Ou-
vrées
116 producers

Volnay produces the most refined red wines on the Cote de Beaune. Vineyards run right up to the village.

Volnay and Pommard are the southernmost regions for the top red wines, but although they are adjacent, the communes have different styles. Volnay is the epitome of elegance, with precisely delineated red fruit flavors that at their best have a remarkable crystalline quality. Pommard has softer, lusher fruits, sometimes considered to be a touch rustic. What is responsible for the difference between the elegance of Volnay and the breadth of Pommard?

Volnay is one of the smaller communes; perhaps that is why there is more consistency to style and quality. It sits on a limestone base, with some variety in the types of limestone, but the base is generally light in

Le Village
1 Clos de la Cave des Ducs
2 Clos de l'Audignac
3 Le Clos de la Chapelle
4 Clos de Château des Ducs
5 Le Village
6 Clos de la Rougeotte
7 Clos de La Bousse d'Or

Clos des Ducs

Taillepieds

Bousse d'Or

Champans

100 m

The best premier crus in Volnay are close to the village. Numbers indicate monopoles in Le Village. Clos des Ducs, Taillepieds, and Champans are other top premier crus.

color and relatively crumbly. The best plots in Volnay are close to the village. In fact, a premier cru called simply *Le Village* consists of various plots surrounding the village, but you rarely see Le Village on the label because most of these plots are monopoles whose proprietors use their individual names. Other top premier crus are Taillepieds, Champans, Clos des Chênes, and Caillerets.

At the northern boundary, Volnay joins Pommard, where the limestone-based soils have more clay. This is said to give the wines of Pommard their sturdier character. There's also more iron in Pommard, due to ferrous oxide in the soil. Volnay has finer tannins compared to Pommard. Benjamin Leroux, formerly of Comte Armand in Pommard, says that the differences are quite evident when you make the wine. "With Volnay the tannins are

Pommard
322 ha
  100% red
28 premier crus
  116 ha
Top Crus
Les Epenots
Les Rugiens
205 producers

Pommard produces firm red wines.

Reference Wines for Red Côte de Beaune	
Chorey-lès-Beaune	Tollot-Beaut
Savigny-lès-Beaune	Benjamin Leroux
Pernand-Vergelesses	Rapet Père et Fils, Île des Vergelesses
Corton	Louis Latour, Château Corton Grancey
Aloxe-Corton	Rapet Père et Fils
Beaune	Joseph Drouhin, Clos des Mouches
Pommard	Comte Armand
Volnay	Marquis d'Angerville
Blagny	Robert Ampeau
Saint-Romain	Alain Gras
Auxey-Duresses	Comte Armand, premier cru
Santenay	Anne-Marie & Jean-Marc Vincent

extracted slowly and tend to come at the end of fermentation. You don't have to look for extraction in Pommard, it is there straight away, because the tannins come at the beginning."

White Burgundy

South of Volnay, the tip of the Côte de Beaune is white wine territory. Characterizing the differences between Meursault, Chassagne Montrachet, and Puligny Montrachet is complicated by the wide variety of producer styles in each appellation. Conventional wisdom identifies Meursault as soft, nutty, and buttery, while Chassagne Montrachet has a bit more of a citrus edge, and Puligny Montrachet is taut, precise, and mineral. Changes

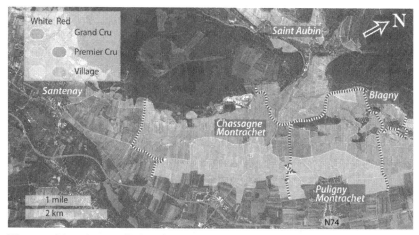

The top white wine appellations lie in a group to the south of Beaune. The line of premier and grand crus runs along the middle and upper slope.

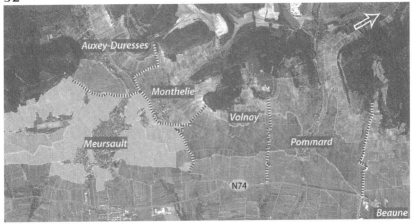

Meursault is almost all white wine, but Volnay and Pommard are exclusively red.

over the past decade or so, especially in Meursault, show that these styles are due only in part to the intrinsic character of each appellation, but "Puligny has more acidity, Meursault is broader," says Philippe Prost at Bouchard Père. "Puligny you have to keep the freshness, Meursault you have to give it energy." Puligny is the most linear, and has the most tension of the three appellations, Chassagne is always a touch broader and softer, while Meursault varies from traditionally broad to its modern impression of gunflint, and tends to be richer.

Meursault

Meursault is the largest of the three appellations. Although it has no grand crus, its top premier crus are excellent, with Les Perrières sometimes approaching grand cru quality. Les Genevrières is also very fine: "for me, it is the little brother of Chevalier Montrachet," says Philippe Prost.

Meursault
396 ha
  96% white
  4% red
19 premier crus
  107 ha
Top Crus
Les Charmes
Les Perrières
Les Genevrières
Porusot
192 producers

Meursault is the largest village on the Côte de Beaune.

The whites used to be rich rather than mineral, although those of the top producer, Coche-Dury, tend towards a savory minerality. Others have now followed Coche-Dury in a more mineral direction, most notably Arnaud Ente and Antoine Jobard. Comtes Lafon makes some of the longest-lived wines of the appellation, halfway in style between minerality and nuttiness, and Jean-Marc Roulot at Domaine Guy Roulot makes elegant wines.

The New Meursault, as I think of it, is as mineral as rich. Is the change to a more mineral focus now the typicity of Meursault, I asked Dominique Lafon. "I think it is typical for the good producers," he holds. At the southwest edge of Meursault is the village of Blagny, whose name appears on Meursault-Blagny premier cru and also in the Hameau de Blagny premier cru of Puligny Montrachet.

Some red wine is produced in Meursault, but the best is a premier cru that is actually labeled as Volnay Santenots. There's also Blagny premier cru red.

Puligny Montrachet

Puligny Montrachet
211 ha
  100% white
  4 grand crus
17 premier crus
  98 ha
Top Premier Crus
Les Pucelles
Les Demoiselles
Les Folatières
Les Combettes
127 producers

Puligny Montrachet can be seen through the gateway into Les Pucelles, its most important premier cru.

Puligny Montrachet is for me the quintessence of white Burgundy: its steely minerality, the precision in the fruits, the sense of backbone—the combination is unique. Some of the premier crus are within a hair's breadth of grand cru quality, with Les Pucelles and Le Cailleret sometimes crossing the line. The hierarchy of Puligny is captured at Domaine Leflaive, where the classic style shows in the village wine, intensifies through the premier crus, and then with Les Pucelles or the grand crus, adds a Rolls Royce sense of power to that steely finesse. The trend to increasing ripeness at most producers means that many premier crus now show richness before minerality, but there should always be tension in Puligny.

Of course, the epitome of white wine is the grand cru Le Montrachet: I am in the camp of those who consider it potentially the greatest white wine in the world (depending of course on the producer). Chevalier Montrachet is usually considered second, followed by Bâtard-Montrachet and Bienvenues-Bâtard-Montrachet. Le Montrachet and Bâtard-Montrachet actually are only partly in Puligny Montrachet, with some of each vineyard across the border in Chassagne Montrachet. Criots-Bâtard-Montrachet is solely in Chassagne.

The unique quality of these grand crus is that subtly shifting balance of power with finesse. Chardonnays from other sources may have one or the other, but I have yet to experience any other wine with both. In terms of the villages, Puligny Montrachet is the closest in style to the grand crus, especially its top premier crus. In fact, village character may show most clearly at this level, as the grand crus can be so powerful as to subdue that steely minerality.

Chassagne Montrachet

Chassagne Montrachet
313 ha
  63% white
  37% red
55 premier crus
  149 ha
Top Crus
Morgeot
Les Champs
Gain
105 producers

Chassagne Montrachet's most important premier cru is Morgeot, with the derelict Abbaye de Morgeot at the center. Including various climats (sometimes used instead of Morgeot), it is by far the largest premier cru.

"Sometimes people ask us what we think is the difference between Chassagne and Puligny, and it's a really difficult question, because there are so many different areas in Chassagne—Morgeot is rich, but other areas are more mineral," says Hubert Lestime at Domaine Jean-Noël Gagnard. It is fair to say that Chassagne is more heterogeneous than Puligny.

The typicity of Chassagne Montrachet is usually considered to lie between Meursault and Puligny Montrachet: not as rich as Meursault but not as linear as Puligny. "Chassagne is always rounder, I've never had a vintage where Puligny is rounder," says Laurent Pillot. "When you plough our vineyards you can see there's more clay in Chassagne." It is fair to say that on average Puligny is more precise, whereas Chassagne has more breadth.

The top premier crus in Chassagne are Morgeot (very large, including some others), Caillerets, Champs Gains, Ruchottes, Chaumées, and La

Le Montrachet is in the middle of the white grand crus, with Chevalier above it, and Bâtard and Bienvenues-Bâtard below it.

Boudriotte. There is more red wine in Chassagne Montrachet than either of the other two appellations; indeed, white wine took over here more recently, as a result of market pressure. This is not always a good thing.

Today, Pinot Noir vineyards tend to be replaced with Chardonnay when it's time to replant. "We think it's a pity the area at the bottom of the village has been replanted; it reduces the reputation of the village because those soils give less minerality. It's a problem to plant white there," says Jean-Marc Blain Gagnard.

Limits of the Côte de Beaune

Adjacent to the great white wine appellations are the satellite appellations at the southern tip of the Côte de Beaune: Saint-Romain, Auxey-Duresses, and Saint-Aubin to the west, and Santenay just south of Chassagne Montrachet. These can be good sources for wines in similar style, albeit less concentrated and complex, but at considerably lower prices than the more famous communes.

The whites of Saint-Aubin are the best known, while Auxey-Duresses and Saint-Romain have become more popular as Saint-Aubin has increased in price. "The vines in Saint-Aubin are relatively young because it used to be Pinot Noir, and much was replanted with Chardonnay thirty years ago. The appellation may have the opportunity to improve as the vines get older," says Damien Colin of Domaine Marc Colin. Now with a clear focus on white, Saint-Aubin is 80% Chardonnay. The terroir is similar to Puligny Montrachet, but the climate is cooler.

Reference Wines for White Côte de Beaune	
Corton Charlemagne	Bonneau du Martray
Pernand-Vergelesses	Rapet Père et Fils, Clos du Village
Savigny-lès-Beaune	Simon Bize
Beaune	Joseph Drouhin, Clos des Mouches
Meursault	Comtes Lafon
Chassagne Montrachet	Louis Jadot, Clos de la Chapelle
Puligny Montrachet	Domaine Leflaive
Saint-Romain	Deux Montille
Auxey-Duresses	Benjamin Leroux
Saint-Aubin	Hubert Lamy
Santenay	Anne-Marie & Jean-Marc Vincent
Bourgogne Aligoté	Pierre Morey

If Saint Aubin is a less expensive alternative to Puligny, Santenay may be a poor man's Chassagne. Indeed, Chassagne runs almost imperceptibly into Santenay, where vineyards lie along a valley with slopes at all angles. If a producer has vines in both, the Chassagne is usually more intense. However, less than a quarter of Santenay is white, and the reds of Santenay are the best known of the satellite appellations, representing a somewhat softer version of Chassagne reds.

Auxey Duresses is about two thirds red, and the style of both reds and whites is a bit on the austere side compared, for example, with Meursault just to its south.

Saint Romain is somewhat different from the other satellites, as it essentially a closed valley, running north-south, with vineyards on the slopes on both sides. Relatively protected by the hills at the end, it tends to be cooler than the other satellites due to higher elevations of 100-400m.

All of the satellite appellations produce white wines that are credible alternative to their more expensive counterparts in the great appellations, albeit less complex, but the reds tend to be less successful. It's really a matter of ripeness, because the reds often fail to reach the roundness that comes from the top communes, leaving them with an austere impression. Of course, that could change with global warming.

Premature Oxidation

The great issue of the day in white Burgundy crosses all appellation boundaries. This is premature oxidation, so prevalent today that it has become known by the abbreviation of premox. Before premox became an issue, a village white Burgundy would probably last for six years or so, a premier cru would not be ready to start for, say, 4-6 years, and would last for more than a decade beyond the vintage, and grand crus would start even more slowly and last even longer. The problem with premature oxidation first became apparent with the 1996 vintage, when soon after 2000, many wines, even at premier cru level, began to show signs of oxidation: deepening color, madeirized nose, and drying out on the palate.

Given significant variability between individual bottles, the immediate reaction was that this was due to a problem with the corks (possibly due to changes in the sterilization procedure). It soon became clear that the answer was not so straightforward, and a variety of causes was proposed, ranging from changes in viticulture, pressing the juice too clean (because this removes anti-oxidants), too much battonage (stirring up the lees while the wine is in barrique), or reduced use of sulfur at bottling.

More than a decade on, however, no one has pinpointed any single cause, so no white Burgundy of more than three or four years old can be considered safe. This greatly shortens the period for drinking: you have to steer between the Scylla of new oak and the Charybdis of premox. Many wines, especially at the premier or grand cru level, have somewhat evident oak on release, and it takes two or three years for this to calm down; sometimes longer, as premier crus with 100% new oak may still display obvious oak after, say, 6 years. So not much time is left before premox might set in. And not only is the window for enjoying wines at their optimum much shortened, but it seems to be different for every bottle.

White Burgundy has become a wine that must be enjoyed young. Even though there is a tendency to reduce new oak, levels are still often appropriate for wines that are expected to last for ten or more years. If the wine needs to be consumed sooner, it follows that new oak should be dialed back more. Too high a proportion of new oak means that many wines now slide straight from showing too much oak into being too tired and old.

Dominique Lafon, who has been at the forefront of efforts to fix the problem, believes that premox is a perfect storm of many factors. "What puzzled us was that it was very random. The first thing we thought was that we had cork failures—I think we did—but it was showing the fragility of the wine," he says. He's changed a variety of procedures to make vinification more reductive, and believes the issue has finally been resolved.

The underlying problem was that the wines did not have enough resistance to oxidation, so the slightest problem with the cork would allow oxidation. This explains the random occurrence. "Even in the cellars here, one in four bottles of white Beaune from 1999 is oxidized, but the others are absolutely fine," Philippe Drouhin told me in 2010, "so what can it be but the cork?" Since producers are unwilling to change to screwcaps, the important thing is to ensure that the wines are more resistant to oxidation.

Is the problem over? "No one really knows where premox is coming from, so no one can really claim they've solved the problem," says Brice de la Morandière at Domaine Leflaive. While it's fair to say that premox is no longer as severe a problem as before, I find that the wines do not age as long as they used to: they seem to tire sooner, even if not showing premox.

Vintages

The most common problem historically in Burgundy has been cool or wet weather, especially at time of harvest, but more recently there have also been problems with heat. The increasingly erratic nature of weather conditions is summarized by Marie-Andrée Mugneret's comment that, "In 2016 we lost 80% of the harvest to frost, in 2017 we needed to do a green harvest to reduce yields." "The first half of the decade through 2014 was cool—2013 was the coolest vintage I've ever made—but since then the years have all been warm," says Jean-Nicolas Méo. 2018 was a large, ripe vintage. "There was no need to sort in 2018," says Jean-Nicolas.

Climate change has increased alcohol levels. "The last four vintages—2015, 2016, 2017, 2018—we had to fight for freshness. Some of my colleagues got 15% alcohol. Years ago they would have been happy to get 11%," says Michel Mallard at Domaine de'Eugenie. Yet chaptalization still occurs in weaker vintages.

While there are distinctions between areas, with local conditions giving different results in the Côte de Beaune and Côte de Nuits, the most important distinction is between red and white wines. Sometimes the best vintages for red wines result in white wines with less acidity and aging potential (a concern increased by the occurrence of premox).

Some pairs of vintages, such as 2015/2016, 2009/2010, or 2005/2006, have a first year with superb red wines, but a second year where whites are crisper and likely to age better. However, uncertainty about the premature oxidation problem means that any white Burgundy more than, say, five years old for village, and eight years for premier or grand cru, is suspect, so notes for older vintages are now really of historical interest only.

2018	***	Hailed by producers as a great vintage, possibly a rival to 1947 (which was very hot, rich, and alcoholic). Another large vintage (although not a large as 2017), with harvest starting very early in August, and grapes reaching high levels of ripeness, so alcohol may be high, sometimes 14% for grand crus. Acidification was common. Reds will be rich, whites could have problems with freshness.
2017	**	Largest crop since 2009, some differences depending on whether producers picked before or after rain was forecast for first week of September. Quality is good, although not as concentrated as 2016 or 2015 for reds, and whites range from very good to outstanding. Both reds and whites often show a tang of acidity on the finish. Early drinking, this is a lovely restaurant vintage.
2016	**	A very small vintage because crop size was reduced by frost and hail; some producers have made only a quarter of normal production. A warm September gave good harvest conditions, and the wines are of excellent quality, lively for the whites and rich for the reds. However, they will be in short supply. Considered a more "classic"

		vintage in terms of structure, more linear than 2015. Reds are well structured, and may last longer than those of 2015. Whites have appealing freshness and precision, and should age well if premox does not set in.
2015	***	A rich vintage. Reds have good structure as well as richness, deep and round, and should age well. They are superficially more opulent than the 2016 vintage. Whites are immediately appealing, but seem to have enough freshness to last better than the 2009 vintage.
2014	*	Storms with hail during growing season reduced crop greatly in many communes, but weather improved after very difficult August. Whites tend to be fruity and easy. Reds are not as rich as 2009, 2012, or 2015, but should be good for short to mid term.
2013		Cold growing season was difficult, but some improvement in September allowed decent harvest for wines that will be good rather than great.
2012	*	Erratic conditions led to low yields of both reds and whites, but quality is surprisingly good.
2011		Difficulties in getting to ripeness make this the least successful vintage of the decade to date.
2010	***	Reds are tighter than the opulent 2009s, with an elegant balance, and potential for good aging. Whites show good acidity, a crisper, leaner style than 2009, but with greater potential for longevity.
2009	***	A great year for reds, rich, ripe and opulent, but a lingering question is whether they will have the tannic structure for extended longevity. Whites were opulent at first, but unlikely to age long as richness is well ahead of acidity. Most have reached their peaks.
2008		Difficult vintage with problems of rain and humidity. Reds show high acidity, whites are on the fresh side.
2007	***	Growing season was too wet, reds suffered from problems with humidity, the whites are better but on the acid side.
2006	*	Reds have a tendency towards austerity resulting from cool conditions leading to high acidity.
2005	***	Reds are on the opulent side but with good tannic structure for long-term development. Whites show classic opulence for a warm year, impression of fat when young, but by now the tendency to earlier aging is making most questionable.
2004	*	Both reds and whites are on the lighter, more acid side, and there are not many of interest today.
2003		Reds tended to be cooked from the outset, and almost all were short-lived. The heat was too much for the whites, which tended to be flabby.
2002	***	Reds are quite rich but well structured, and the best are à point.

		Whites tended to show opulence but the premature aging of white Burgundy means most are now too old.
2001	*	Not a bad vintage at the time, although a bit tannic for reds and acid for whites, but not of serious interest today.
2000	*	Nice enough wines for early drinking, but few survived to the end of the decade.
1999	***	Generous vintage for reds with good supporting structure; the best are still at their peak. Whites showed nice combination of generosity and minerality, but are now too old.
1998	*	Not very interesting at the time and no longer of interest.
1997	*	Pleasant wines for short term drinking at the time.
1996	***	A frustrating year for reds. Billed as vins de garde, they started with strong tannins, but have never come around. The problem is a punishing bitter medicinal acidity that tarnishes the finish. Some grand crus are rare exceptions where concentration of fruits compensates. This was a lovely vintage for whites at the outset: crisp, mineral, and precise, but it was the first vintage where premox became a major problem, cutting short longevity.
1995	**	Reds seemed a little tight at first but in retrospect were generous compared with the following vintage in 1996. They developed in a charming, lighter style, rather than opulent. Whites showed good concentration and weight, but are too old now.
1994		Autumn rains spoiled the harvest, but whites were better than reds.
1993	*	Reds gave quite a charming vintage in a lighter style for mid-term consumption, but the whites were less successful due to lack of concentration.
1992		The best wines were picked before rain spoiled the harvest.
1991		A rare vintage where the whites were quite successful, tending to elegance on Côte d'Or, but the reds never quite made it.
1990	***	A great vintage with good balance of fruit to structure; long-lived for reds. A great vintage for the opulent style of white Burgundy.

Visiting the Region

The Côte d'Or is quite compact, but even so it can take a while to go up and down the N74 (now the D974), so it is a good idea to group visits into villages or adjacent villages. The two bottlenecks in driving around are Beaune and Nuits St. Georges. The best way is to divide producers into three groups: south of Beaune; Beaune to Nuits St. Georges; and north of Nuits St. Georges.

Be prepared for it to take time negotiating the larger towns (Beaune, Nuits St. Georges, Gevrey Chambertin) to find producers, especially Beaune, which is a rabbit warren of small streets.

To get a good perspective on the region, it is useful to visit both larger negociants (mostly located in or around Beaune) and smaller producers (spread around the villages). The N74 is lined with producers who can be visited without an appointment, but these are not usually the most interesting. It is a much better experience to make an appointment.

At the large negociants, a visit and tasting is likely to be conducted by a guide, but at the smaller producers in the villages it will very likely be the owner/ winemaker (more properly the vigneron) who shows you around. (This makes it important to have an appointment: it is a good idea to make this a few weeks in advance.) Seeing winery facilities is common, but you do not usually get taken into the vineyards. Larger negociants have English speaking guides, but some smaller producers may not speak English.

Only the larger negociants or producers have dedicated tasting rooms. At smaller producers, often enough the winery is basically an extension of the family residence. Tastings are usually in the cave, and often exclusively from barrels—bottles may be too precious to open for visitors. Be prepared to taste samples taken from the barrel with a pipette (sometimes involving shared glasses). The etiquette of tasting assumes you will spit. A producer will be surprised if you drink the wine. Usually a tasting room or cellar is equipped with spittoons, but ask if you do not see one (crachoir in French). In smaller cellars, there aren't always spittoons, and sometimes you spit on the gravel floor or into a drain. Visits usually last up to an hour.

There's a long tradition of selling wines directly to consumers in Burgundy—people used to come down from Paris and fill up containers in the past—so most large producers and many family concerns will sell to visitors, but the more important domains whose wines are in high demand, often on allocation, will not do so.

Beaune is the gastronomic center, with restaurants at all levels from bistros to Michelin stars. Le Beneton is the most innovative of the one stars. Jardin des Remparts has recovered its form and has a lovely garden. Loiseau des Vignes has excellent food, and a vast number of wines by the glass, but is spoiled by over-priced wines. Prices at Le Carmin reflect its expensive location in Place Carnot. Among bistros, Ma Cuisine is a

The Hospices de Beaune is the major tourist attraction in the town

The center of Nuits St. Georges is a pedestrian preccinct with shops and cafes.

hangout for wine people with a very long wine list, L'Ecrit Vin has a good atmosphere, but the Bistro de l'Hôtel de Beaune is terribly overpriced.

To the north, the center of Nuits St. Georges has been gentrified with a pedestrian precinct. There are several casual eating places in Nuits St. Georges, but otherwise there are mostly only more formal restaurants to the north of Beaune. Gevrey Chambertin is the only other village of any size until you get to Dijon. There is not much of interest for the tourist between Gevry Chambertin and Dijon, but Marsannay has a plan to introduce a Caveau des Vignerons.

There's also gentrification in the villages south of Beaune, although it's less extensive. The only village where signs to the Centre Ville have much significance is Meursault, which sprawls out around the old Château de Meursault, which is surrounded by shops and restaurants. Pommard has a grand church dominating its square, but restaurants are off to the side by the N74. Volnay and Chassagne Montrachet are each really little more than a church and few houses. Puligny Montrachet, perhaps the best known, is the most chic, perhaps a bit stultified by gentrification. The Place des Marroniers at its core has been reworked and turned into a chic square—alas there are no longer any Marroniers (chestnut trees)—but there isn't otherwise very much in the center. Farther south, Santenay has the liveliest village center, with some cafés in the main square.

With the Château at its center, Meursault is the largest and liveliest of the villages south of Beaune.

Profiles of Leading Estates

Ratings	
****	Sui generis, standing out above everything else in the appellation
***	Excellent producers defining the very best of the appellation
**	Top producers whose wines typify the appellation
*	Very good producers making wines of character that rarely disappoint

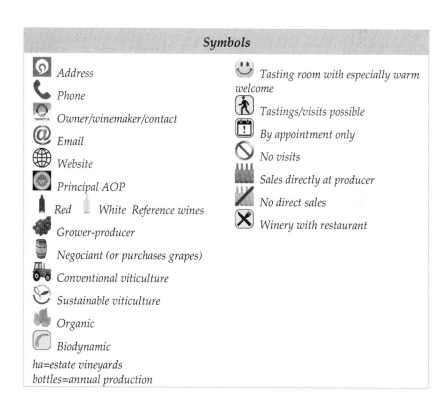

Symbols	
Address	Tasting room with especially warm welcome
Phone	Tastings/visits possible
Owner/winemaker/contact	By appointment only
Email	No visits
Website	Sales directly at producer
Principal AOP	No direct sales
Red White Reference wines	Winery with restaurant
Grower-producer	
Negociant (or purchases grapes)	
Conventional viticulture	
Sustainable viticulture	
Organic	
Biodynamic	

ha=estate vineyards
bottles=annual production

Côte de Beaune

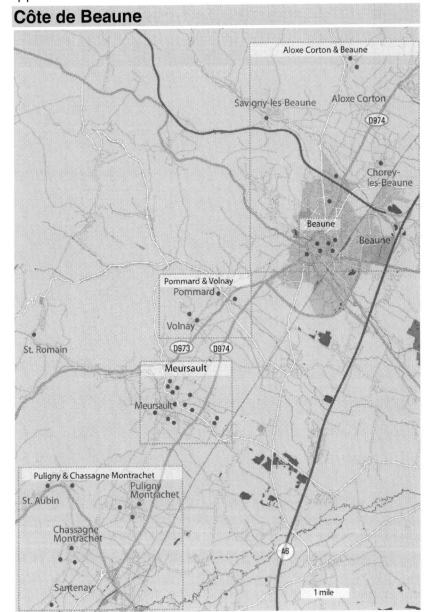

Aloxe Corton & Beaune

Savigny-les-Beaune

Aloxe Corton

D974

Chorey-les-Beaune

Beaune

Beaune

Pommard & Volnay

Pommard

Volnay

St. Romain

D973   D974

Meursault

Meursault

Puligny & Chassagne Montrachet

Puligny Montrachet

St. Aubin

Chassagne Montrachet

A6

Santenay

1 mile

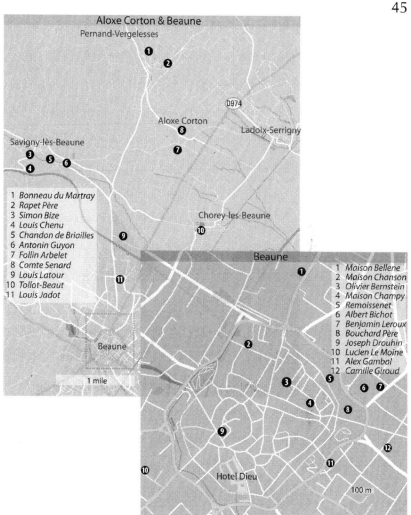

Aloxe Corton & Beaune

Pernand-Vergelesses

Aloxe Corton

D974

Ladoix-Serrigny

Savigny-lès-Beaune

1 Bonneau du Martray
2 Rapet Père
3 Simon Bize
4 Louis Chenu
5 Chandon de Briailles
6 Antonin Guyon
7 Follin Arbelet
8 Comte Senard
9 Louis Latour
10 Tollot-Beaut
11 Louis Jadot

Chorey-les-Beaune

Beaune

1 mile

Beaune

1 Maison Bellene
2 Maison Chanson
3 Olivier Bernstein
4 Maison Champy
5 Remoissenet
6 Albert Bichot
7 Benjamin Leroux
8 Bouchard Père
9 Joseph Drouhin
10 Lucien Le Moine
11 Alex Gambal
12 Camille Giroud

Hotel Dieu

100 m

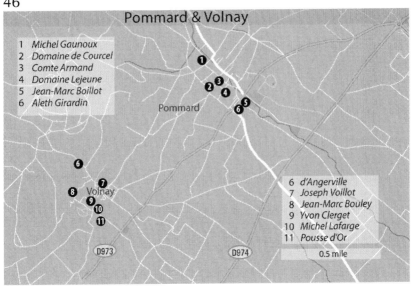

Pommard & Volnay

1 Michel Gaunoux
2 Domaine de Courcel
3 Comte Armand
4 Domaine Lejeune
5 Jean-Marc Boillot
6 Aleth Girardin

Pommard

Volnay

6 d'Angerville
7 Joseph Voillot
8 Jean-Marc Bouley
9 Yvon Clerget
10 Michel Lafarge
11 Pousse d'Or

D973

D974

0.5 mile

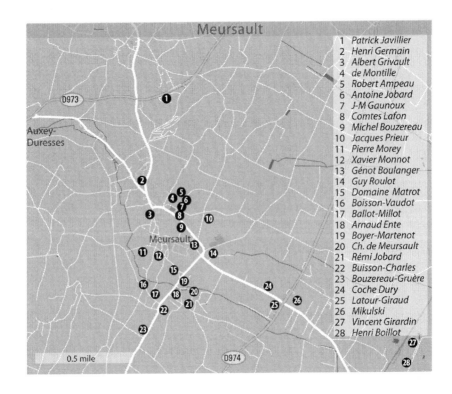

Meursault

1 Patrick Javillier
2 Henri Germain
3 Albert Grivault
4 de Montille
5 Robert Ampeau
6 Antoine Jobard
7 J-M Gaunoux
8 Comtes Lafon
9 Michel Bouzereau
10 Jacques Prieur
11 Pierre Morey
12 Xavier Monnot
13 Génot Boulanger
14 Guy Roulot
15 Domaine Matrot
16 Boisson-Vaudot
17 Ballot-Millot
18 Arnaud Ente
19 Boyer-Martenot
20 Ch. de Meursault
21 Rémi Jobard
22 Buisson-Charles
23 Bouzereau-Gruère
24 Coche Dury
25 Latour-Giraud
26 Mikulski
27 Vincent Girardin
28 Henri Boillot

D973

Auxey-Duresses

Meursault

0.5 mile

D974

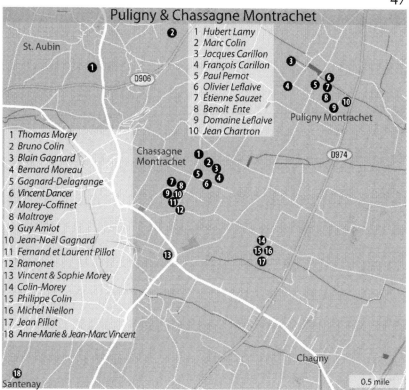

Puligny & Chassagne Montrachet

1 Hubert Lamy
2 Marc Colin
3 Jacques Carillon
4 François Carillon
5 Paul Pernot
6 Olivier Leflaive
7 Étienne Sauzet
8 Benoît Ente
9 Domaine Leflaive
10 Jean Chartron

St. Aubin

Puligny Montrachet

Chassagne Montrachet

1 Thomas Morey
2 Bruno Colin
3 Blain Gagnard
4 Bernard Moreau
5 Gagnard-Delagrange
6 Vincent Dancer
7 Morey-Coffinet
8 Maltroye
9 Guy Amiot
10 Jean-Noël Gagnard
11 Fernand et Laurent Pillot
12 Ramonet
13 Vincent & Sophie Morey
14 Colin-Morey
15 Philippe Colin
16 Michel Niellon
17 Jean Pillot
18 Anne-Marie & Jean-Marc Vincent

Chagny

Santenay

0.5 mile

Domaine Guy Amiot et Fils **

Chassagne-Montrachet
1ᵉʳ Cru Clos Saint Jean
2008
Domaine Amiot Guy et Fils

�’ *13, Rue Du Grand Puits, 21190 Chassagne-Montrachet*

📞 *+33 03 80 21 38 62*

Fabrice Amiot

@ *domaine.amiotguyetfils@wanadoo.fr*

🌐 *www.domaine-amiotguyetfils.com*

Chassagne Montrachet

Chassagne Montrachet, Vieilles Vignes

Puligny Montrachet, Les Champs Gains

🚫🍴🍇🖐 *10 ha; 60,000 bottles [map p. 47]*

"I would describe our philosophy for winemaking as traditional not modern, in the sense that we favor long aging, at least two years," says Fabrice Amiot, who works with his brother Thierry, the winemaker, at this family domain. The family originally had a laundry business in Paris, but bought the house and surrounding vineyard (Cailleret) in the 1920s. By the 1930s they owned more vineyards, and Pierre Amiot became one of the first growers in the town to bottle his own wines. Domain Guy Amiot was created in 1985 as part of a move to expand to markets beyond France. The tasting room is in the original house, on one side of a covered courtyard surrounded by winery buildings.

"The domain has a lot of old vines because it was grandfather who really developed the vineyards," Fabrice says. "All our holdings are in Chassagne, we have all the aspects of Chassagne, and there is a plot in Puligny." The domain's reputation rests on its whites, which include eight premier crus in Chassagne, Les Demoiselles in Puligny, and Saint Aubin, not to mention 0.1 ha in Le Montrachet. Many of the vineyards were leased out until they reverted to the domain in the late 1990s. The domain has expanded beyond the Côte d'Or by buying a vineyard of old vines Aligoté in Bouzeron in 2015. "We could afford to buy it, because it's not expensive and it's very close," Fabrice explains. The wine is very good, with the old vines really showing.

Elegant is the word most often used to describe the style. "Oak is much less than ten years ago, Thierry has reduced new oak to less than 35-30%, and there is a better expression of terroir," Fabrice says. The Vieilles Vignes Chassagne comes from a dozen plots in the village, with an average age of 50 years; it's attractive with a fine granular texture. Les Vergers, from 70-year old vines at the top of the slope, has a little more weight. Les Macherelles is spicier, and Les Champs Gains in smooth, silky, and more complex with faint herbal undertones. Cailleret makes the finest impression of all the Chassagne premier crus. Les Demoiselles from Puligny Montrachet is more linear, with great fruit purity. The comparison defines the difference between Puligny and Chassagne Montrachet. Reds from Santenay and Chassagne Montrachet account for about half of production; the style is precise and linear.

Domaine Robert Ampeau et Fils

6, Rue Du Cromin, 21190 Meursault

📞 +33 03 80 21 20 35

Michel Ampeau

@ michel.ampeau@wanadoo.fr

Meursault

Blagny, La Pièce Sous le Bois

Meursault, Les Charmes

9.5 ha; 50,000 bottles [map p. 46]

Robert Ampeau marches to the beat of a different drum: the concept of the current release has no meaning here. The imperatives of winemaking, or to be more precise, of commercializing the wines, are, to say the least, unusual. Wines are released when they are ready, or perhaps more to the point, when the domain feels like selling them. Both reds and whites from the mid 1990s are on sale now, giving consumers the opportunity to start with mature wines. Tastings start where others leave off: on my most recent visit, we tasted wines from 2002 to 1976. Production is 60% red and 40% white. Since Robert's death in 2004, Michel Ampeau has been making the wines.

There are holdings in ten premier crus, including four in Meursault. The wines are meant to age, and have reached an interesting stage of maturity when released. Since current releases haven't really reached the era of pre-mox, it's impossible to say if that will be a problem for the whites, but typically they peak around fifteen years of age and hold until twenty. I suspect that the traditional style of winemaking in an oxidative manner will avert any problem.

The style of the whites is rich and full, although Michel says he is an early picker. Meursault shows a classically nutty flavor spectrum, Meursault La Pièce Sous le Bois adds hints of honey and spices, and the Charmes premier cru adds a subtle hint of minerality. The complexity of Meursault Perrières shows why it is a candidate for promotion to grand cru, with seamless layers of flavor. This is the epitome of the classic style of Meursault. Puligny Combettes is a textbook example of purity and precision. The general style of the whites shows an intriguing combination of minerality and development.

The reds combine a sheen to the palate that masks the fruit density, with the structure of supple tannins in the background. A sense of liveliness gives an impression of being a decade younger than the real age. Savigny-lès-Beaune and La Pièce Sous le Bois from Blagny age much longer than you might expect for those appellations, in the general soft, earthy style of the house. Auxey-les-Duresses Les Ecussaux adds faintly herbal notes. Beaune Clos du Roi shows a smooth opulence, Pommard is broader but still sophisticated, while the Volnay Les Santenots premier cru tends to earthiness. Reds age easily for 30 years.

Wines from the great appellations show great typicity and ageability, but the surprise and the bargain are the wines from lesser appellations: and the domain is also remarkable for its ability to produce high quality in lesser years; vintages such as 1994 or 1997 show well more than 20 years later.

Domaine du Marquis d'Angerville ★★

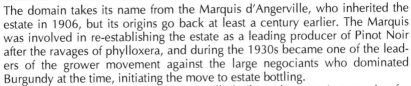

📍 *Rue De Mont, 21190 Volnay*

📞 *+33 03 80 21 61 75*

✍ *Guillaume D'Angerville*

@ *info@domainedangerville.fr*

🌐 *www.domainedangerville.fr*

◉ *Volnay*

🍾 *Volnay, Les Caillerets*

🍇 *15 ha; 55,000 bottles*

[map p. 46]

The domain takes its name from the Marquis d'Angerville, who inherited the estate in 1906, but its origins go back at least a century earlier. The Marquis was involved in re-establishing the estate as a leading producer of Pinot Noir after the ravages of phylloxera, and during the 1930s became one of the leaders of the grower movement against the large negociants who dominated Burgundy at the time, initiating the move to estate bottling.

After 1952, his son Jacques d'Angerville built up the estate's reputation for the sheer precision and elegance of its wines. It's a measure of the commitment to Pinot Noir that a low-yielding, small-berried clone developed from their vineyards is now known as the d'Angerville clone. Jacques was succeeded by Guillaume d'Angerville in 2003.

Most of the holdings are in Volnay, with a roll call of premier crus, headed by the monopole Clos des Ducs, adjacent to the domain, which occupies a splendid nineteenth century maison, just behind the church in Volnay. Other top holdings include Caillerets and Taillepieds. The wines always had a wonderful taut precision under Jacques d'Angerville, but seem since then to have become broader and less focused. One change in winemaking has been the introduction of a small proportion (up to 20%) of new oak. Guillaume has expanded his operations by purchasing two estates in the Jura in 2012, followed by another in 2014: wines are labeled as the Domaine du Pélican.

Domaine de Bellene

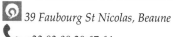

39 *Faubourg St Nicolas, Beaune*

+33 03 80 20 67 64

Nicolas Potel

contact@domainedebellene.com

www.domainedebellene.com

Beaune

Nuits St. Georges, Les Boudots (Maison Roche de Bellène)

Meursault, Les Forges

22 *ha; 70,000 bottles*

[map p. 45]

Nicolas Potel has a chequered history as a both a grower and negociant. His father, Gérard Potel, managed the Domaine de la Pousse d'Or, but after his death in 1997 and the subsequent sale of the estate, Nicolas established his own negociant business. Maison Nicolas Potel became well respected, but was sold to the large negociant Labouré-Roi in 2004.

After leaving in 2007, Nicolas founded a double business, Domaine de Bellène, making wine from its own vineyards, and Maison de la Roche Bellène, a negociant. The domain has its headquarters on the main road going north out of Beaune: behind the double doors it's quite startling to discover vast premises running back from the road. The domain is much smaller than the negociant, which has a separate winery.

Why have both a domain and a negociant? "I come from a domain, it's my background. I was a negociant by force. When I sold the negociant (Maison Potel) I'd started the domain, but my customers wanted me to continue as a negociant." What's the difference between them? "The wines have different goals. You don't have the same control over the vineyard with the Maison. The wines already have an imprint coming from the growers. I'm not going to impose a style on them. The Maison has an easier style, a bit rounder, something that will drink in the next 3-4 years. About 60-70% of the wines are the same every year, but the rest come from sporadic purchases. The domain is biodynamic. Winemaking is minimalist."

But for both domain and maison, the stylistic objective is "a lean style, not too fat or heavy." Nicolas explains that his focus is switching to the domain. "The domain is still growing but the Maison is contracting, it's a matter of balance, they are run separately."

Olivier Bernstein **

MAZIS-CHAMBERTIN
GRAND CRU
BY OLIVIER BERNSTEIN

2007

📍 *4 rue Jean Belin, Beaune*

📞 *+33 03 80 22 49 48*

Olivier Bernstein

@ *contact@olivierbernstein.com*

🌐 *www.olivierbernstein.com*

Beaune

Gevrey Chambertin, Cazetiers

7 ha; 25,000 bottles

[map p. 45]

"It's interesting to have someone like me here, in the most conservative region of France, as I'm not from here, I'm not obliged to make wine," says Olivier Bernstein, who comes from a musical background, but became a micro-negociant in 2007. Olivier makes 3 premier crus, 7 grand crus, and village Gevrey Chambertin in a renovated building in a back street of Beaune. Production focuses on reds from the Côte de Nuits. Quantities are small but not miniscule. "There are 4-8 barrels of each wine, I like to have at least four barrels, I don't want to bottle one barrel, that's a nonsense," Olivier says. The boundary between negociant and domain has blurred as Olivier was able to buy 2 ha in 2012, but this doesn't make much difference as he farms all the plots himself anyway. "So I don't really like to be called a negociant," he says.

Winemaking is modern, with maturation entirely in new barriques, although Olivier says, "It's not the new wood that's interesting for me, it's the oxygenation." Except for Chambolle Lavrottes, vines are 40-80 years old. "We only have very old vines because they are much better than recent plantings." The style is finely structured, with Lavrottes the lightest, Gevrey Chambertin remarkably pure, Clos de la Roche and Clos de Bèze very tight when young, and fleshiness only just showing on Clos Vougeot behind that tight, precise house style. These beautifully balanced wines should come into their own about six years after the vintage.

Domaine Simon Bize

*

⟁ *12 Rue Chanoine Donin, 21420 Savigny-lès-Beaune*

📞 *+33 03 80 21 50 57*

✉ *Chisa Bize*

@ *contact@domainebize.fr*

🌐 *www.domainebize.fr*

◉ *Savigny-lès-Beaune*

🍷 *Savigny-lès-Beaune, Les Fourneaux*

🍾 *Savigny-lès-Beaune, Les Vergelesses*

📅❗🍺

🚜 *22 ha; 100,000 bottles*

[map p. 45]

The Bize family arrived in Savigny in the middle of the nineteenth century. Simon Bize worked at other domains, and little by little built up his own domain. His son took over after the first world war; and his wife (known as Grandma Bize) was a dominant influence. Estate bottling started in 1926, but complete estate bottling only happened a generation later. Patrick Bize started in 1978, and took over in 1988; he expanded the domain with additional vineyards, and built a new cuverie. Under his leadership—sadly he died in 2013—the domain became a reference for Savigny.

You enter in a charming courtyard that appears almost residential, but behind is a huge warehouse facility with an extensive barrel room underneath. Vineyards are mostly in Savigny-lès-Beaune, where there are six premier crus in red and one in white. There's also a little Corton and Corton Charlemagne, and Latricières Chambertin. Overall production is 70% red.

Reds are vinified as whole clusters in large wooden vats (there is some destemming in some years), fermentation is relatively warm, élevage lasts about a year, but there is no new wood. Whites are pressed, go into stainless steel to settle, and then into barriques to ferment. Although vinification is traditional, the style of the reds is modern, almost slick, with a crowd-pleasing suppleness, and never any evident tannins; even lesser vintages leave an opulent impression. I find the reds more successful than the whites.

Domaine Jean-Marc Blain Gagnard   *

○ *15 Route de Santenay, 21190 Chassagne Montrachet*

☏ *+33 03 80 21 34 07*

Jean-Marc Blain

@ *domaine-blain-gagnard@wanadoo.fr*

Chassagne Montrachet

Chassagne Montrachet, Morgeot

Chassagne Montrachet

8 ha; 72,000 bottles [map p. 47]

Jean-Marc Blain is proud of the genealogy of his family, with several domains that have descended from the old domain of Delagrange-Bachelet. Jean-Marc married Claudine Gagnard, youngest daughter of the Gagnards of Domaine Gagnard Delagrange (see mini-profile), and they created their domain in 1980 with vineyards from Claudine's family. Their son Marc-Antonin is now involved, makes the wine at Gagnard Delagrange, makes wine under his own name from some small family plots, and also founded a domain in 2014 in Beaujolais together with his sister, Blain Soeur et Frère.

Blain-Gagnard is located in the old cellars of Delagrange-Bachelet. "We are a typical family domain with holdings broken up into about 40 plots, in 15 different appellations," Jean-Marc says. Production is 60% white (9 cuvées) and 40% red (6 cuvées). "Our style is traditional, producing vins de garde. Our wines need 5-6 years, they have purity and good tension, although they are getting richer because of global warming." Actually, I think Jean-Marc underrates the appeal of his wines when they are young.

White Chassagne Montrachet is just over half of production. Coming from 6 plots all around the village, it includes 30% of grapes from premier crus. "It's a representation of all Chassagne," Jean-Marc says. It's fresh and fruity, with a textured palate showing stone fruits with a touch of citrus that characterizes the house style. Puligny comes from a single plot (in lieu-dit Rue aux Vaches) and shows greater tension and purity. In Chassagne premier crus, Clos St. Jean from calcareous terroir is deeper but more delicate, Boudriotte (within Morgeot) is more upright but covered by a smooth sheen, and Morgeot itself shows more powerful stone fruits with a phenolic texture. Caillerets is more subtle and complete, with a mix of tension and granularity. The tiny production of Criots Bâtard Montrachet is finer and tighter yet, while Bâtard Montrachet is broader and richer, but more restrained at first. All whites spend 11 months in barriques, with the same 15% new oak for village wine and premier crus, but 30% for grand crus. Reds age for 15-18 months in oak.

In reds, the village Chassagne shows typical lightness. Clos St. Jean—"always the lightest and most delicate, this is the Volnay of Chassagne"—has a sense of precision. Morgeots is deeper—"this is a vin de garde par excellence"—and has a sense of power. Volnay Pitures is tighter and purer, Volnay Champans has more lifted aromatics approaches a crystalline purity.

Domaine Jean-Marc Boillot ★★

La Pommardière, Route d'Autun, 21630 Pommard

+33 03 80 22 71 29

Lydie Alzingre

pommardiere@wanadoo.fr

www.jeanmarc-boillot.com

Pommard

Puligny Montrachet

14 ha; 250,000 bottles
[map p. 46]

This domain started with a family division. Jean-Marc Boillot had made 13 vintages at the family domain, when he left in 1984 after a disagreement with his father, Jean Boillot, because he was unable to make the sort of wines he wanted. After four years as winemaker at Olivier Leflaive, while also making his own wine from a couple of rented hectares, he became independent.

He now has half the vineyards from his paternal grandfather, Henri Boillot, plus some vineyards from his maternal grandfather, who was Etienne Sauzet. The domain is run from his grandfather's house in Pommard. Holdings are split more or less equally between Puligny Montrachet (including four premier crus and some Bâtard Montrachet) and reds from Pommard, Beaune, and Volnay. The style is undeniably rich and powerful (and interestingly has been so successful that the family domain, now called Henri Boillot after Jean-Marc's brother, subsequently moved in the same direction). Whites see 25-30% new oak, reds get 50% new oak.

For me, the style comes off better in whites than reds, where sheer power can overwhelm the delicacy of an appellation such as Volnay. The Pulignys tend to be powerful rather than mineral. Whether red or white, this is very much a domain in the modern idiom. In 1998 Jean-Marc extended his activities into the Languedoc, where he produces IGP d'Oc wines under the labels of Domaine de la Truffière and Les Roques.

Domaine Bonneau du Martray ***

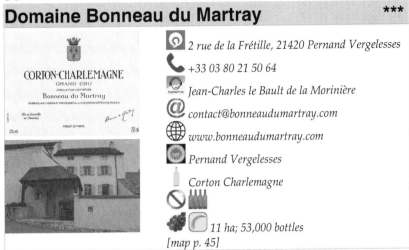

CORTON-CHARLEMAGNE
GRAND CRU
APPELLATION CONTROLÉE
Bonneau du Martray

2 rue de la Frétille, 21420 Pernand Vergelesses

+33 03 80 21 50 64

Jean-Charles le Bault de la Morinière

contact@bonneaudumartray.com

www.bonneaudumartray.com

Pernand Vergelesses

Corton Charlemagne

11 ha; 53,000 bottles

[map p. 45]

The most aristocratic domain in Corton, Bonneau du Martray has a single block of 11 ha between Pernand and Aloxe Corton. The domain has no other vineyards, and makes just two wines. The winery is located in the center of Pernand-Vergelesses, where its buildings have been renovated and there is a stylish tasting room underneath. Jean-Charles le Bault de Morinière abandoned his architectural practice in Paris to take over Bonneau du Martray only in 1993, although he was present for all vintages after 1969.

"You can find Corton Charlemagne producers all around the hill and this produces big differences in the wines according to exposition, slope, style of producer," he says, "We have all the variations between Pernand and Aloxe." The single cuvée of Corton Charlemagne is an assemblage from 90% of the estate; the rest is a red Corton coming from four blocks. Jean-Charles is an enthusiast for biodynamics. "The texture is different, it sits on the mid palate, there is a more mineral style, more clarity, purity, volume." The Corton Charlemagne is barrel fermented, spends 12 months in élevage with about a third new oak, and is transferred to stainless steel with all the fine lees for 6 months. "My wines show well in the year after bottling, then they shut down. In the past they used to shut down so much you could not see anything. They still shut down but since 2005 they have been more approachable and understandable, they never become invisible. They open up after 3-4 years," he says.

Given the history of the domain in one family for two hundred years, it created a shockwave when it was announced in 2016 that the domain was being sold to American businessman Stanley Kroenke, owner of Screaming Eagle in Napa Valley; apparently there was no family member interested in continuing the succession. There will be a little less wine in the future, as 3 ha were then leased to DRC, because the domain was felt to be too large to handle in continuing its biodynamic principles.

Domaine Bouchard Père et Fils

15 Rue du Château, 21200 Beaune

+33 03 80 24 80 24

contact@bouchard-pereetfils.com

www.bouchard-pereetfils.com

Beaune

Beaune, Grèves Vigne de l'Enfant Jésus

Beaune, Clos St. Landry

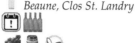

132 ha; 3,000,000 bottles [map p. 45]

"It was magic when Joseph Henriot bought us," says Philippe Prost, wine-maker at Bouchard from 1992 to 2012. "The purchase was the first week of July 1995, and one week later Joseph turned up and said, 'Philippe, I've bought you some grand crus, Bonnes Mares, Echézeaux, and Clos Vougeot'." Bouchard has been expanding ever since, starting with the purchase of Ropiteau Mignon in 1998, which brought 32 ha in Meursault, including many premier crus. It is now one of the largest negociant-growers, with vineyards all over the Côte d'Or.

Dating from 1731, this is one of the oldest estates in Burgundy. (Another member of the family founded Bouchard Aîné in 1750; it is a separate producer now owned by Jean-Charles Boisset.) The Bouchard family remained in control for more than two centuries, but at the end of the period, the wines were distinctly under performing. After the sale to Henriot Champagne, it was revived by new investment, including the construction in 2005 of a new gravity flow winery just north of the city.

The domain is housed in the Château de Beaune, a fifteenth century fortress within the walls of the old city of Beaune (with very impressive cellars underneath). Bouchard is the largest owner of premier and grand crus on the Côte d'Or, and these total two thirds of the estate holdings. Estate grapes account for a third of production overall.

Among the best-known wines are some of the premier cru vineyards in Beaune, the Clos St. Landry (a monopole which produces one of the rare whites from Beaune), and Vigne de l'Enfant Jésus (from the center of the Grèves premier cru, a red with more power than usually found in Beaune). Whether due to the new cellar—"with gravity-feed you don't get the bitterness that can come from pumping," says Philippe—or other changes, the reds have become much finer: Beaune Grèves is firm, Volnay Caillerets has the crystalline purity of the appellation, Le Corton is deep and earthy but delicate, but all have a hallmark silkiness on the palate. The whites also show a very fine texture, sometimes inclining to a saline minerality. Meursault Genevrières is the standout among premier crus. There is never more than a subtle touch of oak. "The maximum is 15% new oak for whites because we want to be discrete," Philippe says. Reds are mostly 35%, and up to 45%.

Domaine Michel Bouzereau et Fils ★★

🔾 5 Rue Robert Thénard, 21190 Meursault

📞 +33 03 80 21 20 74

📇 Jean-Baptiste Bouzereau

@ michel-bouzereau-et-fils@wanadoo.fr

🌐 www.michelbouzereautfils.com

⊙ Meursault

Meursault, Les Tessons

📅 ⛴

🍇 ⚒ 12 ha; 65,000 bottles

[map p. 46]

French inheritance laws explain why there are so many Bouzereau domains in Meursault. "Bouzereau has been important in Meursault for seven generations, although it's only four generations we've been concerned exclusively with viticulture. In my grandfather's time we had four domains, now we have five domains with the name Bouzereau. I have my grandfather's domain, but the vines have been shared at each generation, of course, so we have all the appellations," says Jean-Baptiste Bouzereau.

Domaine Michel Bouzereau has 14 appellations, 11 in white and 4 in red. A splendid modern underground cave was constructed in 2008. Jean-Baptiste says, "I look for elegance and finesse, and to harvest mature but not too mature to keep freshness." There is 15-30% new wood, with higher levels used for premier crus. The whites are Meursault and Puligny, the reds are Volnay, Pommard, and Bourgogne. The three lieu-dits from Meursault show a range from the breadth of Tessons to the tension of Limousin (which is just next to Puligny). The three Meursault premier crus show greater breadth, with complexity increasing from Charmes and Genevrières to Perrières, the last two along the lines of what a Meursault grand cru might offer if one existed. The Puligny premier crus, Champs Gain and Caillerets, are more tightly wound. What you see here across the whole range is how purity of the fruits highlights the characters of the individual terroirs.

Domaine Henri et Gilles Buisson   *

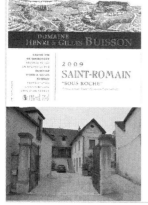

📍 *Impasse Du Clou, 21190 Saint-Romain*

📞 *+33 03 80 21 22 22*

Franck Buisson

@ *contact@domaine-buisson.com*

🌐 *www.domaine-buisson.com*

Saint-Romain

St. Romain, Le Jarron

20 ha; 85,000 bottles

The Buissons have been making wine in Saint Romain for eight generations, but the domain was established when Henri Buisson decided to start bottling his own wines in 1947 instead of selling them to the negociants. The domain continued under his son Gilles, and now is run by two grandsons, winemaker Frédéric and marketing manager Franck. The winery is in the heart of the village, nestled under the rocky hills that surround Saint-Romain. "We've been here for generations, and we've expanded by buying the neighbors," explains Franck as he points to several surrounding buildings that are now part of the domain. This is the most important, and one of the best, domains in the appellation, with its 11 ha in Saint-Romain making up over 10% of the small AOP.

The first estate vineyards were in Saint Romain, where there are cuvées from separate lieu-dits. "We thought of doing an assemblage for a village Saint-Romain," says Franck, "but we prefer to use some grapes in the blend to make a good Bourgogne rather than to make a weak Saint-Romain." Saint Romain is a little over half of production overall, and each of the three cuvées in Saint Romain (one red and two white) carries the name of a lieu-dit. Vineyards elsewhere in the Côte de Beaune include Meursault and Corton, and some Bourgogne near Saint-Romain.

Production is two thirds red to one third white. All wines spend about a year in barrique, depending on vintage. New oak ranges from 20% for Saint Romain to 60% for Corton. The style is clean and pure, and tends to elegance, sleek for the reds, linear and precise for the whites. The Saint-Romain red Sous Roche shows a light, nutty character, a little reminiscent of Chassagne Montrachet. Corton-Renardes is sleek and elegant. In whites, Saint-Romain Perrières comes from a partly north-facing plot with thin soils, and shows a linear style of yellow fruits, more saline than mineral. Sous Château comes from the other side of the hill, on soils with more clay facing full south, and is more textured with a broader palate, but still reflecting the purity of house style.

The focus has been on organic viticulture since the 1970s; the extreme manifestation is the production of the Absolu cuvées, one red and one white, from Saint Romain, which have no added sulfur. The crisp, sleek style is accentuated in the Absolu cuvées.

Domaine François Carillon *

⚲ *2-4 Place de l'Église, 21190 Puligny-Montrachet*

📞 *+33 03 80 21 00 80*

👤 *François Carillon*

@ *contact@francoiscarillon.fr*

🌐 *www.francoiscarillon.com*

▣ *Puligny Montrachet*

▣ ✎

🍇 🕐 *16 ha; 220,000 bottles [map p. 47]*

When the Louis Carillon domain was split between brothers François and Jacques in 2010 after 24 years of partnership, Jacques stayed in the old cellars but changed the domain name to Jacques Carillon (see profile), while François set up his own domain just across the street. He created his own marque but the barriques are stamped with Carillon 1611 to show his pride in the family history of winemaking. The Louis Carillon domain became famous for its white wine, but actually started growing Chardonnay only in 1960.

Vineyards are mostly in Puligny Montrachet (some coming from Louis Carillon but augmented by purchases to increase the size of the domain from its initial 5 ha), with some small plots in Chassagne and Saint Aubin, but the only holding larger than a hectare is the village Puligny. There are 19 white cuvées from estate vineyards, and some grapes are purchased for the three red cuvées.

"We look for purity of style and elegance, we want wines that go with food," says Maître de Chai, Thomas Pascal. "We respect each vintage, there is no chemical transformation. We use five different tonneliers to get a light touch in the wood, we don't want the signal of the oak in the wine."

The style is relatively understated, starting with the Bourgogne, which comes from vines just outside the Puligny appellation; with 12% new oak it makes a fresh citric impression. St. Aubin, even at premier cru level, seems a bit angular by comparison. The Puligny village wine has more sense of minerality, but still staying in a fresh mineral direction. Premier cru Champs Gains makes a more subtle, elegant impression, with some stone fruits showing on the palate. Folatières makes a richer impression and becomes more savory. Combettes is the first in the line really to show any direct impression of new oak, with greater breadth on the palate. "Combettes gives us all by itself what we search for, elegance and power," Thomas says. Perrières, which has the maximum new oak of the house at 25%, is the only cuvée that really seems to need much time to be ready after release.

All the wines spend 11 months in barriques, followed by a few months in cuve to maintain freshness, before they are bottled. There is some experimentation with oak here, including smaller and larger barrels, and a vertical cask resembling an egg with the top cut off. The objective is to mature the wines without undue external influence.

Domaine Jacques Carillon

*

1 Impasse Drouhin, 21190 Puligny-Montrachet

+33 03 80 21 01 30

Carillon Jacques

carillon.jacques@free.fr

www.jacques-carillon.com

Puligny Montrachet

5 ha; 30,000 bottles

[map p. 47]

"I worked with my father and brother until 2010 when we split the domain. We haven't changed anything in the style because I made the wines at Louis Carillon and I haven't changed," says Jacques Carillon. I remember the old Louis Carillon domain as a reliable source of white Burgundy, perhaps rarely scaling the heights but always offering well-made reflections of the vintage. The domain took its modern form with Louis's father, then his sons came into the domain in the eighties, Jacques to make the wine and François to manage the vineyards. After 24 years, the domain was split between Jacques and François, each of whom now has their own domain. Continuing the tradition of the Louis Carillon domain, Jacques remains in the old cellars, although the name on the label has changed to Jacques Carillon.

Jacques has stayed with the vineyards inherited from Louis Carillon, mostly in Puligny, plus some Chassagne village. All are white, except for the St. Aubin Pitangerets, presently red, but likely to be replaced with Chardonnay when the vineyard comes up for replanting. "My grandfather and father planted red in St. Aubin when it was impossible to sell the whites," Jacques says.

Wine ages in barriques for a year with minimal battonage and racking, before aging in a further six months in vats before bottling. "We use little new oak, 15% for village wines and 20% for premier crus. We don't want the aromas of oak in the wine," Jacques says. Bienvenues Bâtard Montrachet is an exception that comes from such a small plot (0.12 ha) that there are usually only a couple of barriques (one is new).

The Puligny village wine is attractive and fruity; "it's an assemblage of 7 lieu-dits from all around, so it's really representative of the appellation," Jacques says. The Chassagne is softer and broader. In Puligny premier crus, Champs Canet moves in a slightly nuttier direction, perhaps reflecting its location on the border with Meursault. Perrières sees the first signs of minerality, flavorful and moving in a more savory direction. "It's always rich and broad, and it could end short, but the acidity gives it length," Jacques says. Les Referts shows more sense of tension, not as rich as Perrières, but more mineral, and perhaps the most typical of Puligny. Bienvenues Bâtard shows that unique Grand Cru combination of power and tension. The style is understated, but relatively broad.

Domaine Jean-François Coche Dury   ★★★★

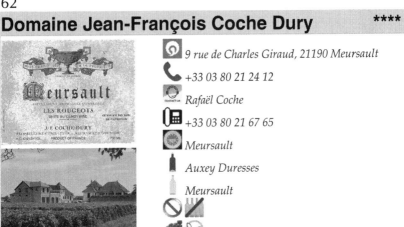

🔵 *9 rue de Charles Giraud, 21190 Meursault*

📞 *+33 03 80 21 24 12*

📧 *Rafaël Coche*

🖨 *+33 03 80 21 67 65*

🔴 *Meursault*

🍾 *Auxey Duresses*

🍾 *Meursault*

🚫 ⚒

🍇 ⏱ *10 ha; 45,000 bottles*

[map p. 46]

One of the great names of white Burgundy, Coche Dury is difficult to taste in depth, partly because quantities are so small, partly because Jean-François Coche verged on reclusive. Jean-François retired officially in 2010, with his son Raphaël taking over. This remains a hands-on operation; Raphaël turned up for our tasting direct from the vineyards. The house on the road through Meursault is surrounded by vines; you can see the church a couple of hundred yards away. Round the back is a second building that has just been extended.

Raphaël is the fourth generation. "My great grandfather worked at a domain in Meursault and started to make his own wines after returning from the 1914 war. He continued to have a day job and accumulated vineyards. When my father (Jean-François) started in the 1970s, there were many good opportunities to buy vineyards and he expanded the domain—today this would not be possible because vineyards are so expensive. Jean-François started by setting up his own domain, but when my grandfather retired in 1985, his vineyards came to Jean-François." This was when the domain was named Coche-Dury. Vineyards come from the old Coche family holdings plus those brought by Jean-François's marriage to Odile Dury in 1975. About half are in Meursault, with the rest spread around Puligny Montrachet, Auxey-Duresses, Monthelie, and Volnay. Appellation Meursault is the largest holding at just over 4 ha.

The style has not changed since Raphaël took over. "Élevage is always for 18 months; we are not going to change it. After the first winter, the wine is soft, then it takes on the permanent character. The whites are structured, with tannins if you like." 25% new oak is more or less the same for all the village wines, premier cru, and grand cru. There is very little battonage. The style here is steely and intensely mineral, right through the range. Going past the smoke and gunflint, the layered palate offers the richness of the Côte d'Or, with precisely delineated fruits, and evident but beautifully integrated oak. The modest alcohol level contributes to elegance.

The village Meursault shows the style to powerful effect, and it intensifies in the Meursault lieu-dit Chevalier (if you can find it). (Chevalier and Rougeots are the only two lieu-dits identified as such on the label: other lieu-dits within Meursault may be bottled separately, but just labeled as Meursault.) The difference between Meursault and Puligny is clear from the Enseignères lieu-dit from Puligny, which is more linear and precise. By contrast, the Caillerets premier cru from Meursault has more breadth but less precision. Genevrières is more backward and structured. "It always has that tannic impression," Raphaël says. The most powerful of the premier crus, always needing more time, Perrières shows the most penetrating minerality. Corton Charlemagne has the greatest concentration and roundness; "it's the softness of Charlemagne," Raphaël says.

As good as it gets for white Burgundy, Coche Dury whites are always expensive. Under the negociant label of Domaine & Selection, there is a Meursault from the Vireuls lieu-dit produced by Coche Dury, at slightly more reasonable prices. When is the right time to drink the whites? "The minimum is after five years but they are formidable after ten years. For Corton Charlemagne they will be even better at fifteen years," Raphaël says. For the reds everything is destemmed. The Bourgogne Rouge comes from two parcels close to the house, the Auxey Duresses is charming, and the Meursault is more reserved.

Domaine Bruno Colin

3 Impasse des Crets, 21190 Chassagne Montrachet

+33 03 80 24 75 61

Bruno Colin

contact@domainebrunocolin.com

www.domaine-bruno-colin.com

Chassagne Montrachet

Chassagne Montrachet

9 ha; 90,000 bottles [map p. 47]

Colin-Deléger was one of the most reliable estates of Chassagne Montrachet (see mini-profile), where Bruno worked with his father Michel from 1993 until the domain was divided between Bruno and his brother Philippe when Michel Colin retired in 2003. Philippe's wines are well thought of, but haven't achieved as high a reputation as Bruno's: see mini-profile.) Sources are supplemented by purchasing some grapes.

Located in the old buildings of the original premises in the heart of the village, Bruno focuses on Chassagne Montrachet, including 8 premier crus, plus 2 Puligny premier crus and some St. Aubin. The 15 white cuvées make up 60% of production. There are 6 red cuvées, including the only one of the 30 estate parcels to be larger than a hectare (in Chassagne). Premier crus account for 14 of the 21 cuvées.

When Bruno was involved in making the wines at Colin-Deléger, the style was never to excess; the wines were always solid representations of their appellations, but Bruno's style seems to have become more elegant now. Bourgogne Chardonnay, which comes from around Chassagne, predicts the house style, inclined to citrus fruits but relatively soft. Chassagne village is a little more textured, broader on the palate, and a fraction nutty. In premier crus, Chaumées jumps in style to show a strong minerality. "It always makes a more woody impression," says Antoine Laisney at the domain. Morgeots has a more understated style, with a more subtle impression of minerality. Its sense of finesse extends to Maltroye, which is less mineral, and softer and delicate.

Moving away from the center of Chassagne towards the grand crus, en Remilly is more linear, setting a saline minerality against a citrus palate. The sense of linearity intensifies with Puligny Truffières, which is fin tight with gunflint minerality in the background. The peak is reached with Les Demoiselles (suspended until 2018 vintage because of replanting all 7 rows), and Chevalier Montrachet, which leans more towards Chassagne than Puligny, setting white flowers against a subtle, nutty, textured background.

Élevage for whites is 12 months in 350 liter barrels with 10-15% new oak. "We switched to larger barrels in 2015 because they are better for everything, we use barriques only when there isn't enough wine to fill a 350 liter barrel," Antoine says. Reds include Bourgogne Pinot Noir, the deeper Santenay Vieilles Vignes, fruiter Chassagne Vieilles Vignes, Maranges Fussières with more lifted aromatics, the earthy Santenay Gravières, and Chassagne Maltroye, which has the most grip and structure of all.

Domaine Marc Colin et Fils

**

GRANDS VINS **2008** DE BOURGOGNE

PRODUIT DE FRANCE

Santenay

LES CHAMPS CLAUDE

APPELLATION SANTENAY CONTRÔLÉE

MARC COLIN ET SES FILS

ÉLEVEURS À SAINT-AUBIN · CÔTE-D'OR · FRANCE

Gamay, 21190 Saint-Aubin

+33 03 80 21 30 43

Damien Colin

contact@marc-colin.com

www.marc-colin.com

Saint-Aubin

Saint-Aubin, en Remilly

17 ha; 130,000 bottles

[map p. 47]

Starting with 7-8 ha, Marc Colin began to make wine with his brother Jacques around 1970, and created the domain in 1979. Marc retired in 2008, and the domain is now run by his sons Damien and Joseph, and their sister Caroline. (The domain was larger until brother Pierre-Yves, who had been the wine-maker together with his father, took out his 6 ha share to run separately as Domaine Pierre-Yves Colin-Morey.)

Winemaking is centered in some old buildings in the main street of St. Aubin, and a bit farther along is a modern tasting room. The Colins own about half the vineyards, and the other half is rented. About 80% is Chardonnay, with the rest split between Aligoté and Pinot Noir. There are 12 different cuvées from St. Aubin, and also Chassagne and Puligny Montrachet. "As we look more and more for finesse, freshness, and minerality, we have reduced new oak and battonage," Damien says. "St. Aubin has 15% new oak, whereas eight years ago it was 30%. St Aubin is cooler so we always have freshness and minerality. Puligny is sometimes like St. Aubin but can be more floral. Chassagne is usually a bit fatter."

The house style is elegant and precise. The St. Aubins are unusually fine for the appellation, but the Puligny shows a touch more tension, and the Chassagne is indeed fatter. It would be good policy to drink St. Aubin and the Chassagne lieu-dit first, while waiting for the Puligny and Chassagne premier crus to come around.

Domaine Pierre-Yves Colin-Morey ★★

4, rue de la Murée, 21190 Chassagne Montrachet

+33 03 80 21 90 10

Pierre-Yves Colin-Morey

contact@pierreyvescolinmorey.fr

Chassagne Montrachet

Saint Aubin, Le Chatenière

7 ha; 85,000 bottles

[map p. 47]

While he was making wine with his father at the family domain of Marc Colin, Pierre-Yves started the Colin-Morey negociant in 2001 with his wife Caroline (formerly Morey). Then in 2005 the family domain was divided and he started to make wine from his 6 ha share. All the wines go under the label of Colin-Morey. The domain vineyards are mostly in St. Aubin, with some in Chassagne Montrachet, but the negociant wines (which amount to about a third of all production) extend over all the white wine appellations of the Côte du Beaune. In 2014, Caroline inherited 7 ha in Chassagne Montrachet and Santenay, and makes wine from them under the separate label of Caroline Morey.

Pierre-Yves is simply fascinated by white wine. The St. Aubins are fine examples of the appellation as his vineyards are all on the slopes; there's a gradation in interest going from the lieu-dits Pucelle to the Perrières or en Remilly premier crus, which are very good value. The lieu-dit Les Ancegnières from domain vineyards in Chassagne Montrachet performs above appellation level. The Champs Gains premier cru in Chassagne is always excellent.

Grapes are pressed as whole bunches, wines are matured mostly in 350 liter barrels rather than the usual 228 Burgundy barriques, and the wines stay on their lees without battonage for a year. There's about 30% new oak on average, but it can be evident when the wines are young, and it's best to give it time to resolve. The style has become increasingly mineral in recent years, with an increase in minerality going from St. Aubin (where the top premier crus are close in style to Chassagne), to Chassagne Montrachet (a touch softer and more textured than Puligny) to Puligny Montrachet (the most intense). Pierre-Yves is generally considered to be one of today's rising stars.

Domaine Comte Armand ***

Place De L'Église, 21630 Pommard

+33 03 80 24 70 50

Paul Zinetti

epeneaux@domaine-comte-armand.com

www.domaine-comte-armand.com

Pommard

Pommard, Clos des Epeneaux

10 ha; 40,000 bottles [map p. 46]

One of the key domains in Pommard, Comte Armand carries as a subtitle, Le Domaine des Epeneaux, reflecting its holding of the monopole of Clos des Epeneaux, one of the best premier crus in Pommard. The same family has owned the domain since before the Revolution; the present Comte Armand is a lawyer in Paris.

The domain was devoted exclusively to Pommard until it expanded in 1994 by purchasing vineyards in Volnay and Auxey-Duresses. The wines increased in elegance under winemaker Benjamin Leroux, who took over winemaking in 1999 (when he was 23), and stayed until 2014, when he left to make his own wine as a micro-negociant. Paul Zinetti took over, but says, "The only thing that changed is me, we want continuity."

The top wine here is always the Clos des Epeneaux, which expresses the generosity of Pommard. In fact, the wine is a blend: "The magic of the *clos* is that you can do an assemblage from four different areas," Paul says. The quarters are divided by location (upper versus lower) and age of vines (35- to 90-years). Each part is vinified separately, and assemblage occurs at the end of élevage. Typically all the lots go into the final blend, but occasionally one is declassified. Tasting barrel samples shows that each brings its own character: the youngest vines give wine that is tight and fresh, the plot of 55-year old vines in the lower part gives more aromatics, turning from red to black fruits, 65-70-year old vines on the calcareous terroir at the top give more aromatic lift with an impression of elegance as well as power, and this sample is perhaps the most complete in itself, while the oldest vines, from the lowest part, give less aromatics but more structure. Tasting the blend, assembled from samples half way through élevage in a beaker, shows that greater complexity, with black fruit aromatics balancing chocolaty tannins.

When lots are declassified, there may be a Pommard Premier Cru *tout court*, which shows a flatter profile than the Clos des Epeneaux. Outside Pommard, the Volnay is fine, and Volnay Fremiets is more elegant compared to the village wine. The red Auxey-Duresses is an unusual example of a wine from that appellation with real character along the lines of Pommard, but less elegant, with its concentration partly explained by the old age (35-60-years) of the vines. The Auxey-Duresses premier cru (a blend of two premier crus) is powerful and ripe. New oak varies from 10% for Auxey-Duresses to 25% for the Volnay and Pommard premier crus. The domain is at the top of its game.

Domaine Comte Senard *

1 rue des Chaumes, 21420 Aloxe-Corton

+33 03 80 26 41 65

Lorraine Senard-Pereira

office@domainesenard.com

www.domainesenard.com

Aloxe Corton

10 ha; 45,000 bottles

[map p. 45]

The domain was founded in 1857 with a couple of hectares, and is still in the hands of the founding family. Lorraine Senard Pereira, the fifth generation, took over from her father Philippe in 2005. The domain is still headquartered in Aloxe Corton, where it's right in the center of the village, opposite the church. Oriented towards oenotourism, there is a tasting room and shop, and a table d'hôte for lunch). It's a good place to go if you want to understand Corton and Aloxe Corton. The old cellars here date from the 13th or 14th century and are interesting to visit, although they are no longer used; wine has been made in a modern facility in Ladoix since 2012.

The vineyards have remained the same for generations, and are almost all in Aloxe-Corton and Corton (including six climats); most production is red. The domain is in fact in the center of grand cru Corton, and the Clos de Meix monopole, the flagship of the domain, runs right up to the cellars. Walking out to the vineyards, you see the elevation, with a view over the surrounding vineyards and countryside.

There are two interesting white cuvées. The Aloxe-Corton white is not Chardonnay but is Pinot Gris (called Pinot Beurot locally), coming from a plot of very old vines. (It's legal to produce Pinot Gris from existing vines, but not to replant it, so quantity is declining and is now down to 600 bottles per year.) A little spicy, it shows more exotic notes and aromatic lift than Chardonnay, and should be drunk within about six years after release. It's quite a transition to the white Corton, which comes from Chardonnay planted 25 years ago on a strip of limestone running through Clos de Meix, and is close to the mineral style of Corton Charlemagne. The whites have 50% new oak, but it's not obvious.

Reds go from the elegant mineral impression of the village Aloxe-Corton to the richer impression of premier cru Valozières (both have one third new oak), while the grand cru Corton shows more rounded fruits with greater depth and a glossy sheen from Clos du Roi, more sense of richness and completeness from Clos dui Meix, but both maintaining the elegance of the house style. Aged in 50-60% new oak, these are never over-extracted wines. A classic representation of Pinot Noir from the Côte de Beaune, they can be started soon after release, but age quite slowly.

Domaine de Courcel ***

🌐 *Rue Notre Dame, Pommard, 21630*

📞 *+33 03 80 22 10 64*

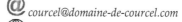
Yves Confuron

@ *courcel@domaine-de-courcel.com*

🌐 *www.domainedecourcel-pommard.fr*

Pommard

Pommard, Epenots

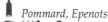 *11 ha; 30,000 bottles [map p. 46]*

"The wines are the equivalent on the Côte de Beaune of Domaine de la Romanée Conti on the Côte de Nuits," according to eminent French wine critics Bettane and Desseauve. The distinctive approach to winemaking was introduced by Yves Confuron, who has been the winemaker since 1996. "Yves developed a method—well his father was involved at the domain in Vosne Romanée—for carbonic maceration à la froide. We believe it is a wonderful method to extract everything from the grapes," explains Alain Bommelaer, whose wife Anne is one of four siblings who are the present owners of the estate. It has been in the hands of the Courcel family for 400 years. The domain has a splendid residence in the main square in Pommard, just across from the church; next to it is the winery, with old caves underground.

"The other thing Yves insisted on was to have extremely ripe grapes. People don't do this in general because we are always afraid here of the weather, and we need to harvest before it turns bad. We want to have extremely ripe grapes because is no destemming—well, just a little to get some juice to start with—and you can't do this unless the stems are ripe." Winemaking starts with cold maceration under carbon dioxide for a few days before fermentation is allowed to begin. After fermentation, maceration continues for three weeks under a blanket of carbon dioxide. The wine goes into casks after 4-5 weeks. The main difference between cuvées is the duration of maceration.

"Only old oak is used. We keep the stems, so we don't want any more tannins from the wood," Alain adds. "Most wine is drunk too young, we all know this, this is why we make a point of keeping back some bottles. One of the major mistakes in Burgundy in the late 1980s was to make wines immediately drinkable, supposedly good after three years. This is why we like our method of winemaking, we think it brings out the specificity of terroir."

The domain focuses on Pommard premier crus (although there is also a Bourgogne), and there is a view that some of them justify grand cru status in Courcel's hands. The same powerful style resonates from the Bourgogne, through the Pommard premier crus, to the Grand Clos des Epenots. Even the Bourgogne has a sense of tannic grip to the palate. Pommard Epeneaux, which comes from the oldest vines, planted in 1936, is aromatically complex, with an impression of rich black cherry fruits. Rugiens is a real vin de garde with less immediate fruits and greater sense of structure. Grand Clos des Epenots is not a wine for the fainthearted, with a powerful structure that takes time to resolve to allow flavor variety to show. These are wines for the ages.

Domaine Vincent Dancer **

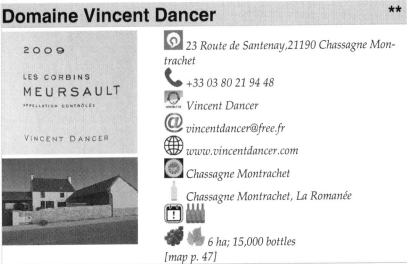

2009

LES CORBINS
MEURSAULT
APPELLATION CONTRÔLÉE

VINCENT DANCER

23 Route de Santenay,21190 Chassagne Montrachet

+33 03 80 21 94 48

Vincent Dancer

vincentdancer@free.fr

www.vincentdancer.com

Chassagne Montrachet

Chassagne Montrachet, La Romanée

6 ha; 15,000 bottles
[map p. 47]

Since the domain was founded in 1996 with vineyards inherited from Vincent's mother in Chassagne and his father in Puligny Montrachet, Vincent has built a reputation as a rising star; indeed, the wines are on their way to achieving cult status. Vincent grew up in Alsace, but after studying engineering went to Burgundy, where his family owned plots that were being rented out. He took them over and founded the domain, which continues with just the original parcels.

All holdings are very small, including lieu-dits and premier cru Les Perrières in Meursault, two parcels in Chassagne's top premier cru, Morgeots (La Romanée and Tête du Clos), and a plot in Chevalier Montrachet so small as to make only one barrel. Vincent is reserved to the point at which detailed information is hard to come by, but he's proud of being the first producer in Chassagne to become organic, and he practices a minimalist approach with no battonage, fining, or filtration. New oak is about 25% for the village wines, 50% for the premier crus, and is 100% for the single barrique of Chevalier Montrachet.

The great reputation here is for the whites, where the new wave style is poised between minerality and opulence; going from the lieu-dits in Meursault to the premier cru in Chassagne, the balance shifts towards greater texture and more intensity. There are also reds from Chassagne (from Morgeots, no less), and from Pommard and Bourgogne. The domain is difficult to visit.

Maison Joseph Drouhin ★★

○ 7, Rue d'Enfer, 21200 Beaune

📞 +33 03 80 24 68 88

Frédéric Drouhin

@ maisondrouhin@drouhin.com

⊕ www.drouhin.com

Beaune

Beaune, Clos des Mouches

Chassagne Montrachet, Marquis de Laguiche

73 ha; 3,600,000 bottles

[map p. 45]

Joseph Drouhin started as a negociant in Beaune in 1880. When his son Maurice took over in 1918, he began the move to becoming a negociant-grower by buying vineyards in Beaune's Clos des Mouches and in Clos Vougeot. Today one of the larger negociant-growers, and one of the few still in the old city of Beaune, Drouhin remains located in its old cellars, some dating back to the twelfth or thirteenth centuries. The firm is presently run by four siblings of the fourth generation. Drouhin has also invested in Oregon, where it produces both Pinot Noir and Chardonnay in Willamette Valley. Winemaker Véronique Drouhin oversees the harvest in Beaune and then flies to Oregon to make wine there.

The range in Burgundy extends from the entry-level Laforêt Bourgogne (both red and white) to the top Grand Crus of both Côte de Beaune and Côte de Nuits. Wines come from around 90 appellations, all across the Côte d'Or, and stretching to Chablis and to Beaujolais. Vinification is traditional, with partial destemming (decreased since 2005), fermentation in open-topped containers, and pump-over or punch-down depending on conditions. Oak is handled lightly, almost always using less than 30% new wood. The Drouhin style is elegant, yet clearly devoted to bringing out the fruits. Clos des Mouches is always a textbook example of Beaune, for either red or white. Drouhin started producing Chassagne Montrachet from the core holding of the Marquis de Laguiche, based on a handshake; for years the wine was labeled only as Chassagne, but more recently has been labeled as premier cru Morgeot. Otherwise, the top whites are the Pulignys, and the top reds are the grand crus from Gevrey Chambertin.

Domaine Arnaud Ente ★★★

 *12, Rue De Mazeray, 21190 Meursault*

📞 *+33 03 80 21 66 12*

 Arnaud Ente

📠 *+33 03 80 21 66 12*

🌐 *Meursault*

🍾 *Meursault*

 *3 ha; 20,000 bottles*

[map p. 46]

Arnaud Ente is sometimes described as a rising star in Meursault, but as evidenced from the price of his wines, he is now solidly established with something of a cult following. Although there are vineyards in the family, they have been run by other members. Arnaud started working at Coche Dury, then in 1991 began producing wine from vineyards rented from his father in law. Individual vineyard holdings are tiny, with nothing as much as a hectare, and most well under half a hectare. This tiny domain is run by Arnaud, his wife Marie-Odile, and two workers.

Initially the wines were made in an opulent style from grapes picked quite late, but since 2000 a policy of earlier picking has focused more on bringing out minerality (and also results in moderate alcohol). Impressions of gunflint and salinity are reminiscent of Coche Dury, but the palate still has a more opulent sheen.

The affordable wines are Aligoté, Bourgogne Blanc, and Meursault, mostly vinified in demi-muids. The village Meursault comes mostly from the clos of En l'Ormeau, where production is divided into three cuvées: Meursault AOP, Clos des Ambres (old vines), and La Sève du Clos, from very old (around 100 year) vines. There is also some Meursault premier cru Goutte d'Or and a Puligny Les Referts, as well as a little Volnay premier cru. Oak is fairly restrained these days, down to 20% new barriques for the top cuvées compared with 35% in the early years, reflecting the change of focus.

Domaine Jean-Noël Gagnard *

⊚ 9, Place Des Noyers, 21190 Chassagne-Montrachet

📞 +33 03 80 21 31 68

☎ Caroline Lestime

@ contact@domaine-jean-noel-gagnard.com

🌐 domaine-gagnard.com

⚫ Chassagne Montrachet

🍾 Chassagne Montrachet, l'Estimée

🍾 Chassagne Montrachet, Les Masures

⊘ 〰🍇🍂 11 ha; 50,000 bottles [map p. 47]

Right in the center of Chassagne Montrachet, the family residence is on one side of the courtyard, and you go down to the old cellars underneath for the tasting. Jean-Noël had an accident in 2015 and hurt his leg, so he had to retire. His daughter, Caroline, is the winemaker, and her husband Hubert came to join her at the domain in 2016. Hubert also runs a shop (called Vignes et Verges) in the village where people can taste the Noël-Gagnard wines and other organic wines. "The shop is focused on everything organic," he says.

"The domain goes back several generations, before the Revolution. We are focused on Chassagne with three communal wines and six premier crus." Red wine is about 20% of production. "We don't want to do everything in white, it's more famous, but we want to keep the character of Burgundy." In addition to Chassagne, there are wines from Santenay and the Hautes Côtes de Beaune. The domain mostly rests on long-term holdings, with many of the vineyards acquired by Jean-Noël in the 1960s. Many of the plots are very small. The latest acquisition was in premier cru Les Chaumées: "it's only five rows but they are pretty long rows."

The style is light and elegant in the modern idiom, with a focus on freshness. "We use oak for sure, but not in excess, we should not even taste the oak, it is for the oxygenation, we use only 30% new oak on average, a little bit more for the grand cru, less for the Hautes Côtes or village wine. Battonage is quite limited, the more battonage the more richness there is, and that is not what we are looking for, we are looking for tension and elegance." The style of the whites is restrained, with a slight citrus or mineral edge to offset against the light impression of oak; the reds follow the house style of elegance.

There's increasing emphasis on expressing individual terroirs. Two Chassagne village wines come from different plots. "Les Masures is not very far from Les Chaumes but we find it much more complex." In premier crus, there are multiple cuvées from within Morgeot. "Jean-Noël mixed Boudriotte and Petit Clos to make a Morgeot, but Caroline decided to separate them to bring out the terroir. The idea is to go even farther in the process of separating the vineyards," Hubert explains.

Maison Alex Gambal   *

14, Boulevard Jules Ferry, 21200 Beaune

+33 03 80 22 75 81

Alex Gambal

info@alexgambal.com

www.alexgambal.com

Beaune

Beaune, Grèves

Saint-Aubin

4 ha; 60,000 bottles

[map p. 45]

There's an unexpectedly modern warehouse building behind the extended façade on the ring road around Beaune, although the cellars underneath date from 1800. The building was originally part of Bouchard Aîné, and then was sold off and became an art gallery; Alex Gambal bought it in 2003 and renovated the building to become a gravity-feed winery. An American who came to Beaune because of his interest in wine, and leaned the business by working with broker Becky Wassermann, Alex has been slowly making the transition from negociant to grower. "I started in the business in 1997 as a classic negociant buying semi finished wine, then the next year I started buying grapes. Then I started buying vineyards. We now have 4 ha which are just about a third of our production. I'm planning to add 8 ha which would triple the domain," Alex says.

There's a wide range of wines from Bourgogne to premier and grand crus from all over the Côte d'Or, with a little more white than red. Everything is destemmed, then fermentation with indigenous yeast is followed by élevage of up to 16 months. New oak is 10-15% for Bourgogne, 20-25% for village wines, a third for premier crus, and 50-100% for grand crus. "But the percentage of new oak is not so important as the barrels you are using, it's a matter of how the oak and toast interact with the juice," Alex says. Style tends to a light elegance rather than power, but always with a sense of underlying structure.

Alex sold the domain in 2019 to Jean-Claude Boisset (owner of Domaine de la Vougeraie and other estates), but it continues to run independently.

Domaine Henri Germain et fils   *

 4 Rue des Forges, 21190 Meursault

📞 +33 03 80 21 22 04

Jean-François Germain

@ domaine.h.germain-et-fils@orange.fr

Meursault

Chassagne Montrachet

Meursault, Limozin

🍇🕐 8 ha; 30,000 bottles

[map p. 46]

"The domain is very recent, started by my parents in 1973 with only 1.5 hectares," says Jean-François Germain. The official address takes you to a courtyard with the bureau on one side, and his parents' house on the other. The winery is 100 yards away, around a corner in the next street. Behind the ordinary looking garage doors is a long courtyard with some old buildings lining one side, and a vineyard at the end. There are very old caves underneath.

Production is three quarters white, with 13 separate cuvées, focusing on Meursault village, lieu-dits, and premier crus. "All whites get the same 20% new oak whether it's Bourgogne or premier cru, and there's no battonage," says Jean-François. The lack of battonage contributes to the impression of elegance in the house style. The Bourgogne comes from vineyards around Meursault and has an unusually fine impression for the level of appellation. The village wine moves in a more citrus direction with some hints of minerality. Coming from mid slope, the lieu-dit Chevalier is more inclined to minerality, and from the bottom of the slope, lieu-dit Limozin is fatter. The premier crus are more complex, moving from the silky elegance of Poruzot, to the more mineral character of Charmes, and the more powerful impression of Perrières. Moving to Chassagne, the Morgeot comes from a single parcel and is quite fat by comparison with Meursault.

The same policy of equal treatment applies to the reds, which get 18 months élevage. Usually everything is destemmed—only an unusually rich vintage will see some stems included. The style is relatively soft, increasing in intensity and roundness from the Bourgogne to the Chassagne to the Meursault lieu-dit Clos des Mouches. Beaune Bressandes is the finest of the reds.

Domaine Albert Grivault ***

7, Place Du Murger, 21190 Meursault

+33 03 80 21 23 12

Claire Bardet

albert.grivault@wanadoo.fr

Meursault

Meursault, Clos du Murger

6 ha; 35,000 bottles [map p. 46]

The domain occupies a lovely maison, graciously set back from the main street of Meursault. It feels like a residence in the town, but walking out of the back of the house into the courtyard behind, winery buildings are on either side, and the Clos du Murger is immediately behind. The caves date from 1865.

"The domain has the name of my grandfather," explains Michel Bardet. "He bought the Clos des Perrières, which was the most famous vineyard in Meursault at the time, just after phylloxera, and established a domain of 12 ha. Because of difficulties with estate taxes, my mother sold some of the estate to Alexis Lichine and to Bize-Leroy's father. Before I became involved, I was an engineer (at Honeywell Bull). Slowly I phased out as an engineer and came to run the domain together with my sister." Today the domain has the monopole of Clos des Perrières, part of Les Perrières ("we are the largest proprietor"), and a vineyard in the village. There is also a hectare of Clos Blanc in Pommard.

The white wines are Bourgogne, Meursault Clos du Murger, Perrières, and Clos des Perrières). "Clos du Murger is a marque. Because my mother left one part of the Clos du Murger unplanted for thirty years, it lost the right to the Meursault appellation." So today the village Meursault comes from the old vines planted in two thirds of the Clos du Murger, and the other third (planted in 2001) is used for the Bourgogne Blanc (but an application has been made to restore it to Meursault AOP). The two top wines of the domain are Perrières, which comes from the major part of the 1.7 ha holding—"We sell some Perrières to Leroy, and we had to use biodynamics for the parcel, it was very complicated"—and Clos des Perrières (just 1 ha). Clos des Perrières was replanted between 1986 and 1989. The only red is the Clos Blanc of Pommard.

The style is restrained, even austere at premier cru level in cool vintages. The Bourgogne has no new wood, there is a little for the Meursault, the premier crus have 20%. The Bourgogne has unusual elegance for the appellation level, the Meursault Clos du Murger is more stony, Perrières is fine and silky, and Clos des Perrières is more tightly coiled. "Meursault does not have a grand cru, but if it did it would be Perrières or certainly Clos des Perrières," Michel says. "Les Perrières has 50-year-old vines, but you see more intensity in Clos des Perrières. Someone who wants to drink the wine immediately will miss the point, Clos des Perrières doesn't reach its peak until 15 years." Indeed, Clos des Perrières may be one of the most ageworthy whites in Burgundy; the 1985 was still vibrant and lively in 2017.

Maison Louis Jadot

**

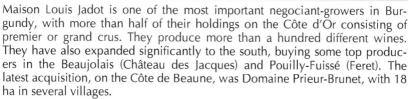

21, Rue Eugène Spuller, 21200 Beaune

+33 03 80 22 10 57

Pierre Henry Gagey

contact@louisjadot.com

www.louisjadot.com

Beaune

Chambolle Musigny, Les Baudes

Puligny Montrachet, Clos de la Garenne

140 ha; 10,000,000 bottles

[map p. 45]

Maison Louis Jadot is one of the most important negociant-growers in Burgundy, with more than half of their holdings on the Côte d'Or consisting of premier or grand crus. They produce more than a hundred different wines. They have also expanded significantly to the south, buying some top producers in the Beaujolais (Château des Jacques) and Pouilly-Fuissé (Feret). The latest acquisition, on the Côte de Beaune, was Domaine Prieur-Brunet, with 18 ha in several villages.

The firm originated as a negociant in 1859, and was run by the Jadot family until it was purchased by their American importer, Kobrand, in 1985. The old cuverie in the center of Beaune was replaced in 1995 by a modern building on the outskirts, which was expanded further in 2010.

Most (60%) of Jadot's production in the Côte d'Or is from estate vineyards; the rest is purchased as grapes from more than 200 growers (on rare occasions they buy finished wine; sometimes they will exchange wine with a grower in order to get a barrel of a specific appellation.) Jacques Lardière was in charge of Jadot's winemaking since 1970 and believes in minimal intervention. "The impression that you can determine quality by controlling winemaking is crazy, you need to have the confidence to work with Nature and allow the terroir to express itself. It is man who makes the mistakes," he says. One of Burgundy's major figures, Jacques retired in 2012, and is now making the wines at Jadot's latest venture, the Resonance Vineyard in Oregon.

Domaine Antoine Jobard ★★

 2, Rue De Leignon, 21190 Meursault

 +33 03 80 21 21 26

 Antoine Jobard

@ *antoine.jobard@orange.fr*

 Meursault

Meursault, en la Barre

 6.5 ha; 40,000 bottles
[map p. 46]

The Jobards go back five generations in Meursault, but the two Jobard domains of today date from the division of the Pierre Jobard domain in 1971 between two brothers. One half was first known as Domaine François Jobard. When François's son Antoine joined in 2002, the name was changed to François and Antoine Jobard, and then in 2007 it was changed to Antoine Jobard when François nominally retired. François was famous for his reserve; Antoine is more forthcoming.

The domain is adjacent to the lieu-dit En La Barre (which can be relied upon to outperform the village level). The domain is exclusively white wine, and all Meursault except for one very small parcel in Puligny Montrachet. The cuvées in Meursault include two lieu-dits, and four premier crus. (There was some red in Blagny, but it's been replaced with Chardonnay.) Under François, the reputation of the domain was for bucking the trend to big, buttery Meursaults and producing a taut, mineral style. Fashion has now caught up, so the Jobard Meursaults are more in the mainstream.

Élevage is long (18-24 months), but uses little new oak, "maximum 20%," says Antoine. There is little battonage. "We make wines that are more reserved," is Antoine's description. The minerality of the style gives an impression moving in the direction of Puligny, yet there is a glossy sheen to the palate, with a sense of richness at the end. I especially like en la Barre for its balance of minerality and opulence; the premier crus are more opulent.

Domaine Rémi Jobard ★★

2009
Meursault 1er Cru
les Genevrières
APPELLATION CONTROLEE

⊙ *12, Rue Sudot, 21190 Meursault*

📞 *+33 03 80 21 20 23*

Rémi Jobard

@ *contact@domaineremijobard.fr*

Meursault

Meursault, Les Narvaux

9 ha; 40,000 bottles
[map p. 46]

The domain started with Charles, when he inherited half of the Pierre Jobard domain in 1971, and has been less well known than the domain of his brother François. The domain became Charles & Rémi Jobard when Charles's son Rémi joined in 1991, and has now become simply Rémi Jobard. Rémi has been making the wine since 1993, although Charles still drops in, and the wines have become increasingly elegant.

The main focus of the domain (and its reputation) rests with the estate vineyards in Meursault, where nine separate parcels include three premier crus, but production has been expanded by a small negociant business, and there is also red wine from Monthélie and Volnay. New presses have been installed to allow slower and gentler pressing. Fermentation is unusually slow: "We have a special system in which it's done outside, so the cold weather blocks its progress in October-November," Rémi explains.

Rémi minimizes oak influence by using barrels made in Austria with oak from Austria, Germany, and France. All wines age in a mix of large or small foudres and barriques. Élevage lasts a year in oak, followed by six months in cuve. New oak is 15% for Bourgogne Blanc, 20% for premier cru whites, and 25% for the two reds. "I like wine with lots of purity and energy," Rémi says. "Everything ages in wood, but I look for oak that does not give classic aromas like toast, I want the oak to bring out the natural aromas of the wine."

The Bourgogne Côte d'Or Blanc is something of a baby Meursault, showing purity of lines with fruits veering towards citrus. There are four cuvées from different lieu-dits in Meursault. "They are bottled individually because I've tried assemblage but I prefer the separate cuvées." The style is modern, meaning clean and pure. Sous La Velle is less overt than the Bourgogne, but has more of a sheen to the palate, Luraule (a little-known lieu-dit next to premier cru Gouttes d'Or) is rounder and more powerful, Les Narvaux is smoother and more upright, and Chevalières is the best of the lieu-dits, with more sense of restraint and minerality. In premier crus, Poruzot Dessous makes a broader impression, Charmes moves more towards minerality, and 60-year old vines make Genevrières more structured and reserved. The style is modern, in the direction of an opulent glycerinic sheen rather than the old butter and nuts, and the mineral edge of the New Meursault shows increasingly underneath going up the hierarchy.

Domaine Michel Lafarge
*

Rue de La Combe, 21190 Volnay

+33 03 80 21 61 61

Frédéric Lafarge

contact@domainelafarge.com

www.domainelafarge.fr

Volnay

Volnay, Vendanges Sélectionnées

Beaune, Les Aigrots

12 ha; 55,000 bottles
[map p. 46]

This is one of the most distinctive domains in Volnay. The Lafarge's have been making wine since the nineteenth century, and started estate bottling in the 1930s. The winery is at an unassuming address in a back street of town, and the rambling cellars underneath are ancient. Vineyards are in 38 separate parcels, divided roughly into a third each of Bourgogne, village wines, and premier crus. In addition to Volnay and its premier crus, which are the heart of the domain, there are holdings in Beaune (white as well as red), Meursault, and Pommard. More recently, the Lafarge's have expanded into Beaujolais with the creation of Domaine Lafarge-Vial.

The style here is traditional in making no concessions to the current trend for immediate gratification: vertical tasting shows that these wines need time, as you dig back far enough for the sheer purity of the fruits to be able to shine though. The wines are taut, precise, and elegant when they come around. Although keeping up with the latest thinking in converting to biodynamics, Frédéric Lafarge points out that this is in line with their care for the soil and the vines. "We did not fall for the fad of clonal fashions or the heavy fertilization in the 1960s," he says, "and part of the reason for our quality is that the plants are obtained by selection massale in which each generation has continued the match of terroir and cépage."

All the reds age for 12 months in barriques; new oak reaches 20% for the premier crus. Even the Bourgogne Passetoutgrains, a 50:50 blend of Pinot Noir and Gamay coplanted in a 90-year old vineyard, shows the tight house style, with red fruits behind acerbic tannins. Volnay village wine shows tight cherry fruits with hints of tobacco-like tannins on the finish when young, Beaune Les Aigrots is softer and rounder, but you have to go to the monopole Clos du Château des Ducs from Volnay to get a silky sheen in a young wine. The Lafarge Volnays can typify the crystalline purity of the appellation, but I would not try to drink any except the very lightest vintages within the first decade. The style of the whites is as lean as the reds.

Domaine Comtes Lafon

***

 5, Rue Pierre Joigneaux, 21190 Meursault

📞 +33 03 80 21 22 17

 Dominique Lafon

@ comtes.lafon@gmail.com

🌐 www.comtes-lafon.fr

◉ Meursault

🍾 Meursault, Clos de la Barre

🚫 ⚒

🍇 ◯ 16 ha; 80,000 bottles

[map p. 46]

Dominique Lafon's great great grandfather started the domain. "The big step was when my father took over in 1956, but he was also an engineer, it was not his main job. The vineyards were under a sharecropping agreement, so my father was not managing them himself. I took over in 1984 and stopped the sharecropping. The contracts are for 9 years, so it was 1993 until I took all of them over." The domain has been expanded by splitting the purchase of the Labouré-Roi vineyards with Dominique's friend Jean-Marc Roulot, and Dominique has put his stamp firmly on the domain. "All the work we've done has been focused on a move towards elegance. We use just enough new oak for each vineyard, but I don't want to taste it in the wine. The objective was to get the wines to my taste."

The domain has become one of the reference points for Meursault with a splendid array of lieu-dits and premier crus, but the reds from Volnay show the same hallmark elegance and precision. The village Meursault is a blend of various plots, sometimes including declassified lots from premier crus. Clos de la Barre comes from the vineyard next to the winery and captures the house style. "There's always more tension here," says Dominique. Another lieu-dit, Desirée, is always fatter. Terroir shows itself in the approachability of Bouchères, the roundness of Poruzots, power of Genevrières, steely backwardness of Charmes, and smoky, stony, depth of Perrières.

Lafon also created a domain in Mâcon in 1999. And in addition to the domain in Meursault, Dominique started his own label in 2008, making wine from 4.5 ha of vineyards in Meursault, Puligny-Montrachet, Volnay, and Beaune. This allows him to experiment beyond the confines of the domain. The wines are in a similar style to the domain, but to my palate do not seem to reach the same heights of refinement.

Domaine Hubert Lamy *

SAINT-AUBIN 1ER CRU
En Remilly
2010

20 Rue Des Lavières, 21190 Saint-Aubin

+33 03 80 21 32 55

Olivier Lamy

hubertlamydomaine@gmail.com

www.domainehubertlamy.com

Saint-Aubin

Saint-Aubin, en Remilly

18.5 ha; 110,000 bottles [map p. 47]

The Lamy's have been making wine in St. Aubin since the seventeenth century. The domain is located just off the main street in a workmanlike building, somewhat like an oversize converted garage. Hubert Lamy started bottling his own wine in 1973, when the domain was created with 8 ha; it increased significantly during the 1990s. All wine has been estate bottled since Olivier took over in 1996. Now there are 47 parcels, two thirds in St, Aubin, but there are small holdings also in Puligny Montrachet, Chassagne Montrachet, and Santenay. More than three quarters are Chardonnay. Some parcels of Pinot Noir have been replanted with Chardonnay. "My father started the switch to white wine in 1970," says Olivier, "It's not the terroir, it's not the typicité, it's commercial. But this is a return to the situation of many years ago." There are 5 red cuvées and 16 white, including 7 premier cru St. Aubin.

The style has lightened since Olivier started. "When I was younger I worked at Coche Dury and with Henri Jayer, and wanted to make wines like they do, but if I use the same techniques in St. Aubin, I won't make the same wines." He describes his target now as wines that are "ripe, fresh, and round, which can be a difficult combination. When I was young, I tried to copy Puligny, but my tastes have changed in twenty years and I try to make wine that expresses the terroir of St. Aubin."

Wines age for a year or longer in barriques followed by a year in stainless steel on the lees. New oak has backed off from 30% ten years ago. "Now we are using less and less." The most interesting wines here are white (it was a good decision to focus on Chardonnay). St. Aubin premier cru Clos de Meix has more stone fruits than citrus but plays to freshness, Derrière Chez Edouard is fuller and more structured, Frionnes is tighter with more sense of purity, en Remilly is fine and textured and resembles the Puligny, and Clos de Chatenière comes even closer to Puligny with a steely sense of minerality. The best from St. Aubin is usually the premier cru Les Murgers des Dents de Chiens. The Puligny village wine itself is tight and pure, and Chassagne is broader. Making some of the best wine in the appellation, the domain is one of the benchmarks of St. Aubin, and actually I prefer the St. Aubins to the Chassagnes. The house style shows stone fruits with a characteristic catch of lime at the end, and has focused more on minerality in the past ten years. The tipping point for developing away from primary character is 5-6 years, and most people will want to drink them in that span.

Maison Louis Latour *

18, Rue Des Tonneliers, BP 127, 21204 Beaune

+33 03 80 24 81 00

Anne Charpin

contact@louislatour.com

www.louislatour.com

Aloxe Corton

Aloxe-Corton   Chassagne Montrachet

48 ha; 6,000,000 bottles [map p. 45]

"I don't want our Pinot Noir or Chardonnay to be too light, we want the power. I think some people are too obsessed about acidity, I think people are missing full, rich wines," says Fabrice Latour. "We've always had a relatively rich style, a bit of richness is good, we try not to harvest too early."

Louis Latour is one of the most important growers and negociants in Burgundy, with estate vineyards all over the area, and a large negociant activity. The house is one of the largest holders of grand crus on the Côte de Nuits. Still family owned, the company is presently run by Fabrice, sometimes known as Louis VII. Offices are in the center of Beaune, wines are produced at the winery built in Aloxe-Corton in 1832 with a rather splendid gravity-feed system using wagons on rails to move grapes to open-topped wood vats, and bottling is done at a modern facility on the outskirts of Beaune.

Whites go from Ardèche IGP or Mâcon or Pouilly Fuissé aged in stainless steel, to Côte d'Or villages given 15% new oak, to premier crus with 35-50%, and grand crus with 100% new oak. The unoaked whites are fresh, a jump in style occurs with the Côte d'Or villages, and there's increased sense of depth with the premier crus, where Chassagne Caillerets is broad while Puligny Sous les Puits has more tension. The flagship Corton Charlemagne is full and opulent, in fact the most opulent Corton Charlemagne of all, while Bâtard Montrachet has minerality to cut the opulence.

The Pinot Noir from southern Beaujolais is more exotic than Burgundy, while Mercurey is a pure expression of Pinot Noir in stainless steel, and then the slightly plusher expression of Marsannay, also in stainless steel, brings you to the Côte d'Or. Aloxe-Corton (with 15% new oak) typifies the AOP with a characteristic glossy sheen, there is more earthiness as you move to Beaune premier crus (35% new oak), and minerality in the Chassagne Montrachet Morgeot red. Volnay En Chevret is very fine with a great sense of purity.

Going up the scale in Aloxe-Corton, you see the glossy sheen of the village wine, restrained by more structure in the premier crus, with more overt structure in Corton itself. Château Corton Grancey, which is not a single plot but a blend from four *climats* behind the winery, is the most sophisticated of all. In reds, Louis Latour remains controversial for using pasteurization at bottling, which some critics believe impedes aging, but a vertical of Château Corton Grancey identifies it as one of the more ageworthy Cortons.

Instead of competing for land and grapes in the Côte d'Or, Louis Latour has expanded elsewhere, starting in the 1970s with the Ardèche Chardonnay. Recent plantings include Chardonnay in the Auxerrois and Pinot Noir in Beaujolais. Expansion has included the purchase of Simonnet-Febvre in Chablis, and Domaine Henry Fessy in Beaujolais.

Lucien Le Moine ★★★

NUITS-ST-GEORGES 1ᵉʳ CRU
"LES CAILLES"

LUCIEN LE MOINE

◉ *1 ruelle Morlot, 21200 Beaune*

📞 *+33 03 80 24 99 98*

👤 *Mounir Saouma*

@ *l.m.sas@lucienlemoine.com*

🌐 *www.lucienlemoine.com*

◉ *Beaune*

🍾 *Gevrey Chambertin, Cazetiers*

🍷 *Chassagne Montrachet, Morgeots*

🚫 🛢️ 🚜 *0 ha; 30,000 bottles*

[map p. 45]

Located just outside the town center, from outside the property looks a little run down, but the interior has been handsomely renovated, practical rather than flashy, but with a certain contemporary flair. Lucien Lemoine is the creation of Mounir and Rotem Saouma, who have been making wine here since 1999. This may be Burgundy's top micro-negociant. The name reflects Mounir's past experience (Lucien, meaning light, is a translation of Mounir, and Le Moine, the monk, refers to when Mounir learned winemaking in a monastery).

There are typically about 80 different wines each year, extending from a basic Bourgogne to the premier and grand crus that form the main focus. Production scale is tiny: just one to three barrels (less than 1,000 bottles) from each cru. The approach to winemaking is direct: let the wine have a slow and very long fermentation, and keep it on full lees for élevage. "We have very cold cellars so we never complete fermentation before ten months after harvest," Mounir explains. There's minimal manipulation at bottling, and the wines often have a little residual carbon dioxide, and so need decanting.

For me, these wines are completely natural, with a wonderful purity of fruit allowing terroir to show itself at every level of the range. The reds are exceptionally refined; the whites are mineral and smoky. They are expensive and hard to find, but an eye opener as to the potential for minimal manipulation. Since 2009 there has also been a winery in the Rhône called Clos Saouma.

Domaine Leflaive ★★★★

7 rue de l'Église, 21190 Puligny Montrachet

+33 03 80 21 30 13

Pierre Vincent

domaine@leflaive.fr

www.leflaive.fr

Puligny Montrachet

Puligny Montrachet, Le Clavoillon

48 ha; 250,000 bottles

[map p. 47]

The atmosphere has certainly changed since I first visited Domaine Leflaive. Twenty-five years ago, I called one morning for an appointment. Anne-Claude answered the phone herself and said, come along this afternoon for a tasting. Today, emails to the domaine get an automated response saying that visits can be arranged only through your local distributor.

One of the leading producers in Puligny Montrachet since the 1920s under Vincent Leflaive, the domaine rose to the summit under his daughter Anne-Claude, who took over in 1990. Anne-Claude was one of the first in Burgundy to convert to biodynamic viticulture (after an experiment to compare wine from vineyard plots treated organically or biodynamically); whether or not biodynamics are responsible, the wines have simply gone from strength to strength.

Sadly Anne-Claude died in 2014, and her nephew, Brice de la Morandière, returned from a career running international companies to take over in 2015. Pierre Vincent came from Domaine de la Vougeraie as winemaker in June 2017. The domain's headquarters are an imposing set of buildings round a courtyard that occupies one side of the Place des Marronniers, but Brice has expanded a facility close by in Rue l'Église, which was the original cellar of Domaine Leflaive, before they moved into Place des Marronniers. Fermentation and first-year aging now take place there, as do tastings.

The domain's style is the quintessence of Puligny: ripe (but never over-ripe) stone fruits, tempered by a steely, mineral structure. New oak is moderate. "At Domaine Leflaive, there is only one method," Brice says. "We haven't changed anything. "One year in barriques is followed by one year in steel. First the wine likes to have the oxygen from the barriques, then it likes to have the mass from the stainless steel." The only difference is the proportion of new oak, rising from 10% for Bourgogne to 15% for village wines, 20% for premier crus, and 25% for grand crus."

The same style runs with increasing intensity from the village wine through the premier crus, a roll call of the most famous names in the appellation, starting with Le Clavoillon (the largest holding and almost a monopole). Clavoillon shows the smoke and gunflint that is classic for Leflaive's Pulignys. Some people consider it a little obvious compared to Les Folatières and Les Combettes, but it can be the most consistent of the premier crus. Les Pucelles is certainly the top premier cru, and can come close to grand cru standard in Leflaive's hands, moving towards smoothness and roundness, but always retaining that quintessential sense of minerality. Moving out of Puligny, Sous le Dos d'Âne from Meursault is sweeter and broader, less austere, with less obvious minerality.

There are four of the five grand crus: Chevalier Montrachet, Bâtard-Montrachet, Bienvenues-Bâtard-Montrachet, and a tiny holding in Le Montrachet itself. Bâtard Montrachet moves to a sense of power, more obvious oak mingling with the stone and citrus fruits: a sense of holding back makes it obvious the wine is too young now. Chevalier Montrachet shows that unique property of the grand crus: it is simultaneously more powerful and has greater sense of tension. Going up the hierarchy, there is greater refinement rather than greater power.

Unfortunately, with the rise to fame the wines have become so expensive that they are for the most part simply out of reach. But at the other end of the range, Mâcon-Verzé (under the subsidiary label of Domaines Leflaive) was added in 2004, followed by a domain in Anjou, Clau de Nell, in 2008. Domaines Leflaive has expanded from 17 ha to 24 ha in Mâcon since Brice took over, and here the élevage is a little different. Wines age in a mixture of concrete and steel. The most recent addition is single-vineyard wines. "We could see interesting differences," Brice says. Single-vineyard wines from Mâcon get about 10% in old barriques, and the transition to the 'Leflaive Method' comes with Pouilly-Fuissé. A west-facing vineyard, Les Chênes is deeper and more textured than Mâcon-Verzé. A single vineyard wine from Pouilly-Fuissé, En Vigneraie, comes closer in style to the wines of Puligny, with stone and citrus fruits texturing the palate. There are also negociant wines, labeled as Leflaive & Associés.

Maison Olivier Leflaive Frères *

🔄 *10, Place Du Monument, 21190 Puligny Montrachet*

📞 *+33 03 80 21 37 65*

✉ *Olivier Leflaive*

@ *contact@olivier-leflaive.com*

🌐 *www.olivier-leflaive.com*

▦ *Puligny Montrachet*

🍾 *Puligny Montrachet*

🙂 🏭 ✖

🍇 🛢 🌀 *19 ha; 650,000 bottles*

[map p. 47]

Officially retired, but in practice evident everywhere, Olivier Leflaive is a force of nature. He was involved in managing Domaine Leflaive from 1982 to 1994, started as a negociant in 1984, and this became his full time activity from 1994. More recently he has acquired vineyards (including an inheritance of some that had been part of Domaine Leflaive). (The domain wines are indicated as Récolte du Domaine on the label).

Given the family history, the focus is on white wine. His first winemaker was Jean-Marc Boillot, who now runs his own domain, and since 1988 Frank Grux has been the winemaker. "In terms of philosophy and character of wine, I was born in Leflaive style which is finesse and elegance," Olivier says. The house style shows good extraction and the wines are flavorful, first showing fruit, but then with a savory edge behind. They are reliable and consistent. In addition to the main focus on Chassagne and Puligny Montrachet, there are also wines from Chablis and some reds from the Côte de Beaune.

Olivier is known as a small, quality negociant, but in fact, including the estate and negociant activity, wine is made overall from around a hundred hectares, so this has grown into a sizeable operation. But Olivier has extensive control of the vineyards, and says firmly, "I am a winemaker, not a negociant." The entrepreneurial spirit has shown itself also in the establishment first of a restaurant in the village square in Puligny Montrachet, and most recently in a hotel.

Maison Benjamin Leroux

5 rue Colbert, 21200 Beaune

+33 03 80 22 71 06

Benjamin Leroux

contact@benjamin-leroux.com

www.benjamin-leroux.com

Beaune

Savigny-lès-Beaune

Chassagne Montrachet, Morgeots

7.2 ha; 120,000 bottles

[map p. 45]

Benjamin Leroux started his negociant company in 2007, but continued to be the winemaker at Comte Armand in Pommard until 2014, when he became a full time negociant. "After fifteen years in Pommard, I have a true idea of what is a domain, I want to do the same thing, but as a negociant," he says. He rents a cavernous space in a large old winery just off the ring road around Beaune, and has now managed to purchase his first vineyards. "Seven years ago, everything came from grape purchases, today it is the strong majority, and ideally in the future it would be half," he says. "Everything is under the same name, I don't distinguish between domain and negociant."

Production is equal white and red, with grand cru about 10%, and premier cru and village about 30% each. "I started with lots of regional villages and where I grew the most was premier and grand cru." There are 30 different wines altogether; the largest cuvées are Bourgogne and Auxey-Duresses, a few thousand bottles each, but others may be as small as only a single barrel. Vinification depends on vintage. "We are wrong if we destem every year and wrong if we always do vendange entière; you have to adjust to the vintage," Benjamin says. The house style for whites shows citrus fruits with faintly piquant lime on the finish and a suspicion of herbal savory notes that will add complexity as the wine ages. The reds are always ripe with good supporting structure, with an approachable, firm style.

Domaine Pierre Matrot ★★

 12, Rue De Martray, Bp 12, 21190 Meursault

 +33 03 80 21 20 13

 Thierry & Pascale Matrot

@ *info@domaine-matrot.fr*

 www.domaine-matrot.fr

 Meursault

Meursault

Meursault

  23 ha; 160,000 bottles [map p. 46]

The estate is now in its sixth generation. It owes its present form to Joseph Matrot, who took over in 1914 and started estate bottling. His son Pierre took over in 1937 and expanded the estate, and Pierre's son Thierry took over in 1976. Today the estate is run by Thierry's daughters, Elsa (winemaking) and Adèle (marketing). "Father has officially retired but continues to take care of the vineyards," Elsa says. The estate has had some changes of name as generations have succeeded one another, to Pierre Matrot, and then since 2009 to Thierry and Pascale Matrot, but policies have stayed the same.

Half the vineyards are red and half are white, but the white includes the Bourgogne Chardonnay, which accounts for about half of all production. (It comes mostly from around Meursault but includes about 20% sourced from elsewhere.) The Matrots have their own view of winemaking, partly reflecting their own traditions, but also modernizing when they feel it to be appropriate. The Bourgogne Chardonnay and the half bottles are all under screwcap. "Screwcaps are more reliable and uniform. A case of bottles under screwcap are all the same, but under cork they are all different. Screwcaps are very good for half bottles because they age more slowly," Elsa explains.

The use of new oak is unusual. "We do the opposite of other winemakers, we use the new oak for the Bourgogne, and then we use the one-year-old barrels for the Meursault and premier crus, which have only barrels of 1-5 years. We don't want the taste of new oak in the premier crus. There is no battonage unless there is a problem with reduction. Too much battonage tires the wine, we prefer minerality and freshness."

Asked to define house style, Elsa explains that the terroirs determine character. The premier crus all come from different terroirs but winemaking is the same. "The Puligny, Meursault, and Blagny premier crus are in a small triangle, but are completely different." In whites, the Meursault tends to minerality; usually this intensifies in Meursault-Blagny which may even acquire a hint of salinity; and Puligny has a fine quality with great purity. The reds are well structured, building from Maranges to Auxey Duresses to Meursault, all a little tight at first and needing time after release to soften, with Blagny Pièce sous le Bois the most generous and rounded—"this is the signature of the domain."

Domaine Hubert de Montille **

 Rue Pied de la Vallée, 21190 Volnay

📞 +33 03 80 21 39 14

Alix de Montille

@ contact@demontille.com

🌐 www.demontille.com

Volnay

Volnay, Taillepieds

20 ha; 140,000 bottles

[map p. 46]

The great reputation of this old domain started after Hubert de Montille took over in 1947, when it had been reduced to 3 ha in Volnay. A lawyer by profession, he continued to practice law as well as to run the domain. His son Etienne joined in 1983, took over the cellars in 1990, and has been in charge since 1995. The domain has expanded all over the Côte d'Or, and has three quarters of its holdings in premier and grand crus, mostly red.

There's been a softening of style with the change of generations. "Hubert's winemaking style was highly extracted and more austere," says winemaker Brian Sieve at Deux Montille, a negociant activity created to complement the domain by producing white wines. Deux Montille is run by Etienne's sister, Alix (who is married to Jean-Marc Roulot, another famous white winemaker). Alix's interest in white wines extends into Côte Chalonnaise and Chablis.

Wines for both domain and negociant have been made in a single spacious facility in Meursault since 2005 (previously the domain was vinified in Volnay and the negociant in Beaune). "There are no style differences between the negociant and the domain: everything is handled in exactly the same way," Brian explains. There's extensive use of whole clusters for reds; new oak varies from 20-50%, and is usually higher for the Côte de Nuits. The domain is known for the purity of its wines, and the style is precise and elegant, showing textbook illustrations of differences due to terroir.

Domaine Pierre Morey **

 13 rue Pierre Mouchoux, 21190 Meursault

 +33 03 80 21 21 03

 Anne Morey

@ contact@morey-meursault.fr

 www.morey-meursault.fr

 Meursault

 Meursault, Les Tessons

  10 ha; 50,000 bottles

[map p. 46]

"The domain is very old," says Anne Morey, who has been making the wine since 1998. "The Morey family arrived in France in the fifteenth century, and started in Chassagne. They moved to Meursault just after the Revolution." Production is two thirds white and a third red. "We work four villages, Puligny, Meursault, Pommard and Monthelie, and make 7 white and 5 red wines." The cuverie was extended in 2010 to allow gravity-feed winemaking. "We want to produce vins de garde, with long élevage sur lies, we keep lots of lees. Malo occurs late because we have very cold cellars."

Whites are fermented in barrique, with 40-50% new wood as the maximum for grand crus. Battonage is done only up to malolactic fermentation. For the reds everything is destemmed. "But I have the impression that you deprive the grapes of something by destemming, I dream of being able to adjust destemming to the vintage and to use a proportion of vendange entière."

The reds are precise and the whites tend to a tight, steely character, not surprising as Anne's father Pierre was winemaker at Domaine Leflaive as well as running his own domain. In addition, there is a negociant activity, Morey-Blanc, which is almost entirely white, and was started in 1992, to replace vineyards when the contracts expired on plots rented from Lafon. Today this is being cut back a bit. "It can be frustrating not to work the vines," Anne says, but the style is similar to Pierre Morey itself.

Domaine Paul Pernot ★★

2002

Grands Vins
de Bourgogne

Puligny-Montrachet
1er Cru Les Pucelles

Alc. 13.5% by vol   Mise en bouteille à la Propriété par   750 ML
WHITE BURGUNDY WINE

Paul Pernot et ses Fils
Propriétaires à Puligny-Montrachet (Côte-d'Or)
APPELLATION CONTRÔLÉE

⊙ *7 place du Monument, 21190 Puligny-Montrachet*

☎ *+33 03 80 21 32 35*

👤 *Michel Pernot*

@ *contact@domaine-pernot.com*

🔵 *Puligny Montrachet*

🍾 *Puligny Montrachet, Champ Canet*

🍇 ⏱ *22 ha; 60,000 bottles*
[map p. 47]

Paul Pernot is still running the domain that he founded in 1959. The Pernot's have been in Puligny for a long time. "My great grandfather was already here even before we were involved with wine. Wine comes from both my mother's and father's sides," Paul says. "I have two sons who work with me. Michel does marketing, Jean-Marc does winemaking and viticulture. My third son thinks the métier is too difficult." Paul is still closely involved: the day after our visit, we encountered him driving out in his Mercedes convertible to check on the work in the vineyards. First impressions at the domain are somewhat traditional: it occupies a series of old warehouse-like buildings along a vast courtyard just off the main square of Puligny. Paul Pernot comes across from the family house for the tasting, which is held in a cavernous space used for stockage.

Vineyards are mostly in Puligny, with some in Meursault-Blagny and in Chassagne, and some premier crus in Beaune. There are splendid holdings in Puligny, where cuvées include one village wine, and several premier and grand crus. "We have many parcels but we don't make lieu-dits, just one cuvée," Paul explains. "Usage of new oak is very light, but we have lots of barriques of 2-3 years age." The village Puligny is a marker for the village, with a characteristic linear purity, and a touch of steel. Champs Canet is broader, showing a more evident touch of oak, while Chalumeaux is fuller, with the fruits more in evidence. Clos de la Garenne (the cru is shared between Pernot and Duc de Magenta), is waiting to uncoil with time. More restrained, Folatières is holding back, and needs longer. There are a lot of old vines here: Garenne (60 years), Chalumeaux (70 years), and Folatières (55 years).

Les Pucelles is the most complex premier cru aromatically. The two grand crus typify the difference between Puligny and Chassagne Montrachet, as Bienvenues Bâtard Montrachet (all within Puligny) is precise, while having the depth of the grand cru without being at all heavy, while Bâtard Montrachet (coming from a plot on the Chassagne side) is broader. This is often felt to be one of the keynote domains of the village.

Domaine Fernand et Laurent Pillot ★★

⊙ *2, place des Noyers 21190, Chassagne-Montrachet*

📞 *+33 03 80 21 99 83*

👤 *Laurent Pillot*

@ *contact@vinpillot.com*

🌐 *www.vinpillot.com*

▣ *Chassagne Montrachet*

🍾 *Beaune, Boucherottes*

🍷 *Chassagne Montrachet, Les Chênes*

☺ ﹏ 🍇 ⟳ *15 ha; 70,000 bottles [map p. 47]*

This dynamic domain makes wine from 64 different plots. There's a tasting room in the family house in Chassagne, but the winery is just outside the village in a practical building near the N74. A new extension has a stylish tasting room overlooking the vineyards. Laurent Pillot has been making the wines since 1994. He turned up for our tasting on his tractor, from the vineyards, which are quite spread out. The original Pillot vineyards are mostly in Chassagne, with some in Meursault and St. Aubin, but Laurent's wife, Marie-Ann, inherited half of the Pothier-Rieusset domain in Pommard, and later they bought the other half. This is very much a family business; Laurent's son Adrian has just joined.

Chassagne Montrachet is the focus for whites, with the village wine coming from several plots in the center ("we sell off grapes from some of the plots at the edge"), lieu-dits, and five premier crus. The house style shows that sense of purity of fruits more commonly associated with Puligny. Palates show complex stone fruits with a subtle touch of oak. "My father likes to have just a slight taste of the barrel," Adrian says. "This is typical of our style. Usually we buy one third new oak and we sell the 3-year barrels." New oak runs from 25% for village wines to 40-60% for premier crus, depending on the cru.

The Les Chênes lieu-dit in Chassagne is close to premier cru quality, Les Vergers premier cru shows a touch more concentration and greater purity, Champs Gains is a little broader, Morgeot is the fattest, Vide Bourse is distinctive as the most delicate and elegant, and Grandes Ruchottes brings out that soft Chassagne style with more depth and power. Laurent looks for elegance. "We work with coopers to extract tannins during barrel production, so that we get elegance in the wine," he says.

The reds are precise. "Normally I destem most of the grapes," Laurent says, "although in 2015 more whole clusters were used because the grapes were so ripe." The Volnay is a blend from all the plots in Volnay, "about a quarter come from premier cru, but the plots are too small to separate." Beaune Boucherottes has a sense of purity and precision that recalls Volnay; with greater fruit concentration pushing the tannins back, Pommard Charmots adds weight to the precision of the red cherry fruits.

Domaine Jean-Marc Pillot   *

2004

CHEVALIER-MONTRACHET

GRAND CRU
Appellation Chevalier-Montrachet Contrôlée

JEAN-MARC PILLOT

WHITE BURGUNDY WINE   PRODUCT OF FRANCE   ALC 13.5% BY VOL.

750 ml   MIS EN BOUTEILLE PAR JEAN-MARC PILLOT

Le Haut des Champs, 21190 Chassagne-Montrachet

+33 03 80 21 92 96

Jean-Marc Pillot

jeanmarc.pillot@wanadoo.fr

www.chassagne-montrachet.com

Chassagne Montrachet

Chassagne Montrachet, Macherelles

Chassagne Montrachet, Les Vergers

12 ha; 70,000 bottles

[map p. 47]

The domain's official address is in fact the family residence in Chassagne, but if you turn up there, Jean-Marc's mother gives you directions to find the winery, which has been located since 1988 in a modern building in Le Haut Champ, just down the road off the RN6. Originally there was one Pillot domain, but in 1988 Jean Pillot split it with his brother Fernand. Jean worked with his son, Jean-Marc, who took over in 1991, and now Jean-Marc's son, also named Jean-Marc, has been working with his father for seven years. The domain has equal plantings of black and white grapes. "The unusual proportion of reds goes back to my grandfather who had more red; and my father believed that the history showed well for reds and there are some terroirs, such as St. Jean, better suited to reds," explains Jean-Marc.

The whites have an approachable style. The village wine has 25% new oak, but 2-year oak is the oldest. Premier crus have up to 30% new oak. Élevage is 12 months in wood and 6 months in cuve, with battonage. The fruits on the village Chassagne are somewhat obvious, then become less overt on the premier crus, with Champs Gains, Maltroye, Les Vergers, and Macherelles showing stone fruits. The two classiest premier crus are Morgeot, which is more restrained, but shows greater sense of depth and texture, and Les Caillerets, which shows the greatest purity. Even barrel samples, a few months before bottling, seem more or less ready to drink.

Reds have 20% new oak for village wines and 25% for premier crus. The reds are typical for Chassagne, quite approachable, and making a light impression, from the direct fruits of the Santenay Champs Claude or Chassagne Vieilles Vignes, to the lightly structured impression of Macherelles, and the fine sense of purity and precision in Morgeot. The top red is the Clos St. Jean, rounder and more structured, supporting Jean Marc Senior's point.

Domaine de La Pousse d'Or

*

Rue De La Chapelle, 21190 Volnay

+33 03 80 21 61 33

Benoît Landanger or Marleen Nicot

marleen@lapoussedor.fr

lapoussedor.fr

Volnay

Volnay, Clos de la Bousse d'Or

18 ha; 90,000 bottles

[map p. 46]

I remember the wines of Pousse d'Or from the early nineties as among the most elegant in Volnay, with an indefinably delicate expression of Pinot Noir. Then with Gérard Potel's death in 1997 the domain somewhat fell out of view. Patrick Landanger, who had been an engineer and inventor, bought the domain. He started by employing a general manager, but "he was told that if he wanted to regain confidence he would need to make the wine himself. So he went to oenology school... The first vintage he made was 1999, which was well received," explains commercial manager Marleen Nicot.

There's been major investment in a new building that houses a gravity-feed winery, with three levels built into the side of the hill. Patrick is still inventing, as seen in a new glass device that has replaced bungs in barrels (so topping up is required less often).

Production is focused on red wine. The heart of the domain remains the premier crus from Volnay, but Patrick has expanded, first by purchasing two vineyards in Corton, and then by adding a village wine and four premier crus in Chambolle Musigny. The only white comes from Puligny Caillerets; it is less interesting than the reds. For all the premier crus there is one third new oak, one third one-year, and one third two-year; grand Crus have 40-45% new oak. Larger barrels (350 liter) are used for the white wine. The wines from Volnay give a precise yet intense expression; the Chambolles seem a little rounder and more feminine.

Domaine Jacques Prieur   *

⊙ *6, Rue Des Santenots, 21190 Meursault*

📞 *+33 03 80 21 23 85*

✎ *Edouard Labruyère*

@ *domaine-jprieur@prieur.com*

⊕ *www.prieur.com*

◉ *Meursault*

🍾 *Clos Vougeot*

🍷 *Meursault, Clos de Mazeray*

🍇🍷 *21 ha; 100,000 bottles*

[map p. 46]

The domain was founded by a couple in the silk business in Lyon; they gave it to their nephew, Jacques Prieur, who became a significant figure in Meursault. In 1988, most of his children decided to sell their share to the Labruyère family. "We come from Moulin-à-Vent where we have owned 14 ha for 7 generations," Edouard Labruyère explains. "I was a courtier in Bordeaux until I came here to run the domain in 2008. My goal was clear. Jacques Prieur is fantastic in terms of terroir—we own 9 grand crus and 14 premier crus. I asked the team to make wines that represent the terroir. The signature of Prieur was too evident in the bottle, we were more known by the label than the terroir. I wanted to change that." Behind the stone façade is a modern cuverie, with separate facilities for red and white. "We modernized everything in 2009, no renovation had been made since 1958."

Production is half red and half white. Meursault Clos de Mazeray is the only village wine in the portfolio. Vinification is traditional, with limited destemming and fermentation in open wood vats. Ageing is 18-24 months with no racking. "I stopped battonage for whites in 2008. I believe we have enough natural richness, I didn't want to add more fat." The reds of the Côte de Beaune have an unusual elegance, while those from the Côte de Nuits tend to be sterner. The whites are relatively sturdy, but good representations of their appellations. Labruyère also owns Château Rouget in Pomerol.

Domaine Ramonet

 *4, Place-des-Noyers, Chassagne-Montrachet, 21190*

📞 *+33 03 80 21 30 88*

Jean-Claude Ramonet

@ *ramonet.domaine@wanadoo.fr*

Chassagne Montrachet

🍾 *Chassagne Montrachet, Les Boudriottes*

🚛 🚜 *17 ha; 100,000 bottles*

[map p. 47]

This old-line domain has long been considered by many to be the best in Chassagne Montrachet. Pierre Ramonet purchased his first vineyards in the 1920s and 1930s, and then built up the domain after the second world war; it passed to his grandsons, Noël the winemaker, and Jean-Claude vineyard manager, in the 1980s. Conscious of its fame, the domain goes its own way and does not take criticism kindly: requests to visit can be rebuffed.

Ramonet has an important diversity of holdings, with six premier crus in Chassagne Montrachet, and four grand crus. There is also village wine from Puligny as well as Chassagne, and small amounts of premier cru from Puligny and St. Aubin. Vinification is traditional, but there is unusually extended lees contact and no battonage. New oak is stated to be around a third for the premier crus, but tastes stronger in the wines. Through the nineties these wines had a powerful yet balanced expression of Chassagne in a relatively creamy style, showing a characteristic sweetness of oak and fruits on a rich and viscous palate.

While I did not have problems with premox in the 2000s, the wines seemed to become heavier, with more phenolic overtones, giving the impression of a heavier-handed use of oak. Now they seem to have lightened up, with more mineral impressions to Boudriottes and Morgeots, which for me are the two most typical premier crus (and the largest holdings). Although there are some reds from Chassagne and from three of the premier crus, they have never been as interesting as the whites.

Domaine Rapet Père et Fils   *

2 Pl. de la Mairie, 21420 Pernand-Vergelesses

+33 03 80 21 59 94

Vincent Rapet

vincent@domaine-rapet.com

www.domaine-rapet.com

Pernand Vergelesses

Savigny-lès-Beaune, Les Fourneaux

Pernand Vergelesses, Clos du Village

20 ha; 80,000 bottles

[map p. 45]

Located right by the church in the center of the village of Pernand-Vergelesses, this is a very old domain, going back at least to the mid eighteenth century. Originally its vineyards were all around the village; that remains true of the whites, which come from Pernand-Vergelesses, its crus, and Corton Charlemagne, but today the reds are scattered all over the Côte de Beaune, coming from Pernand-Vergelesses, Aloxe Corton, Savigny-lès-Beaune, and Beaune. Around 1980 when Vincent's grandfather died, the vineyards weren't in great shape, so most of the domain was replanted, using a mixture of clones and selection massale; the domain has increased just a little in size since then.

Vincent takes a thoughtful approach to viticulture and vinification. When asked how things have changed since he took over, he says that working the soil is better, there's better canopy management, and vendange vert is done when necessary. A sorting table was introduced in 2004, there's no pumping in the cuverie, and nitrogen is used when bottling the whites to avoid premox. There's a real focus on improving each stage to get quality in viticulture and vinification. "The style of the grand années remains the same, it's the style of the minor years that has changed," he says. "The wine used to require three years, now it's drinkable straight away." The whites can be quite full; there's always some proportion of whole cluster for the reds, giving a structured background to the generally silky style.

Remoissenet Père et Fils

*

📍 *20, rue Eugène Spuller, 21200 Beaune*

📞 *+33 03 80 26 26 66*

@ *brepolt@remoissenet.com*

Beaune

🧍 🍾 🛢 🚜 *14 ha; 200,000 bottles*

[map p. 45]

Remoissenet is a classic Burgundian negociant, with minimal vineyard holdings, but a very large range of cuvées from all over the Côte de Beaune and Côte de Nuits. Founded in 1877, it was run for the last thirty years under family ownership by Roland Remoissenet from an old building in Beaune, with a cuverie outside the city. Remoissenet was known for its extensive holdings of old vintages, slowly released on the market at quite reasonable prices. When Roland retired in 2005, the company was sold to New York financiers. Supposedly over a million bottles of old vintages were included in the sale.

The last years of the family regime were marked by a noticeable decline in quality, and the wines gave an impression that they were going through the motions, but under the new ownership the firm has begun to revive and also to purchase some vineyards on its own account. As a negociant, everything depends on the quality of purchases and vinification; a major asset is Remoissenet's longstanding relationship with Baron Thénard, the largest holder of Le Montrachet, which has been their top wine for many years. In fact, the whites have always been regarded as better than the reds.

Domaine Guy Roulot ***

 1 Rue Charles Giraud, 21190 Meursault

 +33 03 80 21 21 65

Jean-Marc Roulot

@ roulot@domaineroulot.fr

Meursault

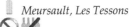 Meursault, Les Tessons

15 ha; 85,000 bottles

[map p. 46]

The domain was established by Jean-Marc Roulot's parents in the fifties, but, "I wanted to be an actor—I went to Paris—it wasn't entirely successful but it didn't work so badly, I was a professional actor for ten years. When my father died we employed a régisseur, then my cousin Grux managed the vintages until 1988, and then I came back to run the estate," Jean-Marc explains. "I still spend 20% of my time acting, but it's no different from having another estate; it takes less time than making Beaujolais."

The domain is famous for its focus on the lieu-dits of Meursault. "My father had no premier crus, but he wanted to distinguish the different lots—he was one of the first to do this—and the style was defined by the decision to separate the cuvées." Jean-Marc has lengthened élevage to 18 months, with 12 months in barrique followed by 6 months in cuve, all on the lees. "The wine needs something to eat." There's no new oak for Bourgogne Blanc or Aligoté, village is 15-18%, and premier crus are 25-33%. The domain increased by 3 ha when Jean-Marc obtained half the vineyards of the old Labouré-Roi domain.

The focus is on Meursault, with 6 lieu-dits and 4 premier crus, but there are also Bourgogne, Auxey-Duresses, and Monthelie (in red as well as white). Aided by an emphasis on early picking, the style is crisp and elegant, with moderate alcohol. "In 2009 we were among the first in the vineyard. I don't like high alcohol, I'm very comfortable with 12.5-12.8%."

Domaine Étienne Sauzet ★★

 11 rue de Poiseul, Puligny Montrachet, 21190

 +33 03 80 21 32 10

 Benoit Riffault & Emilie Boudot

 etienne.sauzet@wanadoo.fr

 www.etiennesauzet.com

 Puligny Montrachet

Puligny Montrachet, Les Champs Canet

 9.5 ha; 100,000 bottles

[map p. 47]

When Etienne Sauzet founded the domain in the 1930s he was a negociant in gateaux as well as a vigneron. "It's bizarre but his deuxième métier allowed him to buy vines. It was common in that period when things weren't too good to use the second job to buy vines," explains Benoît Riffaut, who married Etienne's granddaughter; management of the domain jumped a generation when he took over in 1974. Now his daughter and son-in-law are involved. He's supposed to retire next year but plans to carry on unofficially. "It's impossible to stop when you are used to this métier. I won't be in charge but I'll be here," he says. The domain has a complicated organization because it was divided among three siblings in 1991, and formally functions as a negociant buying grapes from the various parts, but little by little the original vineyards are being reincorporated into the domain.

All cuvées come from Puligny, except for the Bourgogne, which comes from vines just outside the appellation. The village wine comes from 7 plots spread around the village, and there are 9 premier crus—"that's our specialty," says Benoît. Backing off from new oak has changed the style a bit: today it is often 20-25%, and the maximum is 30% for the grand crus. "Vanilla and aromatics of oak are artificial for us," says Benoît. I remember vanillin in the wines from two decades ago, but today the style shows a steely minerality, with emphasis on richer stone fruits as opposed to citrus increasing up the hierarchy.

Domaine Tollot-Beaut et Fils   *

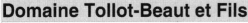 Rue Alexandre Tollot, 21200 Chorey-les-Beaune

📞 +33 03 80 22 16 54

Nathalie, Jean-Paul & Olivier Tollot

@ domaine@tollot-beaut.com

Chorey-lès-Beaune

Savigny-lès-Beaune, Les Lavières

24 ha; 150,000 bottles

[map p. 45]

The domain was founded in Chorey-lès-Beaune just around the time of phylloxera. Very much a family affair, it's run today by a group of family members headed by Nathalie Tollot. With the sale of the other large individual producer in Chorey (Château de Chorey), Tollot-Beaut is really the only major producer dedicated to Chorey. For many years Tollot-Beaut was synonymous with good value wines from the appellation, but in fact the Chorey and generic Bourgogne account for only about half the vineyards. Other holdings extend into Savigny-lès-Beaune, Beaune (including premier crus Grèves and Clos du Roi), and Aloxe Corton (including small plots of Corton grand cru and Corton Charlemagne).

The Chorey-lès-Beaune red, which is the principal cuvée, is an assemblage from all three areas of Chorey. The best wine from Chorey comes from the lieu-dit of Pièce du Chapitre, a monopole of Tollot-Beaut since 2001. Most of the other holdings outside Chorey are small enough that the wines represent individual plots. All grapes are destemmed, but vinification varies with the year. Prefermentation maceration is used only in good years. Cultivated yeasts are used in difficult years, indigenous in good years. All wines are treated the same, with 16-18 months in barrique; the proportion of new oak depends on the cuvée, extending from around 20% for village wines to 60% for grand crus. I've always found the style to be very reliable, with no disappointments.

Domaine Anne-Marie et Jean-Marc Vincent *

 3 rue Sainte-Agathe, 21590 Santenay

📞 +33 03 80 20 67 37

Jean-Marc Vincent

@ vincent.j-m@wanadoo.fr

Santenay

Santenay, Passetemps

Santenay, Beaurepaire

6 ha; 30,000 bottles

[map p. 47]

The cellars date from the fourteenth century, but this is a new domain. The vineyards belonged to the family, but they were not vignerons. "Jean-Marc's father was an engineer in Colmar. Jean-Marc didn't want to follow that and went to oenology school at Dijon in 1993. We were in Nuits St Georges before we came here, we didn't know what we were getting into," says Anne-Marie, a fraction ruefully. Established eighteen years ago, this remains a very hands-on operation: Anne-Marie had a second job until 2000, and the first real employee was hired only in 2009. "When we started all the equipment was old and we had to replace everything, but we did it slowly," Anne-Marie recollects. For the first two years, grapes were sold to negociants, but since then all production has been estate-bottled.

There are separate cellars for whites and reds in the heart of the village (the old cellars were purchased by Ann-Marie's grandfather in 1950). There's the same élevage for all cuvées, with about 25% new oak. The whites have an intriguing blend of fruits and herbs when young, which strengthens to a delicious savory quality as they age. The reds are round, with a touch of tannin showing for the first couple of years, and the premier crus are quite Beaune-like. You might think that given their delicious quality when young, these wines don't need to age, but they do benefit from time in the bottle, becoming deeper with time, and peaking a few years after the vintage. All the wines come from estate grapes, except for the Montagny white, from purchased grapes.

Côte de Nuits

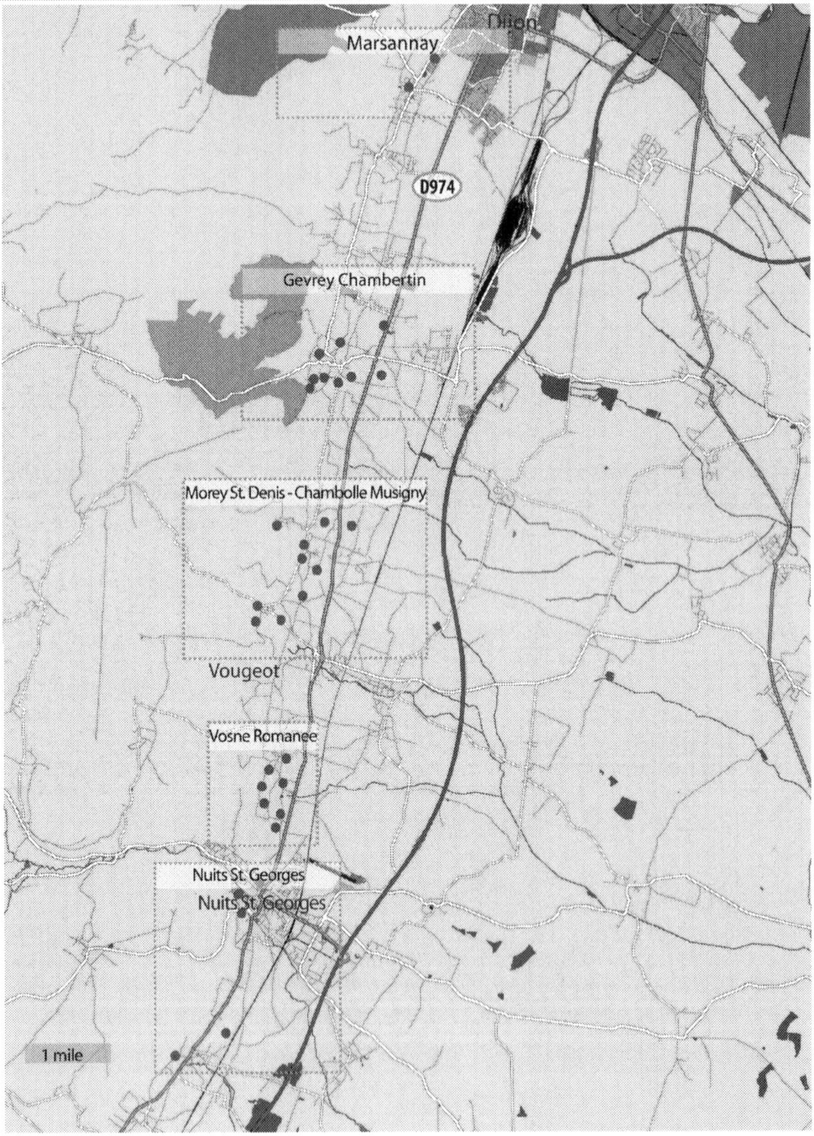

Dijon

Marsannay

D974

Gevrey Chambertin

Morey St. Denis - Chambolle Musigny

Vougeot

Vosne Romanee

Nuits St. Georges

Nuits St. Georges

1 mile

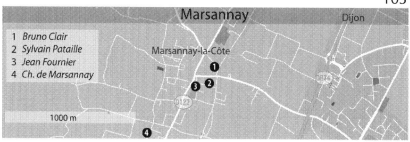

1 Bruno Clair
2 Sylvain Pataille
3 Jean Fournier
4 Ch. de Marsannay

Marsannay

Dijon

Marsannay-la-Côte

1000 m

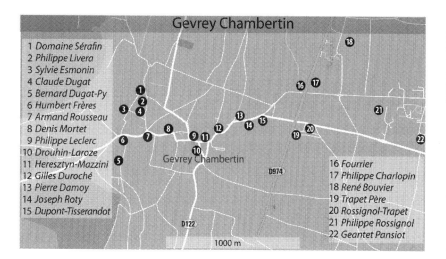

Gevrey Chambertin

1 Domaine Sérafin
2 Philippe Livera
3 Sylvie Esmonin
4 Claude Dugat
5 Bernard Dugat-Py
6 Humbert Frères
7 Armand Rousseau
8 Denis Mortet
9 Philippe Leclerc
10 Drouhin-Laroze
11 Heresztyn-Mazzini
12 Gilles Duroché
13 Pierre Damoy
14 Joseph Roty
15 Dupont-Tisserandot

16 Fourrier
17 Philippe Charlopin
18 René Bouvier
19 Trapet Père
20 Rossignol-Trapet
21 Philippe Rossignol
22 Geantet Pansiot

Gevrey Chambertin

1000 m

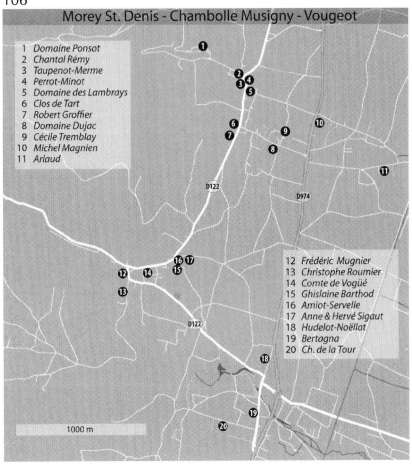

1 Domaine Ponsot
2 Chantal Rémy
3 Taupenot-Merme
4 Perrot-Minot
5 Domaine des Lambrays
6 Clos de Tart
7 Robert Groffier
8 Domaine Dujac
9 Cécile Tremblay
10 Michel Magnien
11 Arlaud

12 Frédéric Mugnier
13 Christophe Roumier
14 Comte de Vogüé
15 Ghislaine Barthod
16 Amiot-Servelle
17 Anne & Hervé Sigaut
18 Hudelot-Noëllat
19 Bertagna
20 Ch. de la Tour

D122
D974
D122

1000 m

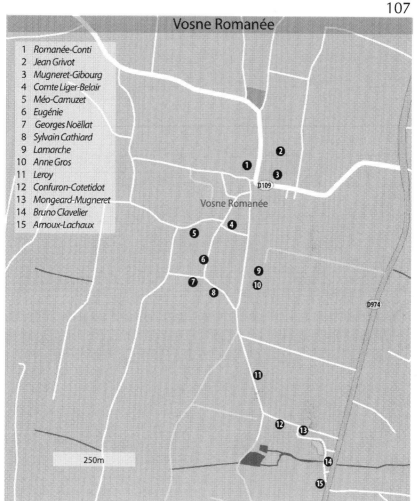

Vosne Romanée

1 Romanée-Conti
2 Jean Grivot
3 Mugneret-Gibourg
4 Comte Liger-Belair
5 Méo-Camuzet
6 Eugénie
7 Georges Noëllat
8 Sylvain Cathiard
9 Lamarche
10 Anne Gros
11 Leroy
12 Confuron-Cotetidot
13 Mongeard-Mugneret
14 Bruno Clavelier
15 Arnoux-Lachaux

Vosne Romanée

D109

D974

250m

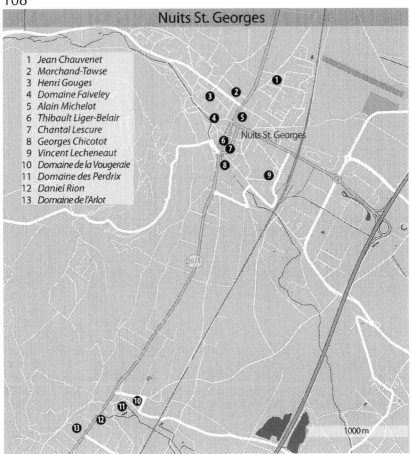

Nuits St. Georges

1 Jean Chauvenet
2 Marchand-Tawse
3 Henri Gouges
4 Domaine Faiveley
5 Alain Michelot
6 Thibault Liger-Belair
7 Chantal Lescure
8 Georges Chicotot
9 Vincent Lecheneaut
10 Domaine de la Vougeraie
11 Domaine des Perdrix
12 Daniel Rion
13 Domaine de l'Arlot

Nuits St. Georges

1000 m

Domaine Amiot-Servelle

**

 34 Rue Caroline Aigle, 21220 Chambolle Musigny

 +33 03 80 62 80 39

 Prune Amiot

 domaine@amiot-servelle.com

 www.amiot-servelle.com

 Chambolle Musigny

Chambolle Musigny

  8 ha; 20,000 bottles

[map p. 106]

The activity of the family in Chambolle Musigny started in the 1920s, and Domaine Servelle-Tachot was created in the 1950s. The name changed to Amiot-Servelle when Christian Amiot and his wife Elisabeth (née Servelle) took over in 1989. Their daughter Prune, who has a degree in oenology, joined the domain in 2011. Tastings take place in a small cave just below the family residence in the center of Chambolle Musigny.

This is very much a domain of the village, with most of the vineyards in Chambolle Musigny coming from the Servelle side, including five premier crus, culminating in Les Amoureuses. There are also wines from the Amiot side, including Morey St. Denis and grand cru Clos St. Denis from the neighboring village, as well as Charmes Chambertin. There are both red and white Bourgogne, coming from the other side of the N74. The Bourgogne is almost the only white; sometimes there is an exchange of berries with a producer in Puligny Montrachet.

The approach to vinification is conventional, with increasing use of new oak going up the appellation hierarchy: Bourgogne is 10% new oak, village is 20%, premier cru is 30%, Amoureuses is 50%, grand cru is 75%. Élevage is 15-18 months. "There is no rule about whole bunches," Prune says. "We look at the grapes, if they are really ripe it could be 100%."

The style here is very expressive of the two villages, with a great sense of purity of fruits, showing as a mixture of red and black cherries. The difference going from Bourgogne to village to premier cru is a greater sense of black fruits and more texture. The tannins are always silky but they are so fine that the village Morey St. Denis and Chambolle Musigny can be started soon after the vintage; the Chambolle is finer than Morey St. Denis. The premier crus have more structure, with a sense of silky tannins on the finish, which needs more time to resolve. Les Plantes gives a finer sense of Chambolle compared to the village wine, and Les Charmes adds weight.

Domaine de l'Arlot

Route Nationale 74, 21700 Premeaux-Prissey

+33 03 80 61 01 92

Geraldine Godot

contact@arlot.fr

www.arlot.com

Nuits St. Georges

Nuits St. Georges, Clos de l'Arlot

Nuits St. Georges, Clos de l'Arlot

15 ha; 60,000 bottles

[map p. 108]

Clos de l'Arlot was part of negociant Maison Belin until it was bought in 1987 by insurance giant AXA, in collaboration with winemaker Jean-Pierre de Smet. When Jean-Pierre retired in 2006, AXA took complete control. Olivier Leriche became the winemaker, then in 2011 Jacques Devauges arrived, and when he left for Clos de Tart in 2014, Geraldine Godot took over. Buildings are located around a gracious courtyard right on the N74, with old cellars underneath.

Most of the vineyards are in two monopoles: 7 ha Clos des Forêts St. Georges is just up the road; and 4 ha of Clos de l'Arlot surround the winery. Across the N74 is the Clos du Chapeau that produces a Côtes de Nuits Villages. The other holdings are smaller parcels in Vosne Romanée Les Suchots and Romanée St. Vivant. There are no village wines: the line goes straight from the regional Côtes to the premier (and grand) crus.

The domain is unusual in producing white wine on the Côte de Nuits. About half of the Clos de l'Arlot now produces white wine. The wine from the younger vines, and from plots with atypical terroir, is declassified to Nuits St. Georges, La Gerbotte. "La Gerbotte is very fresh, Clos de l'Arlot is more complex," Geraldine says. Vinification is similar, with élevage in 20% new oak, but Clos de l'Arlot shows more finesse.

The reds start with the light, fresh Clos du Chapeau, and then jump to the elegance of Clos de l'Arlot, which often strikes me as stylistically close to the reds of Beaune. There's almost as big a jump going to the next wine of the lineup. "Vosne Romanée Suchots comes after Clos de l'Arlot and before Clos de Forêts because the tannins of Suchots are very fine and Forêts is more muscular," Geraldine explains. Les Suchots has something of the minerality of Clos de l'Arlot, but with greater fruit density. This is where the transition from red to black fruits occurs in the range, and where the identity of the Côte de Nuits becomes clear. Clos des Fôrets is more obviously structured with blackberry fruits, rather firm, but still showing the freshness of house style. "We don't have to extract a lot, the tannins are here already," Geraldine says. Romanée St. Vivant shows grand cru breed, interpreted through the domain's fresh style, finer rather than more powerful. One consequence of the fresh style is that most wines stay around 13% alcohol.

Domaine Arnoux-Lachaux   **

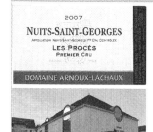

 3, Route Nationale 74, 21700 Vosne-Romanée

 *+33 03 80 61 09 85*

 Florence Lachaux

 info@arnoux-lachaux.com

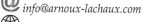 *www.arnoux-lachaux.com*

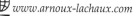 *Vosne Romanée*

 Nuits St. Georges, Clos de Corvées Pagets

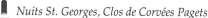

  *14 ha; 70,000 bottles*

[map p. 107]

This started as Domaine Robert Arnoux, in 1858, and was considered to be a typical domain of Vosne Romanée, with strong wines, well structured and concentrated: robust was a common description. Pascal Lachaux, Robert Arnoux's son-in-law, has been running the estate since 1993, and in 2007 changed the name of the domain to Arnoux-Lachaux. There are grand cru holdings in Romanée St Vivant, Echézeaux, Latricières Chambertin, and Clos Vougeot, and some top premier crus, including Suchots, Reignots and Chaumes in Vosne Romanée, and others in Nuits St Georges.

Pascal states his objective as being to make elegant wines, and made a revealing comment when we tasted a 2009 Nuits St. Georges, "This is not typical Nuits St. Georges, it is too elegant." That's the direction of the domain these days. This is aided by the new cuverie, right on the N74, with a stylish tasting room and shop open to visitors. Extending the estate holdings, since 2002 there has been a small negociant activity.

Everything is destemmed, there's cold maceration, and then slow fermentation; part of the change in style here may be due to the fact that fermentation now is slower than it used to be. Wines are aged for 16 months in barriques, with 30% new oak for the village wines, 40-60% for premier crus, and 100% for grand crus. There is no fining or filtration. The leading wines are the Romanée St. Vivant and the Vosne Romanée Les Suchots.

Domaine Ghislaine Barthod

 4 *Rue du Lavoir, 21220 Chambolle Musigny*

 +33 03 80 62 80 16

 Ghislaine Barthod

 domaine.ghislaine.barthod@orange.fr

 Chambolle Musigny

Chambolle Musigny, Les Charmes

7 ha; 30,000 bottles
[map p. 106]

This small domain is tightly focused on Chambolle Musigny, where there are nine premier crus as well as the communal wine. The domain started with Marcel Noëllat in the 1920s, became known as Barthod-Noëllat after the union of the Barthod and Noëllat families, and then changed to Barthod after Gaston Barthod took over in the 1960s; his daughter Ghislaine started making the wines in the early 1990s, and has been fully in charge since 1999. The domain has remained the same, except for the recent addition of the Gruenchers premier cru.

Ghislaine's husband is Louis Boillot, who left his family domain, started to make wine independently in Gevrey Chambertin, and now makes wine in Chambolle Musigny in the Barthod cellars (see mini-profile). The Barthod domain is located in the heart of Chambolle Musigny, with the winery backing right onto the vineyards. Ghislaine and Louis share the same team for managing the vineyards, but winemaking has been independent. Since 2019, their son, Clément Boillot, has taken charge of winemaking for both estates.

All grapes are destemmed at Ghislaine Barthod, then there's a period of maceration before fermentation starts naturally in open-topped wood cuves, with aging following in barriques with up to about 30% new oak for 12-18 months. The regime is the same for all the premier crus. The wines are considered to showcase the characteristic finesse of the commune, with Les Charmes and Les Cras usually at the top of the hierarchy. There is also a Bourgogne Rouge from a vineyard just outside of Chambolle Musigny in Gilly. The wines are definitely taut and elegant, but can be tight when young: even from rich vintages, the communal Chambolle Musigny can still be quite closed several years later.

Domaine Bruno Clair ★★

 5 rue du Vieux-Collège, 21160 Marsannay-la-Côte

 +33 03 80 52 28 95

 Bruno Clair

@ brunoclair@wanadoo.fr

 www.bruno-clair.com

 Marsannay-la-Côte

 Chambolle Musigny, Verouilles

Morey St. Denis

  23 ha; 100,000 bottles

[map p. 105]

"The history of the domain is very complicated, it would take hours," says Bruno Clair with a sigh when you ask how it came to be. "My grandfather created the Clair-Daü domain in 1914, but I started all by myself in 1979 by creating my own domain." It's evident that Bruno greatly respects his grandfather, who was clearly a formative influence, but when he died, the vineyards were divided. One daughter sold all her vines to Jadot, the other kept hers, and Bruno's father gave him his third. That's where the grand crus come from. The other vineyards have since been added by Bruno.

The domain is located in buildings around a charming courtyard in a back street of Marsannay, but vineyard holdings extend south through Gevrey Chambertin, Morey St. Denis, Chambolle Musigny, Vosne Romanée, Aloxe Corton, and Savigny-les-Beaune. There are five premier crus, mostly in Gevrey, as well as two grand crus (Chambertin Clos de Bèze and Bonnes Mares). Vinification is traditional (with no more than 10-20% whole bunches), and new oak is restrained. "I hate to taste new wood, you won't smell it in my wines, it's up to 50% depending on the cuvée."

The style is always smooth and elegant. Fruits show precision, usually more red than black; tannins never stick out. Appellations show their best side; the Morey St. Denis has a silky elegance approaching Chambolle, and the Marsannay has a weight approaching Gevrey. There is refinement right across the range.

Domaine Pierre Damoy ★★

11, Rue du Maréchal-de-Lattre-de-Tassigny, 21220 Gevrey-Chambertin

+33 03 80 34 30 47

Pierre Damoy

info@domaine-pierre-damoy.com

www.domaine-pierre-damoy.com

Gevrey Chambertin

Gevrey Chambertin, Clos Tamisot

12.6 ha; 45,000 bottles
[map p. 105]

The majority of the domain's holdings are in three important grand crus, Chambertin, Clos de Bèze, and Chapelle Chambertin, but the domain was a significant under-achiever until the current Pierre Damoy took over in 1992. The domain is the largest owner in Clos de Bèze, but sells most of the grapes. Its Clos de Bèze is made from an assemblage of berries from parcels at both ends of the appellation; the vines in the northern parcel are younger; the southern parcel, and the adjacent parcel over the border in Chambertin, were mostly planted in 1973-1974.

Pierre Damoy harvests late. "I like ripe berries," he says, although he points out that the late harvest partly reflects the fact that almost all his vineyards are in grand crus. Sometimes there has been a Vieilles Vignes cuvée from a small part of Clos de Bèze. There may also be a Reserve bottling (just two barrels), which is not usually commercialized.

The domain actually started with the purchase of the Clos Tamisot vineyard, which is a village Gevrey Chambertin, and is the most affordable representation of the domain. In addition to the wines from Gevrey Chambertin, there's an unusually refined Marsannay, and a generic Bourgogne that comes from a mix of estate and purchased grapes, and is labeled simply Pierre Damoy (not Domaine). The style tends to be rich and powerful, with quite a bit of new oak usage, ranging from 30% in the Bourgogne, to 50% in Gevrey Chambertin, and 80% or more in the grand crus.

Domaine David Duband

 12 rue du Lavoir, Chevannes, 21220

 +33 03 80 61 41 16

 David Duband

 domaine.duband@wanadoo.fr

 www.domaine-duband.com

 Nuits St. Georges

 Chambolle Musigny, Les Sentiers

 20 ha; 100,000 bottles

Chevannes is in the hills of the Hautes Côtes de Nuits at the end of a narrow twisting road. The domain is on the edge of the little village, in a large modern warehouse-like building built in 2007. It's a practical facility with winemaking on the upper level and a large storage space on the lower level. Wines come from 25 AOPs, varying from 2 to 40 barrels; grapes are purchased for about 25% of production.

David's father created the domain in 1965 when he cut down woods and planted vines on the hillside facing Chevannes. Then he rented vineyards in Nuits St. Georges. David started to make wine in 1991, and took over in 1995. He also makes the wines for Domaine François Feuillet, which has top holdings on the Côte de Nuits, including the old Truchot domain. Wines may be labeled with either name but are the same.

David is frankly unimpressed by very old wines and doesn't see the point of extended aging. "I think that a well made wine with mature tannins can be drunk young. I want the wine to be good when it's bottled, I don't want to make wines that are closed when young." The Hautes Côtes de Nuits has 30% new oak, and the premier and grand crus have 40%. The style is silky with a faint glycerinic sheen, and elegant tannins are usually only just in evidence. Red fruits on the light side favor elegance over power, giving a clean impression. Everything is filtered through the prism of Duband's ultra-modern take on Burgundy.

Domaine Claude Dugat   **

1 place de la Cure, 21220 Gevrey-Chambertin

+33 03 80 34 36 18

Nicolas Dugat

claude.dugat@wanadoo.fr

Gevrey Chambertin

Gevrey Chambertin

6.5 ha; 35,000 bottles

[map p. 105]

It is not often that a mere communal wine from a great vintage is still unready after a decade, but Claude Dugat's Gevrey Chambertin can take years to come around, although promising to showcase a characteristic smooth sheen of black fruits as it develops over its second decade. This small domain, which has something of a cult following in the Anglo-Saxon world, owns 3 ha and rents another 3 ha, and has been managed entirely by Claude and his family. Claude has now retired, and his son Bertrand makes the wine.

The estate is housed in the Cellier des Dimes, a thirteenth century building in the heart of Gevrey Chambertin, just by the church, purchased and restored by Claude's father in 1955. A new cave was constructed in 1976. All the wines come from or near Gevrey Chambertin, extending from a Bourgogne Rouge, through the village wine, two premier crus and three grand crus.

The key to the style here is the low yield, usually below 18 hl/ha, which is a consequence more of small berries than of the number of grape clusters (aided by a proportion of very old vines). The wines have a strong sense of structure resembling the results of whole cluster fermentation, although here everything is in fact destemmed. After fermentation in concrete for about two weeks, the village wine goes into 40-50% new oak, and the premier and grand crus into 100% new oak. When asked about vinification, Bertrand is dismissive. "For me the vines are more important. There are no great winemakers, only great growers," but he adds, "I think Burgundy today makes wines that are too ripe and powerful, I like freshness."

Full of smooth, dense black fruits, the Bourgogne would put many communal wines to shame. The Gevrey Chambertin village wine has the same style, but shows more aromatic lift. Moving to premier crus, the wines become blacker and deeper. At the top of the range, "my three grand crus are like three different people. Charmes Chambertin is jovial and easy, Chapelle Chambertin is larger, more muscular, and Griotte Chambertin is timid and very calm."

All the wines are true vins de garde; they are not for the faint of heart, but definitely require patience. The family's activities are extended by a negociant label, La Gibryotte, which also is confined exclusively to Gevrey Chambertin.

Domaine Bernard Dugat-Py ★★

Rue De Planteligone, B.P. 31, 21220 Gevrey-Chambertin

+33 03 80 51 82 46

Bernard & Loïc Dugat

contact@dugat-py.fr

www.dugat-py.fr

Gevrey Chambertin

Gevrey Chambertin, Coeur du Roy

10.65 ha; 35,000 bottles

[map p. 105]

This domain is much praised by critics in the U.S. for the density and power of its wine, but sometimes criticized in Europe for over-extraction. Bernard Dugat, a cousin of Claude Dugat, has been making wine since 1975, but bottling his own wine only since 1989. The cuverie is located at the foot of the Combe de Lavaux in Gevrey Chambertin, in the remains of the Aumônerie that was constructed in the twelfth century. The winery was renovated in 2004.

Until recently the domain was tightly focused on Gevrey Chambertin, where there are three cuvées of village wine, all rather small: Vieilles Vignes, Coeur du Roy (very old vines of 65-90 years), and the parcel Les Evocelles. There are three premier crus and four grand crus, with the peak being a single barrel of Chambertin. The first white wine of the domain came from a parcel of Morgeots in Chassagne Montrachet purchased in 2004, and Corton Charlemagne was added in 2011. There are other small plots in Vosne Romanée and the Côte de Beaune.

There's always a high proportion of whole clusters, new oak runs 60% or more, and élevage lasts 18 to 24 months. If the wines didn't have so much fruit, they would be quite stern, but as it is, Bernard says a minimum of 6-8 years is required before opening. The huge sense of power comes from low yields rather than extraction during vinification, but certainly the style is enormously rich, with dense black fruits hiding the strong structure. Vin de garde is an under statement.

Domaine Dujac ★★

MOREY SAINT-DENIS
I"CRU MONTS LUISANTS

2008
DOMAINE DUJAC

7 Rue De La Bussière, 21220 Morey-Saint-Denis

+33 03 80 34 01 00

Rosalind Seysses

dujac@dujac.com

www.dujac.com

Morey St. Denis

Morey St. Denis

17.3 ha; 70,000 bottles
[map p. 106]

"Starting in Burgundy I had the disadvantage of not having many generations before me. But I had the advantage of not having three to ten generations before me," says Jacques Seysses, ironically pointing out that being an outsider was balanced by not being overly bound by precedents. He started in 1968 by purchasing a small run-down domain, only 4.5 ha, in Morey St. Denis, which had sold off its grapes. Everything had to be developed from scratch, but the domain has been expanding steadily ever since. After purchasing half of the old Charles Thomas domain in 2005, the winery had to be expanded.

The range now extends from Bourgogne to Grand Cru. Three quarters of the holdings are in premier or grand crus. Jacques's general policy was to use whole bunches for vinification, close to 100% new oak. Belief in tradition extends to cooling the cellar to delay malolactic fermentation until the Spring. After his son Jeremy became involved in 1999, the style softened, with some destemming, and reduced usage of new oak (40-100% today, depending on the cuvée). The general feeling is that terroir shows better as a result of backing off from using complete stems and new oak, but even so, the style can still be a little severe, coming off best with the grand crus where there is the greatest fruit concentration, but the Morey St. Denis can show a lovely balance between crystalline precision and femininity. In addition to the domain wines, the family has a negociant activity, Dujac Père et Fils.

Domaine Sylvie Esmonin ★★

 1 Rue Neuve, 21220 Gevrey-Chambertin

📞 *+33 03 80 34 36 44*

✉ *Sylvie Esmonin*

@ *sylvie-esmonin@orange.fr*

◉ *Gevrey Chambertin*

🍾 *Gevrey Chambertin Vieilles Vignes*

🚫

🍇 *8 ha; 35,000 bottles [map p. 105]*

Sylvie Esmonin was all but born in Clos St. Jacques—when she was a baby she was left in her cot at the end of the row while her parents worked the vines. "It's full of sentiment for me," she says. The domain is on the road along the base of the Clos St. Jacques, with Sylvie's house right at the end of the clos. This is a very hands-on domain: my visit was set for the end of the day because Sylvie was working in the vines during the day. "Working in the vines is my real métier," she says.

The domain is mostly in Gevrey Chambertin, but includes Bourgogne, Côte de Nuits Villages, and some Meursault and Volnay Santenots. "It's a little family domain started by my great grandfather," Sylvie explains. The caves below go deep into the rock and are always cool, so the wines develop slowly: when I visited at the start of July, the previous vintage was just at the start of malolactic fermentation. There's an emphasis on whole cluster fermentation, which is around 30% for communal wines with 5-10% new oak, increasing to 50% for the Vieilles Vignes cuvée of Gevrey Chambertin with a third new oak, and then almost complete for Clos St. Jacques with 100% new oak.

These are very traditional wines. "I don't want to make wines by technique, I work in the same way as my grandparents," Sylvie says. The style is quite dense, increasing in intensity from Gevrey Chambertin to the Vieilles Vignes to the peak of Clos St. Jacques.

Domaine d'Eugénie **

🎯 14 rue de la Gaoillotte, 21700 Vosne-Romanée

📞 +33 03 80 61 10 54

👤 Michel Mallard

@ contact@domaine-eugenie.com

🌐 www.domaine-eugenie.com

▣ Vosne Romanée

🍷 Vosne Romanée

🚫🍴

🍇⬤ 6.5 ha; 20,000 bottles [map p. 107]

The old René Engel domain produced some of the most elegant wines of Vosne Romanée during the 1990s, with village wines as well as the premier cru Brûlées, and holdings also in Clos Vougeot, Echézeaux, and Grands Echézeaux. Created in the early twentieth century by René Engel, who was an oenologist at the university in Dijon, the domain fell into some neglect under his son in the 1970s, and then revived under his grandson Philippe in the 1980s. After the death of Philippe Engel in 2005, the domain was purchased by François Pinault, owner of Château Latour, and the name was changed to Domaine d'Eugénie.

In 2009 the domain moved out of its old house in Vosne Romanée into the Clos Frantin property, which was purchased from Albert Bichot and has been undergoing more or less continuous renovation ever since. There was a change in vineyards. "When we bought this building we swapped some vineyards to get the *clos* outside, which is village AOP, but just next to La Tache," says winemaker Michel Mallard, who came in 2006, and has been stamping his own style on the domain.

Vinification is conventional: a few days cold maceration is followed by fermentation, and then wines go into oak depending on appellation: 40-60% new oak for the village wines, two thirds for the premier crus, and 80% for the grand crus. Regarded as a rising new domain, Domaine d'Eugénie is more a demonstration of the reincarnation of an old domain resulting from unlimited investment. The high price paid to purchase the domain, reportedly €25 million, has been reflected in increased price for the wines.

"The Vosne Romanée village wine is the only blend of the domain," Michel says. It includes younger vines and two specific plots. Its sense of Rolls Royce power epitomizes Vosne Romanée. Clos Eugenie is the new name for the plot outside the winery, and it's a little fuller and rounder, with less obvious fruits and more structure. Premier cru Aux Brulées is more powerful, but smooth and silky in the unique style of Vosne Romanée. Echézeaux comes from a north-facing plot, which explains its sense of restraint and greater structure. Grands Echézeaux is more refined, with real grip from firm tannins. Clos Vougeot comes from an upper plot, and is more opulent with a livelier impression; it's the most precise wine of the domain.

Domaine Faiveley **

8, Rue De Tribourg, 21700 Nuits-Saint-Georges

+33 03 80 61 04 55

Erwan Faiveley

contact@domaine-faiveley.com

www.domaine-faiveley.com

Nuits St. Georges

Clos des Cortons

120 ha; 800,000 bottles

[map p. 108]

Dating from 1825, Faiveley is one of the major domains in Burgundy, with almost half of its vineyards on the Côte d'Or in premier and grand crus, as well as being an important negociant. The source is indicated on the label, as Domaine Faiveley for estate wines, and Joseph Faiveley for wines from purchased grapes. The focus has been on red wines, but the domain has been expanding overt the past decade by purchasing other domains and vineyards, most recently Dupont-Tisserandot in Gevrey Chambertin (see mini-profile) and Chablis producer Billaud-Simon. Faiveley also has significant holdings on the Côte Chalonnaise, especially in Mercurey.

The style of the reds has always been sturdy, but became more extracted and harder in 1993. "For a long time Faiveley was famous for vins de garde for long aging, but we thought it should be possible to produce wines for aging that would be more drinkable young," says Jérôme Flous, explaining that after Erwan Faiveley (then aged 25) took over from his father François in 2004, he started to soften the style. (An abrupt handover seems to be the Faiveley style, as Erwan's father, François, took over from his father in 1976, also at age 25.) A Faiveley vertical shows the old style before 1993, the heavily extracted style until 2006, and since then a more forward fruity style.

Picking today is faster so fruit is fresher, fermentations have been shortened and there is less maceration; pressing is gentler with a new vertical press, and the barriques are higher quality. To compensate for the increased softness, new oak usage has increased: it is up to 15% for village wines, 15-40% for premier crus, and 40-100% for grand crus. The best known wine is perhaps the Clos des Cortons monopole. The strongest suite in reds is a series of premier and grand crus in Gevrey Chambertin, with Les Cazetiers typifying the style. The reds are back on form, and I admit I always found them more interesting than Faiveley's whites before Faiveley started buying significant white grape vineyards. Faiveley's other interests are quite different: Faiveley Transport is involved in producing the TGV.

Domaine Jean Fournier   *

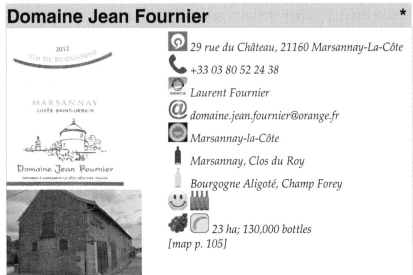

⊙ *29 rue du Château, 21160 Marsannay-La-Côte*

☎ *+33 03 80 52 24 38*

👤 *Laurent Fournier*

@ *domaine.jean.fournier@orange.fr*

▣ *Marsannay-la-Côte*

🍷 *Marsannay, Clos du Roy*

🍾 *Bourgogne Aligoté, Champ Forey*

🙂 ♨ 🍇 ▣ *23 ha; 130,000 bottles*

[map p. 105]

The Fournier family has been growing grapes in Marsannay for generations, but turned exclusively to viticulture when Jean Fournier created the domain in the 1960s. His son Laurent took over in 2003. The old cellars are just off the main road through Marsannay, and now there's a stylish tasting room. Vineyards are mostly in Marsannay, with some small plots in other appellations. Most (80%) are for red wine, but there's also white and a little rosé.

Laurent is committed both to Marsannay and to old varieties. The whites are distinctive in including some unusual blends for Burgundy. The Bourgogne Blanc is two thirds Pinot Blanc and a third Pinot Gris. More aromatic than Chardonnay, it is a lovely aperitif wine. Marsannay Clos St. Urbain is 80% Chardonnay and 20% Pinot Blanc. Laurent is a moving spirit in the association of Aligoteurs—producers who are trying to preserve and improve Aligoté—and he produces three cuvées of Aligoté. Champ Forey Vieilles Vignes is a little tight but with real depth to the fruits. The lieu-dits from Marsannay are 100% Chardonnay, with Les Longeroies rounder and deeper than Clos du Roi.

The rosé is unusually characterful, with a tang of saline minerality. "We make the same aging for whites and rosés, because I want to change the image of the rosé. We age for 18 months for white and rosé—it's expensive for Marsannay but I think it's important." So the rosé is more "serious" than usual for Burgundy. "I don't produce rosé for the summer, it's for gastronomy."

In reds, the Saint Urban blend from about six plots shows fresh cherry fruits. In the lieu-dits, Cloy du Roy, from 40-year-old vines, inclines towards minerality—"the salty character is a feature of Cloy du Roy," Laurent says—while Longeroies, from 40- to 80-year-old vines, is rounder and deeper. The biggest red comes from Ez Chezots (the locals are amused that it is pronounced just like Echézeaux), where the limestone is darker and the plots is windier. The 30-40-year-old vines give a reserved wine that shows its structure more obviously and needs some time. Black grapes are usually 50% destemmed, and the wine ages in a mix of barriques and demi-muids (with a small proportion of new wood) in Austrian oak to limit oak influence.

Domaine Fourrier ***

7 *Route Dijon, Gevrey-Chambertin, 21220*

+33 03 80 34 33 99

Jean-Marie or Vicki Fourrier

@ *domainefourrier@wanadoo.fr*

Gevrey Chambertin

Gevrey Chambertin, Champeaux

10 ha; 50,000 bottles
[map p. 105]

Founded by Fernand Pernot in the 1930s, the domain became known as Pernot-Fourrier when his nephew Jean-Claude Fourrier joined, and then Domaine Fourrier when Jean-Marie Fourrier took over in 1984. The focus is on Gevrey Chambertin, with five premier crus as well as village and grand cru wine. Jean-Marie does not believe in manipulation in the vineyard or winemaking, but says he would call himself more a biologist than a minimalist. He harvests at 100 days after flowering plus or minus five days, and believes that people who harvest very early in warm years or very late in cool years do not necessarily get full ripeness.

His philosophy is also a little different from the usual Burgundian approach. "In Burgundy many producers make a difference in how they handle village, premier cru, and grand cru wines, but this does not make any sense, the difference should rest on the terroir," he says. Jean-Marie uses 20% new oak for all cuvées, more to renew the barrels than to add flavor. All of his vines are old, typically around 50 years.

Grapes are destemmed, there are five days of cold maceration before fermentation, and during aging there is no racking, which keeps a high level of CO_2 and minimizes the requirement for sulfur. The style is fine and precise for Gevrey Chambertin, and there's a clear gradation going from the village wines, which have that slightly hard edge to the palate that's typical of Gevrey, to premier crus such as Goulots, which is more mineral, Champeaux which is earthier, and Clos St. Jacques whose ripe opulence reinforces the impression that it should have been a grand cru. The impression is modern, but continuing to respect Gevrey's typicity.

Domaine Geantet-Pansiot **

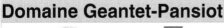

3 Route de Beaune, 21220 Gevrey-Chambertin

+33 03 80 34 32 37

Vincent Geantet

domaine.geantet@wanadoo.fr

Gevrey Chambertin

Gevrey Chambertin, Vieilles Vignes

24 ha; 120,000 bottles

[map p. 105]

This domain was founded relatively recently (in Burgundian terms) when Edmond Geantet married Bernadette Pansiot in 1954 and started to work on 3 ha of Gevrey Chambertin and Bourgogne. The domain increased to 7 ha by 1977 when their son Vincent joined. Vincent has been running the domain since 1989, and Fabien, the third generation, joined in 2006. Vineyard holdings have continued to increase, remaining focused on Gevrey Chambertin, where there are six cuvées extending from village to grand cru, and Chambolle Musigny, where there are two premier crus and a vieilles vignes cuvée. There's still a building with the domain's name on the side on the N74, but production moved in 2013 to a spacious new winery in the quasi-industrial area across the main road to the east of the town.

After destemming and sorting, uncrushed berries go directly into open-topped wooden fermentation vats for a period of cold maceration. Following fermentation, "élevage is the same for all wines in order to show the terroir," Vincent says. There is a third each of new, one-year, and two-year oak barriques. There are 24 cuvées, extending from Bourgogne, Côte de Nuits, Ladoix, and Marsannay, but the focus is on Gevrey Chambertin, extending from village wine to grand. The only white is a Bourgogne Blanc, and there's also a rosé.

The Gevrey Chambertin and premier crus are on the lighter side for the appellation, with that typical tightness of the commune when they are young. In classical manner they require a little time to come around, a couple of years for a light vintage, longer for a strong one. Moving from village wine to premier cru, there is greater elegance rather than more power, with tannins becoming increasingly silky, giving a really fine texture to the black fruits. En Champs is finer than the village wine, Poissenot is finer and also rounder than En Champs, and then grand cru Charmes Chambertin has an aromatic lift showcasing the purity of fruits. "We're looking for fruits and fine tannins, giving finesse," is how Vincent describes his style.

Vincent's daughter has a small negociant business under the name of Emilie Geantet, for which she makes wine in conjunction with her father, with winemaking following the same principles as at Geantet-Pansiot.

Domaine Henri Gouges

**

7 rue du Moulin, 21704, Nuits-Saint-Georges

+33 03 80 61 04 40

Pierre & Christian Gouges

domaine@gouges.com

www.gouges.com

Nuits St. Georges

Nuits St. Georges, Les Pruliers

Nuits St. Georges, Les Perrières

14.5 ha; 50,000 bottles

[map p. 108]

This is one of the most traditional producers in Nuits St. Georges, and the first time I visited, the premises matched my expectations. But a new cuverie was constructed in 2007—in a large courtyard behind the unassuming house—whose existence you would scarcely imagine from the street. Things have not changed with regards to winemaking, however, because "it is the grapes that count." The old cement tanks were moved into the cuverie. The most significant change is that pumping has been eliminated; everything is gravity driven now.

Pierre Gouges says that changes in style are due more to the current age of the vines than anything else; the new cuverie maintains better freshness, so the wine is fruitier, perhaps also due to the lack of pumping. Gouges used to be known for a rather tough style when young, requiring time for the tannins to soften. The changes in the new cuverie have lightened the style, and certainly I notice increased purity of fruit, but although the wines are more accessible, still they are not really intended for early drinking.

Most of the wines come from Nuits St. Georges, including six premier crus as well as the village wine. Les Pruliers is perhaps the most refined, and Les St. Georges the strongest. In addition to the reds, there are also two white wines, from Clos des Porrets St. Georges and Les Perrières, which come from a from a rare albino clone of Pinot Noir observed in the Perrières vineyard. The wines are therefore Pinot Blanc rather than Chardonnay, and the cultivar is now known as the Gouges clone of Pinot Blanc.

Domaine Jean Grivot **

6 rue de La Croix Rameau, 21700 Vosne-Romanée

+33 03 80 61 05 95

Etienne Grivot

domaine.grivot@domainegrivot.fr

www.domainegrivot.fr

Vosne Romanée

Vosne Romanée, Bossières

15 ha; 72,000 bottles

[map p. 107]

The Grivots have an interesting record of buying and selling vineyards advantageously. Coming from the Jura in the seventeenth century, they purchased vineyards at Arcenant (over the mountain from Nuits St. Georges). Just before the Revolution, Joseph Grivot sold these vineyards in order to purchase in Vosne Romanée. In 1919 his son Gaston sold the lesser holdings in order to buy part of Clos Vougeot, running up from the N74 where a splendid entrance gate with a view of the château was built. More recently Jean Grivot purchased a tiny holding in Richebourg. Since 1987, the domain has been run by his son, Etienne.

At almost 2 ha, Clos Vougeot is the largest parcel; parcels in five premier crus of Vosne Romanée and three premier crus of Nuits St. Georges, as well as communal plots, are all under a hectare, sometimes much less. Altogether there are around twenty different cuvées. Vines are replaced individually as necessary, and the average age is around 40 years. Vinification starts with complete destemming, followed by 5 days cold maceration, with fermentation lasting just over two weeks. Élevage lasts 18 months, with 25% new oak for communal wine, 30-60% for premier crus, and 40-70% for grand crus. The style has seemed relatively light in the past, with a spectrum of red rather than black fruits, which can pay off by bringing elegance rather than power to grand crus such as Clos Vougeot, but I find more overt fruits in the young wines of more recent vintages.

Domaine Robert Groffier Père Et Fils   **

Chambertin Clos de Bèze
"Grand Cru"
APPELLATION CHAMBERTIN CLOS DE BÈZE CONTRÔLÉE
RED BURGUNDY WINE
Mis en Bouteille au Domaine
Robert GROFFIER Père & Fils
Propriétaire-Récoltant à Morey-Saint-Denis - Côte d'Or - France

⊙ *3 Route Grands Crus, Morey-Saint-Denis, 21220*

📞 *+33 03 80 34 31 53*

Nicolas Groffier

@ *domaine.groffier@gmail.com*

Morey St. Denis

Gevrey Chambertin

🚫 ⚒ 🍇 🚜 *8 ha; 40,000 bottles [map p. 106]*

"Most of our vineyards are in Chambolle Musigny and most are premier or grand cru. We try to represent the appellation elegance, that's sure, but each cru is different. Sentiers is strong, Haut Doix is more feminine, we try to get the best out of each," says Nicolas Groffier. The domain is located on the main road through Morey St. Denis, but its vineyards are to the south (in Chambolle Musigny) or to the north (in Gevrey Chambertin). It dates back to the nineteenth century, but most of the vineyard holdings were acquired by Jules Groffier in the 1930s; it was his son Robert who started domain bottling after 1973. Nicolas is Robert's grandson.

There's 1 ha of Gevrey Chambertin and 0.5 ha of Clos de Bèze, but the main holdings are three premier crus of Chambolle Musigny, including Les Amoureuses (where Groffier is the largest owner, with three parcels totaling 20% of the cru), and also grand cru Bonnes Mares. Vines are trained in the Cordon Royale instead of the more usual Guyot, in order to reduce yields; the objective is "to seek concentration in the berries and not in the cave."

The Groffiers are late pickers, so the style tends to be full and powerful. Policy on destemming has gone to and fro, and now varies with the vintage; usually there are some whole clusters. Cold maceration is followed by fermentation at unusually high temperature. Since the late 1990s, new oak has been moderate, 20-25% for premier crus, up to 50% for grand crus.

Bourgogne Rouge comes from just on the other side of the N74 from Clos Vougeot, and ages in old barriques. "I could put it in new oak, but that wouldn't serve the purpose, It should drink in 3 years, 5 years maximum, but it's a serious wine, it's well-placed, the separation from Bourgogne to Clos Vougeot is a bit brutal."

Gevrey Chambertin has 30% whole bunches and a little new oak. Fruits are more obvious than the Bourgogne, with the stern character of the appellation showing faintly in the background. The vines in premier cru Haut Doix are 60-years old, and the wine is a beautiful demonstration of the elegance of Chambolle Musigny. "This is the wine that's the most open and easiest to approach that I make." You can see a direct lineage from the Chambolle premier crus to grand cru Bonnes Mares, which is smooth, deep, and seamless, but showing the sense of firmness that characterizes the house style. The rising reputation of the domain has been accompanied by a commensurate increase in prices.

Domaine Anne Gros ★★

2007

ANNE ECHEZEAUX GROS
Appellation Echezeaux Contrôlée
GRAND CRU

LES LOACHAUSSES

DOMAINE
ANNE GROS
Propriétaire Viticulteur - www.anne-gros.com

11, Rue Des Communes, 21700 Vosne-Romanée

+33 03 80 61 07 95

Anne Gros

domaine-annegros@orange.fr

www.anne-gros.com

Vosne Romanée

Vosne Romanée, Les Barreaux

6.5 ha; 35,000 bottles [map p. 107]

The old Louis Gros domain produced some splendid wines in the fifties and sixties, but in the way of French inheritance, the domain became divided into several parts, today represented by Gros Frère et Soeur, Jean Gros, Michel Gros, A. F. Gros, and Anne Gros. After a decade during which production was sold to negociants, Anne Gros and her father François effectively restarted his part of the domain in 1988 (as Anne et François Gros, not to be confused with A. F. Gros!), and then changed the name to Anne Gros in 1998. The best plots are the village parcels and grand crus from Louis Gros. The only whites are Hautes Côtes de Nuits and Bourgogne.

The domain is located around a gracious courtyard in the center of Vosne Romanée, but extends well back into a practical building on the edge of the vineyards. All vinification is in stainless steel and there is 100% destemming. "Je deteste vendange entière (using whole bunches)", Anne says. "I am looking for aromatic precision, and the grapes are uncrushed, so we get the advantages of whole berries without the stems. You need to focus on finesse, if you push too much, the wine becomes square. I want as much extraction as I can, but without getting to the point where tannins become rustic." Village wines usually get 30% new oak, going up to a limit of 60% for grand crus.

The wines are precise and well-structured at all levels. Hautes Côtes de Nuits comes from vineyards at 400m just above Vosne Romanée, and is fresh but well-rounded for the AOP. The Bourgogne Rouge comes from just the other side of the N74, and gets extra roundness from 50-year-old vines. The delicacy of the Chambolle Musigny is a bit of an exception from the line of intense black fruit purity, but Vosne Romanée is classic for the appellation and the domain. The domain passes straight from village wines to grand crus, with Echézeaux round and intense, Clos Vougeot balanced between intrinsic fleshiness and the structure of Côtes de Nuits, and Richebourg remarkable for its finesse and purity.

Anne is married to Jean Paul Tollot (of Tollot-Beaune in Savigny-lès-Beaune) and in 2008 they extended their winemaking into a domain in Minervois. "We wanted to work together, so we decided to have a joint enterprise. And we have three children, so there are family reasons as well as the passion for wine," Anne says.

Domaine Hoffman-Jayer

*

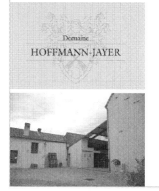

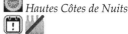

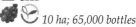

Route Corgoloin, Magny-Les-Villers, 21700

+33 03 80 62 91 79

Alexandre Vernet

domaine@hoffmann-jayer.com

Hautes Côtes de Nuits

10 ha; 65,000 bottles

Under its original name of Jayer-Gilles, this was considered to be one of the most artisanal domains of the Côte d'Or. A cousin of Henri Jayer, Robert Jayer-Gilles created the domain, and his son Gilles took over when he retired in 1998. Most of the vineyards are on the Hautes Côtes; the village of Magny-lès-Villers is at the junction of the Hautes Côtes de Beaune and Hautes Côtes de Nuits, so there are cuvées from both, although the vineyards are in the same village. Unusually for the area, they are planted at the same 10,000 vines per hectare as the top vineyards of the Côte d'Or. Small holdings in Nuits St. Georges and Echézeaux total 1 ha. Not long before he died, Gilles sold the estate in 2017 to Swiss billionaire André Hoffman of Hoffmann-La-Roche, and the name was changed to Hoffman-Jayer. Winemaker Alexandre Vernet says that, "We don't have any plans to expand the domain except perhaps for another white."

The domain was famous for its stern winemaking policy, with 100% new oak for all cuvées, something that few producers could pull off on the Hautes Côtes. Policy remains generally the same under the new ownership, and Alexandre says that, "I want to maintain the artisanal reputation and even to increase it, from moving viticulture to organic to having very long vinification with lots of extract." The only change is that, "I'm reducing new oak a bit for the lower-level wines to make them more immediately approachable."

There are both whites and reds from both Hautes Côtes. In each case, there is a little more power to the Hautes Côtes de Nuits, but the differences is more marked with the reds. The whites both contain 30% Pinot Blanc with 70% Chardonnay and give a finely textured impression. The red Hautes Côtes de Beaune seems more elegant while the Hautes Côtes de Nuits seems more powerful.

The artisanal style is evident in the Côtes de Nuits Villages, which comes from two parcels in Corgoloin. Perfumed black fruits are elegant, but with a definite tannic edge. Nuits St. Georges shows more aromatics and tannins kick in on the finish. In Echézeaux, the aromatics move more towards tobacco, the palate shows precision of black fruits, but tannins really grip the finish. The domain's reputation is for lots of extraction, but although tannins certainly grip the finish when the wines are young, the style is quite perfumed and elegant.

Domaine Hudelot-Noëllat ★★

 5 Ancienne Route Nationale 74, 21220 Chambolle-Musigny

 +33 03 80 62 85 17

 Charles Van Caneyt

@ contact@domaine-hudelot-noellat.com

🌐 www.domaine-hudelot-noellat.com

 Chambolle Musigny

🍾 Vouvray Moelleux, Plan de Jean

 10.5 ha; 60,000 bottles
[map p. 106]

Alain Hudelot formed the domain in 1964, then changed the name to Hudelot-Noëllat in 1978 when he married Odile Noëllat, the granddaughter of Charles Noëllat (whose domain was purchased by Lalou Bize-Leroy in 1998). Alain retired in 2008, and his grandson Charles van Canneyt took over.

There are 15 appellations in the domain, in Chambolle Musigny, Vosne Romanée, and Vougeot. Vineyards include some top premier crus—Vosne Romanée les Malconsorts, Les Beaumonts and Les Suchots—and grand crus Richebourg and Romanée St. Vivant. Many of the vines are close to a hundred years old. Winemaking is traditional, with 15% new oak for village wines, 30% for premier crus, and a maximum of 50% for Romanée St. Vivant.

As you would expect from the focus on Vosne Romanée, the style tends to opulence, but is very refined. Richebourg shows characteristic breadth while Romanée St. Vivant shows typical precision. Tasting a vertical of Romanée St. Vivant identifies that characteristic line of purity, even in lesser vintages. Even in the grand crus, the wines are never heavy. "We are looking for freshness and elegance. The difficulty in 2015 was to keep the balance between richness and acidity. Personally I don't want to do heavy wines."

Charles decided also to add a negociant activity under his own name, beginning with only 7 barrels. Now there are 25 barrels at the negociant, mostly grand crus, premier crus, and some villages, and sometimes Bourgogne. "I try to produce appellations we don't have at the domain." The wines for the negociant are made at separate facilities in Beaune.

Domaine François Lamarche ***

9 Rue Des Communes, 21700 Vosne-Romanée

+33 03 80 61 07 94

Nathalie Lamarche

vins@domaine-lamarche.fr

www.domaine-lamarche.com

Vosne Romanée

Vosne Romanée

11 ha; 60,000 bottles

[map p. 107]

"This has been a family domain for five generations," says Nathalie Lamarche. "Today we are a feminine domain. My cousin Nicole is the winemaker and viticulturalist; I deal with the commercial part." The domain took its present form under Henri Lamarche in the early twentieth century. His grandson, François, was the winemaker until Nicole took over in 2007. Aside from the Bourgogne and a Nuits St. Georges premier cru and Clos Vougeot, all the wines come from Vosne Romanée, mostly premier crus and grand crus. The only white wine is a Bourgogne Aligoté. The vineyards have old vines, and the average age (now around 60 years) is maintained by replacing vines one by one as necessary. The domain is appropriately located in a rather grand house in Vosne Romanée.

The wines have improved steadily since a new cellar was constructed in 1990. New oak is moderate, usually around 30%, but with a maximum of 50% for the grand crus. Élevage is usually 12-15 months. After racking off, wine stays in stainless steel for a few months before bottling. There is no fining and no filtration.

With important holdings in Vosne Romanée and its premier and grand crus, all Lamarche wines are at a high level. The Rolls Royce combination of silkiness and power reaches its peak in the monopole La Grand Rue, which was a wedding present to Henri Lamarche, and has the rare distinction of having been promoted from premier cru to grand cru (with effect from 1991), but a ripe, round style, with fruits supported by supple tannins, runs through the whole range. They do require some time to develop: Nathalie recommends waiting at least five years after the vintage.

The Vosne Romanée village wine is classic: rich, round, ripe with great grip and a touch of aromatics. Malconsorts is not so much deeper than the village wine as more precise, with greater flavor variety as it develops. Suchots is always the top premier cru. Echézeaux has a marginally deeper expression than the Vosne Romanée premier crus. Clos Vougeot is a blend of plots from the upper and lower parts, showing classic opulence in a rich expression of black fruits. Grands Echézeaux is finer and more linear. The seamless quality of La Grande Rue is very much in line with La Tache and Romanée St. Vivant.

Domaine des Lambrays ★★★

31 Rue Basse, 21220 Morey-Saint-Denis

+33 03 80 51 84 33

Jacques Devauges

clos@lambrays.com

www.lambrays.com

Morey St. Denis

Clos des Lambrays

11 ha; 40,000 bottles

[map p. 106]

The domain is effectively synonymous with the Clos des Lambrays, a 9 ha vineyard in Morey St. Denis. References to Cloux des Lambrey go back to 1365. It was divided between 74 owners after the Revolution, but reunited in 1868. The domain owns all but a tiny parcel at the bottom. Clos des Lambrays was classified as premier cru in 1936 because its owner did not submit the paperwork to become a grand cru. The estate was somewhat neglected until a change of ownership in 1979, when Thierry Brouin came as winemaker. He is generally credited with restoring the estate to its former glory; he retired in 2015.

The clos was promoted to grand cru in 1981. The domain also produces two other red cuvées: Les Loups is a blend from young vines of the clos together with plots in two premier crus, and there is a communal Morey St. Denis. There are also two Puligny Montrachets from tiny plots in Caillerets and Folatières. Occasionally there is a rosé (from less ripe grapes selected out during sorting; it is superb, with the quality of the grand cru evident).

Winemaking is traditional, with fermentation of whole bunches irrespective of vintage. I would describe the style as upright. Younger vintages can seem tight, and older vintages soften slowly, with fruits moving from cherries towards strawberries, but not evolving in a savory or tertiary direction in the first couple of decades. The focus is on purity and precision of fruit. Running counter to the modern trend, these are definitely not wines for instant gratification: it remains to be seen how that will play under the aegis of LVMH, who purchased the estate in 2014 for €101 million.

Maison Dominique Laurent ★★

2 rue Jacques Duret, 21700 Nuits-Saint-Georges

+33 03 80 61 31 62

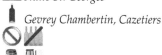

Dominique Laurent

+33 03 80 62 32 42

Nuits St. Georges

Gevrey Chambertin, Cazetiers

7 ha; 300,000 bottles

A pastry chef before he went into wine, Dominique Laurent made his name as a negociant. He became famous for the technique of using 200% new oak, meaning that the wine is racked from new oak barrels into a second set of new oak barrels. Attempts to discuss his methods are firmly rebuffed. "Like any artisan, I have no wish or need to discuss; my experiences and research are secret and from a commercial point of view can't be explained, you understand my position?.. I have even less wish to discuss a subject which has caused me so much criticism from the most stupid people... You'll have to give just another opinion based on tasting." Recently, Dominique appears to have decided that 100% new oak is enough, because he has supplies of higher quality oak; he selects the trees himself in the Tronçais forest.

Insofar as it's possible to form any single opinion, my impression is that sometimes the approach works, and sometimes it overwhelms the wine. An interesting comparison is between the Laurent's Gevrey Chambertin premier cru Clos St. Jacques with the corresponding cuvée from Sylvie Esmonin, from whom he buys the grapes. In 2002, the Laurent wine was richer and rounder, but in 1999 the fruits could not show through Laurent's oak.

Focused on Gevrey Chambertin (although not necessarily making the same cuvées every year), the Laurent wines are always powerful. The style certainly comes over as unusually powerful in, for example, Chambolle Musigny where the usual delicacy of the appellation gives way to overt richness; the richer fruits in, say, Charmes Chambertin, carry the style better, but in Vosne Romanée the combination of Laurent's style with the power of the appellation can be overwhelming.

I think it's fair to say that Dominique's style dominates over appellation, partly because of strong oak, partly because of the use of vendange entière, which together give an acerbic note and overly structured impression to the finish. Since 2006, Dominique has also been making wine with his son Jean from vines rented in Vosne Romanée.

Domaine Philippe Leclerc ＊

9-13, rue-des-Halles, 21220 Gevrey-Chambertin

+33 03 80 34 30 72

Véronique & Philippe Leclerc

+33 03 80 34 17 39

www.philippe-leclerc.com

Gevrey Chambertin

Gevrey Chambertin, en Champs

8 ha; 48,000 bottles

[map p. 105]

Philippe Leclerc has adopted an economic model that would be familiar in the New World, but is quite rare in France. When Philippe took over the family domain in the 1970s, he bought a building right in the center of Gevrey Chambertin, and since then has expanded into neighboring buildings. The building has a tasting room and shop above old caves that are used for stockage and display. The tasting room is almost always open (even on Sundays), and a tasting of 6 wines is offered for a nominal fee. The wines are produced in a cuverie across the street. There's a village wine, a lieu-dit, and four premier crus, all in Gevrey Chambertin, and also a Chambolle Musigny and Bourgogne.

"We are producing wines mostly to sell here in the tasting room, but we are not making wines to drink very young. The goal is that we sell a lot here, almost three quarters is sold here, perhaps one day we will sell it all here. When people make wines (exclusively) to export, they have to make wines that sell very young, but we want to keep the taste of the real Gevrey Chambertin. If you make a very light Gevrey that you could drink immediately, it is not a real Gevrey." All the same, the style has been evolving. "Ten or twenty years ago you had to wait 10 or 15 years to open our wines, now it's 4 or 5 years. The wines are smoother and rounder at an earlier age." the change was fairly abrupt, as indicated by a remark in the tasting room. "We have a Chambolle from 2005, but it is typical of the old style, it is rather full bodied"—so we tasted a Combe aux Moines from 2006 instead.

The Gevrey Chambertin shows a light style for the village wine, and the en Champs lieu-dit (just below the premier crus) is a touch smoother and silkier in the same style. The first impression of roundness to the hard edge of Gevrey comes with the Champeaux premier cru. The real jump in quality comes with Les Cazetiers, where the house style shows as elegant, pure, and precise. Combe aux Moines is more structured and requires longer, not really opening out until around eight years after the vintage. More clay in the soil gives a richer wine at Champonnets.

Domaine Leroy   ★★★★

 15 Rue De La Fontaine, 21700 Vosne-Romanée

 +33 03 80 21 21 10

 Lalou Bize Leroy

@ domaine.leroy@wanadoo.fr

 www.domaineleroy.com

 Vosne Romanée

 Nuits St. Georges

Meursault-Blagny, Premier Cru

 22 ha; 40,000 bottles

[map p. 107]

Maison Leroy was a negociant, but Henri Leroy also acquired a half share in Domaine de la Romanée Conti. Henri's daughter, Lalou Bize-Leroy, ran Maison Leroy and distributed DRC wines until a disagreement caused her to leave DRC in 1992. Domaine Leroy was founded in 1988 by purchasing the vineyards of Charles Noëllat in Vosne Romanée; Takayashima of Japan is a sleeping partner.

Located in an unassuming house in Vosne Romanée, the domain has a small winemaking facility, with open-topped wood fermenters. All wines go into new barriques, as they have the character to stand up to, and indeed, require, new oak. Yields are minuscule here: "25hl/ha is, for me, the absolute maximum for a grand cru," Lalou says. The domain has been biodynamic since its creation: Lalou is a fervent believer to the point of following the lunar cycle to apply the preparations.

Vinification is traditional. "Jamais, jamais, jamais" was the response when I asked if destemming is used. The wines show an intensity and concentration across the range that would put most producers to shame; the character of each appellation is magnified by sheer purity of expression. There was a look of surprise when I asked whether Lalou would call her wines "vins de garde" as though the question was simply too obvious to be worth answering. She also owns Domaine d'Auvenay in Saint Romain, a small domain inherited from her father, which is run on the same principles.

Domaine du Comte Liger-Belair ⋆⋆

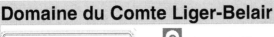

🔵 *Château De Vosne Romanée, 21700 Vosne-Romanée*

📞 *+33 03 80 62 13 70*

📇 *Louis-Michel Liger-Belair*

@ *contact@liger-belair.fr*

🌐 *www.liger-belair.fr*

◉ *Vosne Romanée*

🍾 *Vosne Romanée, Petits Monts*

📅 *10.5 ha; 30,000 bottles*
[map p. 107]

The domain as such was created in 2000 by Louis-Michel Liger-Belair, but the name goes way back into the history of Vosne Romanée, starting with the purchase of vineyards in 1815, when General Liger-Belair returned from the Napoleonic wars. In the mid nineteenth century, Comte Liger-Belair owned parts of La Tâche and La Romanée, as well as parts of several premier crus in Vosne Romanée and elsewhere.

Most of the holdings were sold when the estate was dispersed in the early 1930s; the grapes from what remained were sold off or the vineyards were rented out. Two branches of the family own vineyards and have recently resurrected domains, Thibault Liger-Belair in Nuits St. Georges (see mini-profile), and Comte Liger-Belair in Vosne Romanée.

Comte Liger-Belair is a general, but his son Louis-Michel wanted to be a winemaker and started his domain with the 1.5 ha of his father's remaining vineyards, which include the monopole of grand cru La Romanée. He added another 1.5 ha in 2002. Other vineyards are rented in Vosne Romanée and Nuits St. Georges. The smallest parcel from which a single cuvée is made is 0.12 ha. There's a focus on old vines, with most plantings varying from 60 to 90 years old; the domain may be young, but attitudes are quite traditional: "We don't make Pinot Noir, we make Burgundy."

The style here tends to elegance, almost delicacy, with concern to avoid over-extraction. Since the domain started, there's been a change to longer cold soak before fermentation starts and less maceration after fermentation; pumping-over is used rather than punch-down. Wine is kept on the lees, without racking, once malolactic fermentation has finished. The strength of the wines (mostly from Vosne Romanée, after all) calls for reliance on largely new barriques for maturation.

Domaine Michel Magnien   *

26 Route Nationale, 21220 Morey-Saint-Denis

+33 03 80 51 82 98

Maxime Pinder

domaine@michel-magnien.com

www.domaine-magnien.com

Morey St. Denis

23 ha; 160,000 bottles

[map p. 106]

There are two Magniens. Michel and Frédéric are father and son, but their names on the label have different meanings. Domaine Michel Magnien means the wines come from the estate, which includes 23 cuvées from the Côte de Nuits. Maison Frédéric Magnien refers to the negociant, with grapes coming from around 20 growers, and production a little greater than the domain. The negociant is a bit broader in scope, still more focused on the Côte de Nuits, but including some whites from the Côte de Beaune. Fréderic joined his father in 1993, and started Maison Frédéric Magnien in 1995; Michel has now re-tired and Frédéric makes all the wines at the cuverie on the N74 at Morey St. Denis. Black labels are used for Domaine Michel Magnien, and white labels for Frédéric Magnien. The tasting room was renovated and opened to the public in 2016, but unusually does not sell the latest vintages, and mostly offers vintages from 5 to 10 years old.

Winemaking is identical whether for black or white label. Frédéric does not like the taste of oak in the wine—"we want to taste the typicity of the terroir." Only old barriques are used, and in 2015 clay jars were introduced for matu-ration. More than a hundred clay jars were purchased in 2016. "We think the clay jars make the wine more accessible. We get more oxygenation and finer tannins." A couple of grand crus have been vinified exclusively in clay jars, but most of the premier and grand crus are vinified in a roughly equal mix of old barriques and clay jars.

The house style is light, never highly extracted. Whites show as fresh rather than powerful. For reds, this plays well for the wines of Chambolle Musigny and Morey St. Denis, but the wines are lighter than expected for, say, Vosne Romanée. Even the Vosne Romanée is ready to drink by, say, four years after the vintage. In a generous vintage such as 2015, the wines from Chambolle and Morey St. Denis may be virtually ready to drink on release.

Maison Marchand-Tawse   *

9 *rue Julie Godmet, BP 76, 21700 Nuits-Saint-Georges*

+33 03 80 20 37 32

Pascal Marchand

contact@marchandtawse.com

www.marchand-tawse.com

Nuits St. Georges

Vosne Romanée

Meursault, Les Charmes

12 ha; 120,000 bottles

[map p. 108]

"I'm from Montreal, I came to Burgundy thirty years ago, I was a régisseur in Pommard at Comte Armand, then I was with Vougeraie for seven vintages. In 2006 I decided to create my own label," says Pascal Marchand. "I started by renting premises, and making 5 wines and 1,000 cases." Starting as a negociant, Pascal expanded by forming a partnership in 2010 with Canadian banker Moray Tawse, and the firm became Marchand-Tawse. In 2012 they purchased Domaine Maume in Gevrey Chambertin, which brought premier and grand cru vineyards to the portfolio. Pascal bought his own space in the center of Nuits St. Georges in 2011, with buildings surrounding a handsome courtyard, a large warehouse-like facility on the other side of the street, and extensive cellars underground. He also makes wine in Western Australia under the Marchand & Burch label.

The estate vineyards are about half in Bourgogne, with the rest divided between villages and premier or grand crus. Today production is about half from his own vineyards and half from purchased grapes (where half are premier or grand cru, and most of the rest are communal). Altogether there are about 60 wines, many in small quantities, sometimes only 1-3 barrels. 30% is white; about half is Côte de Beaune and half is Côte de Nuits. At the moment, all the wines have the same label but Pascal says that, "In the long run I want to distinguish between the negociant parts and the wines from our own vineyards." There's a family resemblance between the wines going from Nuits St Georges to Vosne Romanée to Gevrey Chambertin: refinement is the common feature that runs through all.

Domaine Méo-Camuzet **

📍 *11, Rue Des Grands Crus, 21700 Vosne-Romanée*

📞 *+33 03 80 61 55 55*

Jean-Nicolas Méo

@ *information@meo-camuzet.com*

🌐 *www.meo-camuzet.com*

Vosne Romanée

Nuits St. Georges, Les Boudots

18 ha; 130,000 bottles [map p. 107]

Every time I visit Méo-Camuzet, there seems to be a new expansion. The latest has been to expand the hundred-year old cave underneath the courtyard. A previous effort showed a liking for modernization by adding a striking glass front to the old building. From its inception until fairly recently, the domain was rented out, as founder Étienne Camuzet and his successors were not resident in Burgundy. In 1988, Jean-Nicolas Méo took over the estate, reclaimed the vineyards, and started bottling. (He was helped by Henri Jayer, who had been farming many of the vineyards.) Production is divided between the domain (60%) and purchased grapes, which tend to focus on village wines. The label on domain wines says Domaine Méo-Camuzet, while the negociant label says Méo-Camuzet Frères et Soeurs.

The domain has some remarkable holdings: six grand crus and ten premier crus as well as villages and Hautes Côtes de Nuits. The parcel of Clos Vougeot was originally bought by Étienne Camuzet together with the château itself (which he owned until it became the headquarters of the Confrérie). Most of the holdings are in Nuits St. Georges or Vosne Romanée, but individual cuvées don't necessarily show appellation stereotypes. The estate Nuits St. Georges comes from lieu dit Au Bas de Combe, right at the junction with Vosne Romanée. Vosne Romanée is a blend from two plots, three quarters from a cool spot up the slope, one quarter from the center of the village. Typically the harvest is a week later for the Vosne village wine than for Nuits. "Our Vosne is more structured and our Nuits is more feminine, it all depends on the plot," says Jean-Nicolas.

Vinification varies with the cuvée, for example, with varying extents of destemming. Use of new oak has backed off, and now the lesser wines (Bourgogne or Marsannay) have up to 10% new oak, village wines less than 50%, premier crus 50-60%, and grand crus 80%. I find that the estate wines are stronger and more rounded than the negociant wines, but that may be partly because the estate has such splendid vineyards.

The classic cuvées are Vosne Romanée Brulées, planted in the 1930s (in a plot next to Richebourg), Clos Vougeot, and Cros Parantoux (made famous by Henri Jayer). The style is glossy, with the negociant wines showing red cherry fruits, and estate wines moving more towards black fruits. For the top wines, "There's a window after bottling for two years when they are open—although you would miss the soul of the wine—then forget them for another five years."

Jean-Nicolas is a livewire, and since 2014 he's been making Pinot Noir at his Domaine Nicolas-Jay, in Oregon's Willamette Valley. Here he has designed his own winery. The wine is in the Burgundian tradition, but doesn't have the breed of Méo-Camuzet.

Domaine Denis Mortet **

 Rue de Lavaux, 21220 Gevrey-Chambertin

📞 +33 03 80 34 10 05

Arnaud Mortet

@ contact@domaine-denis-mortet.fr

🌐 www.domaine-denis-mortet.com

Gevrey Chambertin

Gevrey Chambertin, Les Champeaux

🚫

🍇 12.5 ha; 70,000 bottles

[map p. 105]

There's a sad history to this domain, which has continued to develop its style in recent years. The domain was founded by Denis Mortet in 1991, with vines he obtained when his father retired. (The other half of the family inheritance became Domaine Thierry Mortet.) The domain more or less doubled in size when Denis took over the Guyot estate in 1993. His focus was on working the vineyards to reduce yields and obtain ripe berries, and the result was that wines tended to be somewhat ripe and powerful in what was often regarded as the new wave style. He was known for bringing as much care and attention to his communal vines as to the grand crus. His well known description was that the wines should be "a pleasure to drink young or old." Denis died young in 2006 after taking his own life as the result of depression.

The wines now are made by his son Arnaud. Holdings include 14 different appellations; the most important are in Gevrey Chambertin, extending from Le Chambertin, several premier crus, and a variety of communal plots (which may be bottled as one or more cuvées). There's a strong use of new barriques, with most of the premier and grand crus seeing 100% new oak; communal wines see about 60% new oak, and even the Bourgogne has 30-40%. Whether because the vineyards are maturing, the work in the vineyards is more detailed, or vinification is more precise, there is general agreement that the wines show increasing finesse.

Domaine Georges Mugneret-Gibourg **

📍 *5 Rue Communes, Vosne-Romanée, 21700*

📞 *+33 03 80 61 01 57*

👤 *Marie-Andrée Nauleau*

@ *dgm@mugneret-gibourg.com*

🌐 *www.mugneret-gibourg.com*

◎ *Vosne Romanée*

🏛 *Nuits St. Georges, Les Chaignots*

⚠ 🍴 🍇 🍷 *6 ha; 30,000 bottles [map p. 107]*

"Mugneret-Gibourg used to be under the radar but now it's been discovered," says one wine merchant ruefully. Originally there were two domains, Mugneret-Gibourg, created in 1933 by the marriage of Jeanne Gibourg and André Mugneret, and Georges Mugneret, created by their son who purchased additional vineyards in his own name. George's daughters, Marie-Christine and Marie-Andrée, took over the domains, and were forced to make wine under both labels until in 2009, "after the stupidity of the French administration, we managed to combine the domains" says Marie-Andrée. Now all the wines are labeled as Domaine Georges Mugneret-Gibourg. Production increased in 2016 when 2 ha was regained after a sharecropping arrangement terminated.

The domain is located in what looks like an ordinary house around a courtyard, but it extends deceptively far back, opening out on to the domain's major vineyard, from which you can see all the way back to the N74. It's presently a matriarchal domain with two sisters and three daughters, but after that, in the next generation there is a boy. It's very hands-on: Lucy Teillaud-Mugneret greeted us when we arrived, then went off to help her aunt Marie-Christine run the bottling line.

Vineyards include Bourgogne, Vosne Romanée and Nuits St. Georges villages, premier crus from Nuits St. Georges and Chambolle Musigny, and grand crus Echézeaux, Clos Vougeot, and Ruchottes Chambertin. Marie-Andrée describes vinification as classic, meaning that there is complete destemming and fermentation with indigenous yeast. "We make the wine in the same way for each appellation because terroir is the most important. The way we make Bourgogne is the same as the way we make grand crus. The only difference is the amount of new oak, of course." There's 20% new oak for Bourgogne, 30% for village, 40% for premier cru, and 75-80% for grand cru.

The style epitomizes the Côte des Nuits, with pure, clean, black fruits tending towards freshness and minerality. The wines are not exactly stern when young—one French critic calls them "introverted," which is a fair description. Certainly these are not wines for instant gratification; they start tight, develop slowly, and need time to come around. Going from the village wines to premier crus, there is increasing refinement and silkiness. The grand crus mark the full range of the domain: Ruchottes Chambertin is all silky elegance, Clos Vougeot is unusually elegant for the appellation but shows a sense of soft opulence, and Echézeaux has a deep and broader structure.

Domaine Jacques Frédéric Mugnier ***

Château De Chambolle-Musigny, 21220 Chambolle-Musigny

+33 03 80 62 85 39

Frédéric Mugnier

info@mugnier.fr

mugnier.fr

Chambolle Musigny

Chambolle Musigny

13.5 ha; 45,000 bottles
[map p. 106]

In the early nineteenth century the Mugniers developed a successful business in liqueurs in Dijon. In 1863 they purchased the Château de Chambolle Musigny, an imposing Château at the foot of the hill, and they acquired the vineyards that form the basis of the domain. All the vineyards were in Chambolle Musigny until their last purchase, the Clos de la Maréchale in Nuits St. Georges, in 1902. This vineyard was leased to Faiveley and reverted to Mugnier only in 2004; now it is their largest single property. The vineyards are not formally organic, but there is no use of fertilizers, herbicides, or pesticides. All the wines are red, except for a white that was introduced at the Clos de la Maréchale.

Frédéric Mugnier was an airline pilot until he started to run the domain full time in 2000. Soon he was forced to expand, building a new cuverie under the courtyard of the Château, when the domain was tripled by the reversion of the Clos de la Maréchale. The Chambolle Musigny and the two premier crus, Les Fuées and Les Amoureuses, are the quintessence of elegance, textbook examples of the "femininity" of Chambolle. The Clos de la Maréchale follows the same style but is more obviously structured. "It took me years to realize that the best way to vinify the different terroirs was to make all the wine exactly the same," says Frédéric, and today all the wines get the same 15-20% new oak. Freddy says he would be happy to be described as a minimalist but would prefer "essentialist."

Domaine Sylvain Pataille   *

📍 *14 Rue Neuf, 21160 Marsannay-La-Côte*

📞 *+33 03 80 51 17 35*

✎ *Sylvain Pataille*

@ *domaine.sylvain.pataille@wanadoo.fr*

⬤ *Marsannay-la-Côte*

🍾 *Marsannay, Clos du Roy*

🏭 ⛟ *13 ha; 50,000 bottles*

[map p. 105]

After studying in Bordeaux, Sylvain Pataille returned to Burgundy and became a consulting oenologist in 1997 (including Roumier and Groffier among his clients); he still consults for several domains, but in 2001 he established his own domain, starting out with a hectare. The domain focuses on Marsannay and its environs, producing red, white, and rosé. In addition to Marsannay, there's AOP Bourgogne from vineyards just to the north in Chenôve (which Sylvain comments had a higher reputation when it used to be known as part of the Côte de Dijon). Most of the vineyards are rented on long term contracts.

Altogether there are 8 reds, 5 whites, and 2 rosés. In addition to communal Marsannay cuvées of all three colors, there are several red cuvées from individual lieu-dits of Marsannay (there are presently no premier crus in the Marsannay appellation, but perhaps Sylvain's efforts will result in some lieu-dits being promoted). Sylvain is a modernist in the context of Marsannay. Vinification is in stainless steel and fiberglass tanks, and élevage usually uses a maximum of 30-35% new oak for 12-18 months. The reds are round, the whites are crisp, and the rosés have unusual character. Sylvain is actually a fan of Aligoté, and his largest vineyard is 3 ha of Bourgogne Aligoté. The best of the lieu-dits in Marsannay are Les Longeroies and Clos du Roy, but the top wine of the domain is L'Ancestrale, a cuvée from a 1 ha plot of vines planted in 1946.

Domaine Henri Perrot-Minot ***

⊙ *54 Route-des-Grands Crus, 21220 Morey-Saint-Denis*

📞 *+33 03 80 34 32 51*

Christophe Perrot-Minot

@ *gfa.perrot-minot@wanadoo.fr*

🌐 *www.perrot-minot.com*

Morey St. Denis

Morey St. Denis, La Riotte

🚫🍴

🍇 *13 ha; 65,000 bottles*

[map p. 106]

I started off on the wrong foot when I visited Perrot-Minot by mistakenly going to the new winery across the N74, but Christophe Perrot-Minot was typically charming about it, and the next day we had a splendid tasting in the cellars of the old domain in the center of Morey St. Denis. Christophe is the fourth generation, and worked as a wine broker before making his first vintage in 1993. The domain originated with Domaine Maume Morizot, which was formed by his great grandfather, but the estate was subsequently divided into four parts in 1973. Christophe is quite hands on, spending his mornings in the vineyards; when I arrived, he had just returned from the green pruning.

The key here is a combination of old vines and low yields, 20-30 hl/ha for everything, even the Bourgogne. Everything is destemmed except for four cuvées: grapes are cut one by one from the central stem—Christophe calls this destructuration. The house style is faintly spicy and nutty with perfumed hints. Smooth palates show round fruits with silky tannins, never any rough edges; the overall impression is ultra-modern, with a silky approachability even in Gevrey Chambertin or Vosne Romanée, but there's structure behind. Yet when I asked Christophe if he regards himself as a modernist, he was a bit indignant. "For me this is traditional, not modern. It's not that I'm looking for drinking young, I'm looking for elegance, balance, and concentration, but it must be natural, it must come from the berries."

Domaine Ponsot ***

📍 *17 à 21 rue de La Montagne, BP 11, 21220 Morey-Saint-Denis*

📞 *+33 03 80 34 32 46*

@ *info@domaine-ponsot.com*

🌐 *www.domaine-ponsot.com*

▣ *Morey St. Denis*

🍷 *Morey St. Denis, Premier Cru*

🍷 *Morey St. Denis, Monts Luisants*

🚫 🍴 🚜 *10 ha; 50,000 bottles [map p. 106]*

William Ponsot established the domain in 1870 with the vineyards that are still at its heart: premier cru Monts Luisants and grand cru Clos de La Roche. Jean-Marie Ponsot took over in 1957, expanding the domain by marriage, and becoming mayor of Morey St. Denis. Laurent Ponsot took over in 1981, and expanded north into Gevrey Chambertin and south into Chambolle Musigny. Ponsot's vineyard in Clos de la Roche was the origin for the now-famous Dijon clones of Pinot Noir. An impressive gravity-feed winery at the top of the hill in the town extends several storeys underground. The range extends from communal Morey St. Denis and Gevrey Chambertin to grand crus.

Owned by Laurent together with his three sisters, the domain encountered an unexpected turn of events when Laurent announced in 2017 that he was leaving after 36 years with his son Clément to form his own negociant (see profile). His sister Rose-Marie is now in charge, and Alexandre Abel was appointed as winemaker in time to make the 2017 vintage.

Winemaking policy has not changed. Ponsot harvests late in order to get maximum ripeness, and usually is the last in the village. Regarded as a fashion, there is no new oak, the wines are not filtered, and there is minimum use of sulfur (for reds a little sulfur is added only at bottling).One of the rare white wines produced in the Côte de Nuits, Mont Luisants is unique in consisting of Aligoté. The vines go back to 1911. "It's not always easy to distinguish as Aligoté from Chardonnay, it's really premier cru white Burgundy," Alexandre says. This wine usually is delicious for its first couple of years and then closes up; Laurent Ponsot said it takes a decade to emerge from its shell. About the only change in winemaking is that Mont Luisants moved to whole cluster pressing in 2017. The other top white is Corton Charlemagne, which can be quite stern when young.

The communal reds are relatively bright in style. In grand crus, Griotte Chambertin is exceedingly elegant, and Chapelle Chambertin has just a touch more weight. The top red is Clos de la Roche Vieilles Vignes, coming from two plots, the largest from the historic parcel of 1872, the rest from a smaller plot lower down. Most of the vines were planted in 1954, but about 15% date from 1938 and another 15% from the 1990s. The style is smooth and velvety, chocolaty in a warm vintage, and brighter in a cool vintage.

Domaine Daniel Rion et Fils **

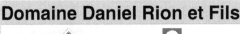

CLOS VOUGEOT
Appellation Clos Vougeot Contrôlée
GRAND CRU
2004
DOMAINE DANIEL RION & FILS
21 PREMEAUX • FRANCE

📍 *Route Nationale 74, 21700 Premeaux-Prissey*

📞 *+33 03 80 62 31 28*

👤 *Pascale Rion*

@ *contact@domaine-daniel-rion.com*

🌐 *www.domaine-daniel-rion.com*

⚫ *Nuits St. Georges*

🍷 *Nuits St. Georges, Vieilles Vignes*

🙂 🍾

🚚 🚜 *15 ha; 100,000 bottles*

[map p. 108]

"The domain started with a few parcels of vines in 1955. Slowly we've added more parcels," says Pascale Rion, who runs the domain together with her two brothers. Driving along the N74, you cannot miss the domain because the adjacent house has "Daniel Rion" in huge letters facing the road. The domain itself is in a large building just off the road. Production is only red wine. One third is regional, a third is in Nuits St. Georges and Vosne Romanée, and a third is in premier or grand crus.

"We try to keep freshness, to have ripe fruits, but not over ripe," is how Pascale describes the style. "We destem 100%. We try to harvest the vineyards so that each is at the same stage of maturity." There is 40% new oak for villages and premier crus. Élevage depends on vintage but is usually 16-18 months.

The style is modern and pure, expressing ripe, round, but fresh, black fruits. Going up the range, the difference is not so much the flavor spectrum as the texture and structure. First the texture becomes finer, then the structure becomes more obvious. There are three different cuvées from Nuits St. Georges: the village wine, a lieu-dit, and the Vieilles Vignes. "We have all the vineyards that my father planted between 1960 and 1967." Moving from the Nuits St. Georges village wine to the lieu-dit, Les Grandes Vignes, the fruits become darker and there is more obvious sense of structure; and with the Vieilles Vignes, the main difference is not in flavor or intensity, but increased refinement of tannins, which are so fine and silky they make the wine more approachable. With the premier crus, Hauts Pruliers is yet more refined, and Aux Rondes Vignes a touch more obviously structured.

Going from Nuits St. Georges to Vosne Romanée, there is an increased sense of reserved power, with more of a glycerinic sheen moving through to the premier crus. Vosne Romanée village wine comes from two plots. "Every year we taste each plot separately, but we always prefer the blend." In premier crus, Beaumonts has increased finesse, Chaumes is more granular, and then coming to the grand crus, Echézeaux has more weight but less refinement, and Clos Vougeot shows its opulence up front. There's a textbook impression of the differences in appellation level all the way from village level to grand cru.

Domaine de La Romanée-Conti ★★★★

 1 Place de l'Église, Vosne-Romanée, 21700

 +33 03 80 62 48 80

 Aubert de Villaine

 secretariat@romanee-conti.fr

 www.romanee-conti.com

 Vosne Romanée

 Richebourg

 29 ha; 80,000 bottles

[map p. 107]

"The typicity of Pinot Noir first is to be Burgundian," says Aubert de Villaine, who has been at the domain since 1965, and indeed DRC is generally acknowledged as the epitome of both Pinot Noir and Burgundy. Ever since the vineyards of Romanée Conti were reunited by Aubert's grandfather, Edmond, who created the Domaine de la Romanée Conti in 1912, and then acquired all of La Tâche in 1933, this has been Burgundy's top domain.

With monopoles of Romanée Conti and La Tâche, and major holdings in Romanée St. Vivant, Richebourg, Grands Echézeaux, and Echézeaux, DRC dominates the grand crus of Vosne Romanée. There is also a small holding in Le Montrachet. The focus is not on power, but on subtlety of expression. "Romanée Conti has a character of softness and length in the mouth that makes it special compared to other wines. But it's a question of taste; some people might prefer Chambertin or La Tâche for their greater body," Aubert explains.

Viticulture is organic, the vineyards are perpetuated by selection massale using stock that goes back to Romanée Conti before it was replanted in 1945, and vinification is traditional (with no destemming). A horizontal tasting here is an exploration of nuances in expression at the most refined level, but it is fair to say that Romanée Conti and La Tâche are sui generis.

Lately DRC has been expanding, first in 2008 by leasing vineyards in three *climats* of Corton from Prince de Mérode, and then by leasing 3 ha of Bonneau du Martray's vineyards in Corton Charlemagne in 2017. The wines are of course fabulously expensive, and unfortunately are now bought more for investment than drinking. Aubert de Villaine also owns a domain in his own name in Bouzeron, where the grape is Aligoté.

Domaine Rossignol-Trapet ★★

📍 *4, Rue De La Petite Issue, 21220 Gevrey-Chambertin*

📞 *+33 03 80 51 87 26*

👤 *Nicolas Rossignol*

@ *info@rossignol-trapet.com*

🌐 *www.rossignol-trapet.com*

Gevrey Chambertin

Gevrey Chambertin, Clos Prieur

13 ha; 55,000 bottles
[map p. 105]

Jacques Rossignol created the domain in 1990 when the original Trapet domain was divided (the other half is Trapet Père et Fils, in the original building, a couple of hundred yards up the N74 from the Rossignol-Trapet domain, which occupies a building constructed in 1994). The domain is run today by Jacques's two sons, Nicolas (the winemaker) and David (viticulturalist). The winery was renovated in 2002 and extended to have more space. There are vast caves underneath.

There are 13 cuvées of exclusively red wine. Most of the vineyards are in Gevrey Chambertin, extending from Bourgogne to grand cru. There are 2 ha in Beaune. Vineyards have changed only slightly since the domain was established. Winemaking is traditional, usually with one third whole bunches, no new oak of Bourgogne, 10-15% for village Gevrey Chambertin and Beaune premier cru, 25% for Gevrey premier crus, and 40-50% for grand crus. Élevage extends from 12 months for Beaune and village Gevrey to 18 months for grand crus.

House style is very much in the tradition of Gevrey Chambertin. The Beaune premier cru Teurons is lighter and purer, the village Gevrey has more direct fruits, and then moving through the series of premier crus, first there is a sense of the fruits becoming brighter, and then the wines become more overtly structured; usually they need a few years after the vintage to come around. Clos Prieur is on the verge of austere, more clay in the soil gives more weight on the palate to La Petite Chapelle.

Moving to the grand crus, the sense of structure becomes more finely textured: Latricières Chambertin is very fine with an earthy palate and sense of minerality, Chapelle Chambertin is more intense and slightly earthier with blacker fruits, while Le Chambertin is on another level, making a different impression, rounder and more supple, and moving in a savory direction. The wines give an impression of no compromise.

Domaine Georges Roumier

***

⊙ *4, Rue De Vergy, 21220 Chambolle-Musigny*

📞 *+33 03 80 62 86 37*

Christophe Roumier

@ *domaine@roumier.com*

🌐 *www.roumier.com*

◉ *Chambolle Musigny*

🍾 *Morey St. Denis, Les Bussières*

🍇 🕑 *14 ha; 50,000 bottles*

[map p. 106]

The domain originated in 1924 when Georges Roumier obtained vineyards in Chambolle Musigny by marriage. The wines have been estate bottled since 1945. His son, Jean-Marie, took over in 1961, and the domain is now run by Christophe, who joined his father in 1981 and took over in 1990. Expanded from the original holdings, the heart of the estate still lies in Chambolle Musigny, and includes vineyards in the two grand crus, Bonnes Mares and Le Musigny (a really tiny holding, giving only 300 bottles), and in three important premier crus, Les Amoureuses, Les Cras, and Les Combottes. The average age of vines is around forty years. There is a little white wine in the form of Corton Charlemagne (only a hundred cases).

The style is on the sturdy side for Chambolle Musigny, and the wines usually require some time to open up: the monopole of Clos de la Bussières from Morey St. Denis, for example, can be positively hard when first released, but give it a decade and it acquires a silky sheen. Some of that initial hardness may be due to the practice of not necessarily destemming—only the village wine is always destemmed, otherwise each vintage is judged separately. A short cold maceration is followed by fermentation under 30 °C and warm post-fermentation maceration. New oak is usually around 25% (perhaps 30% for the grand crus). The corollary of making wines in traditional style requiring time to open out is that they are correspondingly long-lived.

Domaine Armand Rousseau ***

📍 *1, Rue De L'Aumonerie, 21220 Gevrey-Chambertin*

📞 *+33 03 80 34 30 55*

📇 *Éric Rousseau*

@ *contact@domaine-rousseau.com*

🌐 *www.domaine-rousseau.com*

⚫ *Gevrey Chambertin*

🍾 *Gevrey Chambertin*

🚫🍴

🍇 ⌚ *15.5 ha; 65,000 bottles*

[map p. 105]

Armand Rousseau is the doyen of Chambertin, widely acknowledged to set the standard with his premier and grand crus. The domain is the largest single owner of Le Chambertin and has a substantial parcel in Clos de Bèze, as well as holdings in three other grand crus and three premier crus in Gevrey Chambertin. The eponymous Armand Rousseau was involved in the drive to domain bottling in the 1930s; today his grandson Eric is in charge of the domain. Its increasing success in rising into the stratosphere with DRC and Leroy was indicated by the throes of construction when I visited, with the small courtyard being excavated in order to construct a new cave underground. With better capacity for storage, Rousseau won't have to sell all the wine at the vintage.

As is evident from the generally soft style, there is usually at least 90% destemming. Vinification is the same for all wines; the only difference is in the use of new oak. Both Chambertin and Clos de Bèze have their élevage in 100% new oak; Clos St. Jacques is 60-70%. All wines spend 20 months in barrique. "I am completely against over-extraction of color and material. I prefer Pinot Noir with elegance. If you go too far, you eliminate the effects of terroir," Eric Rousseau says. The style here is consistent across the range, with increasing concentration as you go from the village wine to Clos St. Jacques, and then up to Chambertin or Clos de Bèze.

Domaine Sérafin Père et Fils **

 Place du Château, 21220 Gevrey Chambertin

 +33 03 80 34 35 40

 Karine Sérafin

 domaine.serafin@orange.fr

 Gevrey Chambertin

Gevrey Chambertin, Vieilles Vignes

 5.5 ha; 26,000 bottles
[map p. 105]

"The domain mostly consists of the vineyards my grandfather bought," says Karine Sérafin. "He came to France from Poland in 1936, was taken prisoner in the war, and then was employed in the vineyards here after the war. There were lots of abandoned vineyards as a result of the war, and he was able to buy his own vines. Almost all our vineyards date from then, and were planted just after the war. My father turned more to export, and his move to quality was driven by Robert Kacher (the American importer). He purchased two more parcels of premier crus in Morey St. Denis and Chambolle Musigny." Karine's father, Christian, is still making the wines, now assisted by his niece Frédérique Bachotet. The domain is located at the top of Gevrey Chambertin, just below the northeast group of premier crus, opposite the church on the edge of the Place du Château, in buildings that look new but actually date back to the beginning. Most of the 9 cuvées come from Gevrey Chambertin. The domain produces only red wine.

Usage of new oak is high, extending from 50% for the Bourgogne Rouge to 100% for the Cazetiers premier cru and Charmes Chambertin grand cru. In terms of new oak and length of élevage, the wines are divided into Bourgogne, Gevrey Chambertin, Gevrey Chambertin Vieilles Vignes, the premier crus, and then Cazetiers and Charmes Chambertin. The wines are firmly structured, well-rounded with concentrated fruits that may hide the tannins when they are young, but they require time, typically a few years, to develop flavor variety. The purity of the cherry fruits makes a modern impression. Powerful but restrained might be a fair description of the young wines.

Although a big distinction is drawn between the village wine and the Vieilles Vignes—the average age is 70 years, but some are as old as 90 years—there are really no young wines in the domain. The Gevrey Chambertin village wine is the youngest, with vines that are 35-years-old. Les Cazetiers and Charmes Chambertin are close in age to the Vieilles Vignes, which comes from several of the original parcels near the winery. The age of the vines, and perhaps the locations of the parcels close to the premier crus, makes the Vieilles Vignes close in quality to the premier crus.

Domaine du Clos de Tart ***

7 *Route des Grands Crus, 21220 Morey-Saint-Denis*

📞 *+33 03 80 34 30 91*

Jacques Devauges

@ *contact@clos-de-tart.com*

🌐 *www.clos-de-tart.com*

Morey St. Denis

Clos de Tart

🍇 *7.5 ha; 23,000 bottles*
[*map p. 106*]

This splendid domain is synonymous with the largest grand cru monopole in Burgundy, occupying a single plot on the slope running up behind the Maison. It has had only three owners since it was created by nuns in 1141. After the Revolution in 1789 it was acquired by Marey-Monge, and then it was sold to the Mommessin family in 1932. The Mommessins also owned a negociant business (since sold to Jean-Claude Boisset). Clos de Tart went through a difficult period until Sylvain Pitiot became the winemaker in 1996; he retired in 2015. The vineyard unusually is planted with rows in north-south orientation across the slope, and Clos de Tart has its own nursery for selecting vines for propagation by selection massale.

There are two cuvées. Until vines are 25 years old, production is declassified into La Forge des Tarts (labeled as premier cru). In addition, lots may be assigned to La Forge on the basis of blind tasting. Usually La Forge is about a quarter of production, but there have been extreme vintages where there has been much less La Forge or no Clos de Tart. Although this is a genuine clos (entirely surrounded by walls), soils vary extensively, and it is divided into 23 plots, which are vinified separately. Vinification matches the plot, in some cases with complete destemming, in others with partial or entire whole clusters. Only new oak is used. There is no difference in winemaking between La Forge and Clos de Tart, but La Forge is less structured and ready to drink sooner.

Clos de Tart has never been divided in its history, which is a remarkable contrast with the fate of most properties in Burgundy. But it is following a more common path with its sale in 2017 for more than €210 million to François Pinault, one of the richest men in France, who owns Château Latour and other wine properties, including Domaine d'Eugénie in Vosne-Romanée. There is speculation that the style will now change, as it has at Domaine d'Eugénie.

Domaine Trapet Père et Fils ★★

DOMAINE TRAPET PÈRE & FILS
GEVREY-CHAMBERTIN 1ᵉʳ CRU
PETITE CHAPELLE
APPELLATION CONTRÔLÉE
1995
Jean & Jean-Louis TRAPET
75 cl 12,5% vol.

53, Route de Beaune, 21220 Gevrey-Chambertin

+33 03 80 34 30 40

Famille Trapet

message@trapet.fr

www.domaine-trapet.com

Gevrey Chambertin

Gevrey Chambertin

17 ha; 60,000 bottles
[map p. 105]

Located right on the N74 in Gevrey Chambertin, Domain Louis Trapet was established in 1870, and was one of the major suppliers to negociants until estate bottling started in the 1960s. Its extensive holdings made it the most important domain in Gevrey Chambertin, but it was divided in 1993 as the result of inheritance issues. One half was renamed as Domaine Trapet Père et Fils. (The other part gave rise to what is now Domaine Rossignol-Trapet: it can be interesting to compare the styles of the two domains since the holdings are so parallel.)

Trapet Père et Fils is presently run by Jean-Louis Trapet, and has holdings in some of the best terroirs of Gevrey Chambertin, including almost 2 ha of Le Chambertin, with vines going back to 1919. The other grand crus are Latricières Chambertin and Chapelle Chambertin, and there are three premier crus, as well of course as the communal Gevrey Chambertin, which is the largest production of the house. There are also Marsannay and Bourgogne.

Vinification uses partial (typically 70%) destemming, cold maceration before fermentation in open top vats, with 30-70% new oak used for élevage of 15-18 months depending on the appellation. The style is structured, but not especially powerful. At its best, it may be very smooth, but it can be austere when young. There is also a Domaine Trapet in Alsace, as Jean-Louis's wife, Andrée, comes from Alsace and took over her parents' vineyards in 2002.

There is now a small restaurant facility in Gevrey Chambertin, where tastings are held.

Domaine Cécile Tremblay **

8 rue de Très Girard, Morey St. Denis

+33 03 45 83 60 08

Cécile Tremblay

domainetremblay@yahoo.fr

www.domaine-ceciletremblay.com

Morey St. Denis

Bourgogne Grande Ordinaire

4.5 ha; 30,000 bottles

[map p. 106]

This is essentially a new domain. The family lives in Vosne Romanée, but has always rented out its vineyards. When some of the rental agreements ended in 2003, Cécile was able to take back 3 ha of vineyards. In 2009, she purchased vineyards in Bourgogne AOP and Chambolle Musigny, bringing the domain to its present size. In 2021, rental agreements expire on another 3 ha, so the domain will come to about 7 ha. Cécile started by making wine in borrowed facilities at other producers, but constructed a cuverie in a quiet residential street in Morey St. Denis in 2012, just behind the hotel Castel Très Girard. Although the domain is small—"we have two and a half people working here, we do everything"—there are 11 cuvées.

Depending on the vintage, usually there is some whole bunch, about 15% for Bourgogne, a third for village wine, up to 75% for premier or grand crus. Cécile tries to ensure the stems are ripe, but cuts out the biggest stems from whole bunches to avoid astringency. There is no general rule for new oak; generally there's about 50% for grand cru and less for others. Élevage is 15-18 months with no racking, but the small cellar forces them to roll the barrels to move, so the lees get stirred up anyway.

The Bourgogne Grande Ordinaire is a blend of two plots, one in Vosne Romanée, one the other side of the N74 in Chambolle. "It's rare to have Bourgogne in Vosne, so we are lucky to have it." The wine follows the imperatives of Vosne intensity rather than Chambolle delicacy, showing unusual breed and class for Bourgogne AOP. The Chambolle Musigny and Morey St. Denis have less weight but greater refinement than the Bourgogne, with more of a sheen on the Chambolle. The Morey St. Denis comes from a tiny holding. "It's an example of how Burgundy works: three rows and it's already a plot." Vosne Romanée and the premier crus are tighter and more structured, and the structure becomes more obvious moving from the premier crus to Echézeaux. The wines are classic representations of their appellations with a common thread of refinement.

Domaine Comte Georges de Vogüé ***

 7 Rue Ste. Barbe, 21220 Chambolle-Musigny

 +33 03 80 62 86 25

 Jean-Luc Pepin

 +33 03 80 62 82 38

 Chambolle Musigny

Chambolle Musigny

Musigny Blanc

12.5 ha; 36,000 bottles

[map p. 106]

One look at the fifteenth century entrance, and you can see this is a really old domain: ownership has not changed since 1450. Comte de Vogüé is by far the most important holder of Musigny, with 7 of the 11 ha. A small part (0.65 ha) makes the Musigny Blanc, although since 1994, when the vineyard was re-planted, it has been declassified to Bourgogne Blanc. "It seems a bit brutal to declassify grand cru to Bourgogne, but we didn't have any choice," says François Millet, who has been making the wine here since 1986. "We declassify young vines (everything under 25 years) from (red) Musigny into Chambolle Musigny premier cru," he explains, adding, "I don't consider this to be a second wine, it's a younger Musigny." The domain also has a large holding in Bonnes Mares, and some Chambolle Amoureuses and village Chambolle Musigny.

François has strong views on winemaking. "Grapes are destemmed and used as whole berries. I've never used whole bunches. The question I ask is, if we have whole berries, why should I use whole bunches?" And as for oak, "I have chosen to be a winemaker not a forester." There is 15% new oak in Chambolle Musigny, 25% in premier crus, and 35% in grand crus. The best single word to describe the de Vogüé wines is soignée: they give a silky impression of infinite smoothness, ranging from the precision of Chambolle Musigny, to the sheer elegance of the firmer premier cru, the classic seamless Amoureuses, and the weight of Musigny.

Domaine de La Vougeraie ✱

7bis Rue de L'Église, 21700 Premeaux-Prissey

+33 03 80 62 48 25

Sylvie Poillot

vougeraie@domainedelavougeraie.com

www.domainedelavougeraie.com

Nuits St. Georges

Vougeot, Les Cras

Clos Blanc de Vougeot

44 ha; 130,000 bottles

[map p. 108]

One of the newest, and most rapidly growing, domains in Burgundy, Domaine de la Vougeraie brings together several old domains under a new name. The driving force is Jean-Charles Boisset, who together with his sister Nathalie, has become Burgundy's largest producer by acquiring Bouchard Aîné in Beaune, Ropiteau Frères in Meursault, Antonin Rodet in Mercurey, Château de Pierreux in Beaujolais, and J. Moreau in Chablis, and several other houses. These continue to run independently, but Domaine de la Vougeraie amalgamates holdings from four old domains: Claudine Deschamps (the original Boisset family estate in Premeaux, where a new winemaking facility has now been constructed), Pierre Ponnelle, Louis Voilland, and L'Héritier Guyot.

Starting in 1999, winemaker Pascal Marchand went for a powerful style, and then the style is supposed to have lightened after Pierre Vincent took over as winemaker for 2006. He uses 30% new oak for the village wines, 40% for the premier crus, and 50% for grand crus, with an élevage of 18 months. However, I still find the wines to be on the powerful side: the white Clos Blanc de Vougeot, for example, shows a mass of new oak and is all up-front power, compared with the more classic style it used to have when made by L'Héritier Guyot. But you could say the same of many wines in Burgundy, so the fair comment may be that these are definitely wines in the modern style, with something of an influence from the New World.

Mini-Profiles of Important Estates

Côte de Beaune

Domaine Ballot-Millot & Fils

9 rue de La Goutte d'Or, Meur-
sault, 21190
+33 03 80 21 21 39
Charles Ballot
charles.ballot@ballotmillot.com
www.ballotmillot.com

10 ha; 55,000 bottles
[map p. 46]

The roots of this family domain go back to the seventeenth century. Charles Ballot, the fifteenth generation, took over in 2000. Whites are 60% of production, with the heart in Meursault, where there are three top premier crus including Les Perrières, and some lieu-dits. For whites, there is no battonage during aging for a year in barriques with no more than 25% new oak. In reds there are three premier crus from Pommard and also Volnay and Beaune. Reds are destemmed and spend 18 months in barriques, with 15-20% new oak depending on the cuvée.

Maison Albert Bichot

6bis Boulevard Jacques Copeau,
21200 Beaune
+33 03 80 24 37 37
Albéric Bichot
bourgogne@albertbichot.com
www.albertbichot.com

103 ha; 650,000 bottles
[map p. 45]

The company was founded as a negociant in 1831, and took its name from the third generation, Albert Bichot, who established it in Beaune. It was generally an underperformer until Albéric Bichot took over in 1996. It owns several individual estates (collectively described as Domaines Albert Bichot): Long Depaquit in Chablis, Clos Frantin and Château-Gris in Nuits St. Georges, Domaine du Pavillon south of Pommard, Domaine Adélie in Mercurey, and Domaine de Rochegrès in Moulin-à-Vent. Each has its own winery, but the general mandate is that wines should be approachable when young. Wines under the Albert Bichot label come from the negociant and are aged in the large underground cellars in Beaune.

Domaine Henri Boillot

Les Champs Lins, 21190 Puligny
Montrachet
+33 03 80 21 68 01
Guillaume Boillot
henri@boillotvins.fr
www.henri-boillot.com

15 ha; 70,000 bottles
[map p. 46]

The domain started as Jean Boillot, but there was a family split when his son, Jean-Marc, who had made the wine for several years, left in 1984 after a disagreement because he wanted to make wines in a more forceful, modern style (see profile). Jean's other son, Henri took over the domain, and in 2005 renamed it as Henri Boillot. Previously (in 1996) he had created a negociant business, which he still runs. At the domaine, Henri now makes the white wines, and his son Guillaume has made the red wines since 2006. Production is divided more or less equally between red and white. Wines for both domain and negociant are made in a modern facility in Meursault. The same label is used for both, but estate wines are labeled Domaine Henri Boillot, while negociant wines are labeled just Henri Boillot. The style is not as powerful as Jean-Marc Boillot. Oak exposure is about 10% for Bourgogne, 25% for village wines, 60% for premier crus, and 100% for grand crus.

Domaine Bernard Boisson-Vadot

1 Rue Moulin Landin, Meursault, 21190
+33 03 80 21 21 66
Pierre Boisson
fax; +33 03 80 21 66 51

10 ha; 55,000 bottles
[map p. 46]

The Boissons have been making wine in Meursault for two centuries, and from their cellars in the heart of the village, Bernard Boisson and his son Pierre actually produce wine under three labels: Boisson-Vadot, Pierre Boisson, and Anne Boisson. The labels reflect the pattern of family ownership of the vineyards; Bernard and his wife own about half, Pierre and his sister Anne own the rest. Most of the wine is white, from Meursault, including three lieu-dits and the Genevrières premier cru. Élevage is relatively long at 19-22 months, but new oak is moderate, with no more than 25-35%, depending on the cuvée. There is a little red from Auxey-Duresses and Pommard.

Domaine Jean-Marc Bouley

Chemin De La Cave, 21190 Volnay
+33 03 80 21 62 33
Jean-Marc Bouley
jeanmarc.bouley@wanadoo.fr
www.jean-marc-bouley.com

9 ha; 35,000 bottles
[map p. 46]

The name of the domain has been changed to Jean-Marc & Thomas Bouley to reflect the fact that Thomas joined the domain in 2002 and has been in charge since 2012. There has been a Bouley family estate in Volnay for several generations; this domain was created when Jean-Marc founded his own domain in 1974 with 2.5 ha of rented vineyards; ten years later he inherited the family vineyards. Wines are red, from Volnay, Pommard, and Beaune, except for Bourgogne Aligoté. There is usually no destemming. Bourgogne ages in old barriques, village wines get 30% new oak, premier crus 30-50%, with 18-20 months aging.

Domaine Bouzereau-Gruère et Filles

22a Rue De La Velle, 21190 Meursault
+33 03 80 21 20 05
Marie Laure & Marie Anne Bouzereau-Gruère
contact@bouzereaugruere.com
www.bouzereaugruere.com

10 ha; 36,000 bottles
[map p. 46]

Hubert Bouzereau came from a winemaking family in Meursault and Marie-France Gruère from Chassagne Montrachet. They established their estate in 1970, and in 2001 the domain took the name of Bouzereau-Gruère et Filles when their daughters joined; Marie-Anne is the winemaker, while Marie-Laure manages the domain. Most of the cuvées come from the villages or premier crus of Meursault or Chassagne Montrachet, but there are also Puligny Montrachet and Saint Aubin. Production is three quarters white, with a little Chassagne red and two tiny red plots in Corton Bressandes and Santenay. All the plots are smaller than a hectare. The flagship wine comes from 40-45-year-old vines in Blanchots Desssous in Chassagne Montrachet.

Domaine Yves Boyer-Martenot

17 rue de Mazeray, 21190 Meursault
+33 03 80 21 26 25
Vincent Boyer
contact@boyer-martenot.com
www.boyer-martenot.com

10 ha [map p. 46]

The domain goes back four generations, and after a brief period working with his father, Vincent Boyer took over in 2002 and renovated the winery in 2003. His sister Sylvie was involved in marketing at first, and then ran a negociant business before moving on. The domaine has plots in some top premier crus, Perrières, Charmes, and Genevrières in Meursault, and Caillerets in Puligny, and has a focus on single-vineyard wines including four lieu-dits in Meursault. All production is white, and the wines are aged in one third new oak.

Domaine Buisson-Charles

3 Rue De La Velle, 21190 Meursault
+33 03 80 21 22 32
Patrick Essa
dombuissoncharles@wanadoo.fr
www.buisson-charles.com

7.2 ha; 45,000 bottles
[map p. 46]

Michel Buisson was the third generation of winemakers and established the domain in the 1960s; he officially handed over to his daughter Catherine and son-in-law Patrick Essa in 2001. Based in Meursault, the domain has 4 ha of Meursault and its premier crus, but added more vineyards including a hectare in Puligny Montrachet in 2016. All this is white, but there is a little red from premier crus in Volnay and Pommard. In 2001 a negociant activity was added, and this is the source of the Corton Charlemagne and Chablis. New oak is from 20-40% depending on the cuvée.

Maison Camille Giroud

3 Rue Pierre Joigneaux, 21200 Beaune
+33 03 80 22 12 65
Carel Voorhuis
contact@camillegiroud.com
www.camillegiroud.com

11 ha; 75,000 bottles
[map p. 45]

The house started as a small negociant in 1865. In the first half of the twentieth century, it was known for its policy of purchasing wine rather than grapes, relying on the palate of owner Lucien Giroud. After Lucien died in 1989, the policy changed and the house followed a more traditional policy, buying grapes and even some vineyards. In 2001 the house was sold to the Colgins of Napa Valley. David Croix came as winemaker, and was succeeded in 2016 by Carel Voorhuis. The house has become somewhat of a micro-negociant, with its production coming from 30 different appellations.

Maison Champy

12 place de la Halle, 21200 Beaune
+33 03 80 23 75 21
Dimitri Bazas
visites@maisonchampy.com
www.champy.com

22 ha; 500,000 bottles
[map p. 45]

Founded in 1720, this is one of the oldest negociants in Beaune. Ownership has changed in rapid succession. Financial difficulties caused Champy to be sold to Jadot in 1990, then Pierre Meurgey bought it back without its vineyards. More recently it was bought by Pierre Beuchet in 2012, and then sold in 2016 to Advini, a holding company with several wineries in France and South Africa. Champy owns Domaine Laleure-Piot, which is run independently, and also bought the Louis Boillot domain in Volnay, which it renamed as Domaine Clos de la Chapelle. Dimitri Bazas has been the winemaker since 1999, and Champy is still located in its historic cellars in Beaune. I have never found the wines to have much character.

Domaine Chandon de Briailles

Rue Soeur Goby, 21420 Savigny-Lès-Beaune
+33 03 80 21 52 31
François de Nicolay
francois.de.nicolay@
chandondebriailles.com
www.chandondebriailles.com

14 ha; 55,000 bottles [map p. 45]

The manor house and gardens where the domain is headquartered were built at the end of the seventeenth century by the same architect who designed Versailles. This has been a family estate since it was purchased in 1834; present owners Claude and François de Nicolay, the seventh generation, took over in 2001. Vineyards are in the vicinity, which is to say Savigny, Pernand and Aloxe. Most production is red: there is little destemming, and aging takes place in old barriques with almost no new oak.

Chanson Père Et Fils

10 Rue Paul Chanson, 21200
Beaune
+33 03 80 25 97 97
Maxime Montaldi
caveau@domaine-chanson.com
www.domaine-chanson.com

45 ha; 1,000,000 bottles
[map p. 45]

This is an old negociant, established in 1750, and sold to its manager, Alexis Chanson, in 1847. A decline in quality led to its purchase by Bollinger in 1999. Jean-Pierre Confuron was brought in to help with production and Gilles de Courcel to help with commercialization. Wines are still aged in the old cellars in a bastion in Beaune, but there's a modern production facility outside the town. Vineyards include 25 ha in Beaune premier crus, and provide about a quarter of the grapes. Whites are vinified as whole clusters and there is no destemming of reds. Wines age for 12-20 months in barriques with 20% new oak.

Domaine Jean Chartron

8 Grande Rue, 21190 Puligny-
Montrachet
+33 03 80 21 99 19
Anne-Laure or Jean-Michel
Chartron
info@jeanchartron.com
www.jeanchartron.com

14 ha; 100,000 bottles [map p. 47]

This old domain in Puligny Montrachet, founded in 1959, has been led by Jean-Michel Chartron since 2004. Vineyards are mostly in Puligny Montrachet, with a majority in premier and grand crus. There are five premier crus in Puligny, one in Chassagne, and two in St. Aubin. Grand Crus include Le Montrachet. Vineyards are almost all white, with small plots of red in Bourgogne and (unusually) in Puligny Caillerets. In the past, I have generally found the wines to be unexciting, but a heavier style of the early years has been lightened by reducing the reliance on new oak since 2009, which is now 10-40% depending on the cuvée.

Maison Chartron et Tré-buchet

RN 74, 21190 Puligny-Montrachet
+33 03 80 21 32 85
Vincent Sauvestre
contact.france@bejot.com
www.groupegcf.fr

16 ha; 600,000 bottles

The large negociant of Chartron et Trebuchet was founded in 1984 by Jean-René Chartron (of Domaine Jean Chartron: see mini-profile) and Louis Trébuchet (who managed the negociant Jaffelin in Beaune). In addition to producing wines under its own name, it distributed the wines of Jean Chartron. The negociant got into financial difficulties and was sold in 2004 to Victor Sauvestre (who runs Bejot wines, a large negociant Moillard and Corton-André and 260 ha of vineyards in Burgundy, and 270 ha in Southern France). I have never found the wines to be very interesting.

Domaine Louis Chenu et Filles

12, Rue Joseph De Pesquidoux,
21420 Savigny-lès-Beaune
+33 03 80 26 13 96
Caroline Chenu
juliette@louischenu.com
www.louischenu.com

 [map p. 45]

The domain is 90 years old, but started bottling its own wines only when sisters Juliette and Caroline took over from their father Louis in 2007. Located almost entirely in Savigny, the focus is largely on Pinot Noir. The sisters describe their style as "elegant not extracted, refined in that just enough oak is used to provide shoulders for the wine." In whites, the Bourgogne Blanc is close in style to the Savigny-lès-Beaune, both showing a smoky nose with hints of gunflint following on the palate in quite a mineral style. In reds, the style remains elegant, and the Savigny Vieilles Vignes adds a layer of extra richness compared with the Bourgogne. The Aux Clos premier cru shows a more precise edge and greater grip on the palate. But in both reds and whites, the bargain that typifies the elegant house style is the Bourgogne.

Domaine Yvon Clerget

12 Rue de La Combe, 21190 Volnay
+33 03 80 21 61 56
Thibaud Clerget
thibaud@domaine-clerget.com
www.domaine-clerget.com

6 ha
[map p. 46]

This is effectively a new domain, although the Clergets have been making wine here since the thirteenth century. Under Yvon Clerget the wines were workmanlike but not very interesting. There was an inter-regnum after Yvon retired in 2009, and grapes were sold off until his son Thibaud was ready to take over the domain in 2015. Vineyards include four premier crus in Volnay, Rugiens in Pommard, one of Beaune, and Clos Vougeot. The only white comes from a small plot in Meursault. Fort reds, grapes are destemmed and wine ages for 18 months. There are high expectations for success.

Domaine Colin-Deléger

3 impasse-des-Crêts, 21190 Chassa-gne Montrachet
+33 03 80 24 75 61
Michel Colin-Deléger
fax; +33 03 80 21 93 79

1 ha; 5,000 bottles

Michel Colin-Deléger created this domain in Chassagne Montrachet in 1987. The style was always mainstream, never falling into excess of either of the extremes of buttery notes or minerality. When Michel retired, the vineyards were divided between his sons Philippe and Bruno, who now have their own domains, but Michel kept back three small parcels (totaling less than a hectare) from which he still makes wine: En Remilly premier cru in Chassagne, Les Demoiselles premier cru in Puligny, and Chevalier Montrachet grand cru.

Domaine Philippe Colin

ZA du Haut-des-Champs, 21190
Chassagne Montrachet
+33 03 80 21 90 49
Philippe Colin
domainephilippecolin@orange.fr

13 ha
[map p. 47]

When Michel Colin retired in 2003, the Colin-Deléger domain was divided between his son Bruno (see profile) and Philippe. Each got 9 ha, and Philippe has since acquired another 4 ha. Bruno kept the original premises, and Philippe built a new winery on the edge of the village. For a small domain there are a lot of different cuvées, partly representing Philippe's interest in terroir and his wish to represent each plot individually. Most production is white, and there are 7 white crus in Chassagne Montrachet alone. The oldest vines, about 80 years of age, are in Chenevottes. Village wines age in 20-25% new oak, and premier crus get 35%.

Domaine Benoît Ente

4 Rue Mairie, 21190 Puligny Montrachet
+33 03 80 21 93 73
Benoît Ente
domainebenoit-ente@orange.fr
www.benoit-ente.fr

5.2 ha; 35,000 bottles
[map p. 47]

Benoît is the younger brother of Arnaud Ente in Meursault (see profile), making wine from a tiny domain based on old vineyards (planted in the 1950s) he inherited in 1997. His style has evolved from gaining richness through battonage with reliance on new oak to a more minimalist approach; new oak is now less than 30%. He's considered to be a rising star in the village, and only the small size of the domain prevents greater acclaim.

162

Domaine Follin-Arbelet

Les Vercots, 21420 Aloxe-Corton
+33 03 80 26 46 73
Franck Follin-Arbelet
franck.follin-arbelet@wanadoo.fr
www.domaine-follin-arbelet.com

6 ha; 25,000 bottles [map p. 45]

Franck Follin-Arbelet founded this small domain in 1992 with his father-in-law's vineyards. He has premier crus in Aloxe-Corton and Pernand-Vergelesses as well as grand cru Corton and Romanée St. Vivant. The domain is located in old family building in the center of Aloxe-Corton. Reds are destemmed and wines aged in new oak varying from 15% for village wine to 75% for grand cru. The only white is the Corton Charlemagne.

Domaine Gagnard-Delagrange

26 Rue Charles Paquelin, 21190
Chassagne Montrachet
+33 03 80 21 31 40
Marie-Josèphe Delagrange
ma@marc-antonin-blain.com

2 ha; 10,000 bottles [map p. 47]

Domaine Gagnard-Delagrange was created in 1959 when Jacques Gagnard married Marie-Josèphe Delagrange. The domain included several premier crus in Chassagne Montrachet and grand crus. Jacques Gagnard had a restrained style, which he passed on to his grandson, Marc-Antonin Blain-Gagnard, who has been making the domain wines since Jacques died in 2009 (and is now also involved at Domaine Blain-Gagnard: see mini-profile). Many of the vineyards were distributed in the family when Jacques died, but the domain retained 7 ha.

Domaine Jean-Michel Gaunoux

1 Rue De Leignon, 21190 Meur-sault
+33 03 80 21 22 02
Jean-Michel Gaunoux
jean-michel.gaunoux@wanadoo.fr
www.jean-michel-gaunoux.com

6 ha; 40,000 bottles [map p. 46]

Henri Gaunoux was a well known vigneron before and after the second world war. When he died in 1972 the estate was divided between his sons. François established a domain based on the vineyards in Meursault, and Michel founded one with the vineyards from Pommard (see mini-profile). François's son, Jean-Michel, started with his father, but left to form his own domain in 1990, with three premier crus in Meursault as well as the village wine, and reds from premier crus in Pommard and Volnay. New oak is moderate, with 15-30% depending on the cuvée, and aging lasts 15-16 months.

Domaine Michel Gaunoux

Rue Notre Dame, 21630 Pommard
+33 03 80 22 18 52
Alexandre Gaunoux
fax; +33 03 80 22 74 30

7 ha; 40,000 bottles
[map p. 46]

The estate was founded by Alexandre Gaunoux in 1885, Michel Gaunoux joined in 1957, the domain took his name after it was split following Henri's death in 1972, and Madame Ganoux ran it after he died young in 1984, until his children Alexandre and Anne were able to take over in 1990. Pommard is the heart of the domain, with premier crus Rugiens-bas and Grand Epenots, and a premier cru cuvée blended from Les Arvelets, Combes, and Charmots. Various plots in Beaune, including some premier cru, go into the single red cuvée from Beaune. The domain is often described as traditional, but this is misleading because grapes are destemmed and new oak is only 15-20%. The domain is known for holding back some production so as to be able to offer old vintages. Tastings are unusual here, because the domain does not believe in tasting from barrique, and allows only bottled wines to be sampled.

Domaine Génot Boulanger

21190 25 rue de Cîteaux, Meursault
+33 03 80 21 49 20
Guillaume Lavollée
contact@genot-boulanger.com
www.genot-boulanger.com

22 ha; 80,000 bottles
[map p. 46]

The domain was founded in 1974 when Charles-Henri Génot and his wife, Marie Boulanger bought vineyards and a nineteenth century château (at first the domaine was known as Château Génot-Boulanger). In 1995 they expanded from the Côte de Beaune into the Côte de Nuits; subsequently they also started to produce Crémant. In 1998, their grandson François Delaby took over, and he was succeeded in 2008 by his daughter Aude and son-in-law Guillaume Lavollée. There is an unusually wide range of wines, including more than 30 cuvées. Reds are partly destemmed. All wines see 25-35% new oak. The domain now also has a modern production facility in an industrial park near Meursault.

Domaine Aleth Girardin

21 Route D'autun, 21630 Pommard
+33 03 80 22 59 69
Aleth Le Royer
alethgirardin@orange.fr
www.alethgirardin-pommard.com

7 ha; 30,000 bottles
[map p. 46]

The domain was called Armand Girardin until his daughter Aleth Le Royer took over in 1995. She had planned to be a lawyer, but did not like it, and returned to the family domain in 1978. The only change in style is that Armand did not destem, but Aleth destems completely. She also uses cold maceration before fermentation. Most of the vineyards are in Pommard: there are five premier crus, with Rugiens-bas, where the vines date from 1906, the flagship of the domain. The average age of other parcels is 65 years. Vinification and aging are identical for all cuvées, in order to showcase terroir; new oak is usually one third.

Maison Vincent Girardin

5 Impasse des Lamponnes, 21190
Meursault
+33 03 80 20 81 00
Marco Caschera
vincent.girardin@vincentgirardin.com
www.vincentgirardin.com

14 ha; 500,000 bottles
[map p. 46]

The domain was sold in 2012 to La Compagnie des Vins d'Autrefois, a negociant in Beaune. Winemaker Eric Germain has stayed on. Vincent Girardin started with an initial 2 ha that he obtained from his parents in 1982. The family had been making wine in Santenay since the seventeenth century. Expansion focused mostly on the white wines of the Côte de Beaune, which are 80% of estate production, but the negociant activity of Maison Girardin extended the range significantly (and is known for its affordable Bourgogne, Emotion), as also did a large purchase of vineyards in Chénas from La Tour du Bief (which added another 200,000 bottles per year). Production moved in 2002 from the old cuverie in Santenay to a purpose-built facility in the industrial estate east of Meursault. Half of the 42 individual parcels are in Puligny and Chassagne Montrachet. The domain was converting to biodynamics, but backed off, although it still follows many biodynamic practices. There is extensive sorting here—Girardin is one of the few in Burgundy to run to an optical sorting machine—and fermentation is allowed to occur naturally. Use of new oak is claimed to be moderate—10 to 35% depending on appellation—but I find oak to be quite evident in the young wines, which tend to power, sometimes at the expense of finesse: these are strong wines.

Domaine Alain Gras

Rue Sous-la-Velle, Village Haut,
21190 Saint Romain
+33 03 80 21 27 83
Alain Gras
contact@domaine-alain-gras.com
www.domaine-alain-gras.com

14 ha; 80,000 bottles

Alain took over his family vineyards in 1979. Located on top of a hill, the winery has panoramic views over Saint Romain. Vineyards are mostly in Saint Romain (including the recent acquisition of a couple more hectares), but extend to Meursault and Auxey Duresses. Reds are destemmed and get about 15% new oak; whites are fermented as partial whole clusters and get about 20% new oak. This is generally regarded as the top producer in Saint Romain, and the wines are well represented in restaurants in France.

Domaine Antonin Guyon

2 Rue de Chorey, 21420 Savigny-lès-Beaune
+33 03 80 67 13 24
Dominique Guyon
domaine.guyon@wanadoo.fr
www.guyon-bourgogne.com

48 ha; 200,000 bottles
[map p. 45]

A large estate for Burgundy—in fact one of the largest family-owned wineries in the region—the domain started in the 1960s with parcels extending from Meursault to Gevrey Chambertin. During the 1970s Antonin Guyon's sons Dominique and Michel extended the domain by assembling 350 different parcels representing 25 appellations, including a 22 ha block on the Hautes Côtes de Nuits that was assembled from 80 parcels. Dominique's daughter Hombeline manages the estate today, together with her father. There are 4 white cuvées and 16 reds, with a range from village wines to grand crus. White grapes are pressed as whole bunches, fermented in barrique with weekly battonage, and bottled after 12 months (18 months for the grand crus). Reds are destemmed, held for a week of cold maceration, fermented in open-topped vats, and then given a another week of maceration before aging in barriques. There's been some backing off from new oak, with the current maximum now 50% for grand crus.

Domaine Patrick Javillier

19, place de l'Europe (shop)
9 rue des Forges, 21190 Meursault
+33 03 80 21 27 87
Marion Javillier
contact@patrickjavillier.com
www.patrickjavillier.com

10 ha; 70,000 bottles
[map p. 46]

Raymond Javillier built up the domain after the second world war. Patrick took over in 1974 and expanded further, partly by acquisition, partly from his wife's vineyards (the source of the red wines in Santenay). His daughter Marion took over making the red wines in 2008. The domain is best known for its whites, which are sometimes felt to be on the austere side when young, but a change to shorter aging in barriques and more time spent in cuve has made them more approachable. New oak policy is hard to pin down because it varies with conditions. Reds are completely destemmed, there is cold maceration before fermentation, and aging lasts for 18 months.

Domaine Latour-Giraud

6 rue de l'Hôpital, 21190 Meursault
+33 03 80 21 21 43
Jean-Pierre Latour
domaine-latour-giraud@wanadoo.fr

Latour-Giraud takes its name from the marriage in 1958 between a Latour, whose history in Meursault dates from the seventeenth century, and a Giraud, from a family who had owned a distillery in Meursault since 1845. The domain has been run since the 1990s by Jean-Pierre Latour and his sister Florence. The domain is known for its extensive

www.domaine-latour-giraud.com

11 ha; 55,000 bottles
[map p. 46]

holdings in the top premier crus of Meursault, including Charmes, Perrières, and Genevrières (the flagship wine, where Latour-Giraud's 2.5 ha make it the largest owner). White wine is 85% of production. Reflecting the focus on premier crus, the wines tend to be powerful; village wines see 25-33% new oak, and premier crus 40-70%.

Domaine Lejeune

1 Place De L'Église, La Confrèrie,
21630 Pommard
+33 03 80 22 90 88
Aubert Lefas
commercial@domaine-lejeune.fr
www.domaine-lejeune.fr

10 ha; 50,000 bottles
[map p. 46]

The domaine is located in the village square in Pommard. François Jullien de Pommerol, Professor of Oenology in Beaune, introduced estate bottling in 1977 after he inherited this family estate, which had been passed from aunts to nieces for several generations. His son-in-law, Aubert Lefas, has been in charge since 2005. Aside from some Bourgogne, the wines are all red and come from Pommard, with three premier crus. There is no destemming, and there is a small amount of carbonic maceration to start off fermentation. New oak is 25-35%, except for Rugiens and Grands Epenots at 50%.

Domaine Château de la Maltroye

16, Rue de la Murée, 21190 Chassa-gne Montrachet
(33) 03 80 21 32 45
Jean-Pierre Cournut
chateau.maltroye@wanadoo.fr

15 ha; 60,000 bottles
[map p. 47]

The Château de Maltroye occupies an eighteenth century house set back from the road though the village. Its caves date from the fifteenth century. The Picard family purchased the house and the vineyards that came with it in 1940. André Cornut purchased the property in 1993 after a dispute about inheritance, and his son Jean-Pierre took over in 1995. Immediately behind the house are the vineyards of the Maltroie premier cru. Vineyards are in Chassagne except for 2 ha in Santenay, and just over half are white grapes. There's village wine from Chassagne, several premier crus, and Bâtard Montrachet. The whites tend to be rich, too rich and powerful for my palate, which may be due to the use of high proportions of new oak.

Domaine du Château de Meursault

Rue Du Moulin Foulot, 21190
Meursault
+33 03 80 26 22 75
Stéphane Follin-Arbelet
tourisme@chateau-meursault.com
www.meursault.com

60 ha; 300,000 bottles [map p. 46]

Dating from the eleventh century, the château dominates the square in the center of the village of Meursault and is a major tourist site. The ancient cellars underneath are the largest in the region. It stayed in the hands of one family from the nineteenth century through 1973; since then it has belonged to two moguls. André Boisseaux, whose family founded the Patriarche negociant and Kriter sparkling wine, purchased and restored it in 1973. His son, Jacques Boisseaux, was in charge until 2012, when it was sold to Olivier Halley, an owner of Carrefour supermarkets and head of H partners, which owns several wine brands, and also purchased the Château de Marsannay. There has been significant investment, including an optical sorter, which is rare in Burgundy. Stéphane Follin-Arbelet came from Bouchard to be the winemaker. The extensive land holdings all over the Côte de Beaune are split equally between red and white. Whites age for 12 months in 20-25% new oak; reds are destemmed and age for 12-15 months in 25-40% new oak.

Domaine François Mikulski

7 RD 974, 21190 Meursault
+33 03 80 21 25 11
Marie Pierre Mikulski
contact@domainemikulski.fr
www.domainemikulski.fr

10 ha; 50,000 bottles
[map p. 46]

François Mikulski is a first generation winemaker: his mother was Burgundian and his father escaped from occupied Poland in 1939. After spending time at wineries in California, François worked with his uncle, Pierre Boillot, from 1984 to 1991, and then rented the family vineyards to create his own domain. Most of the vineyards today are rented. The original intention was to sell the wine to negociants, but prices were so low at the time that the Mikulskis decided to bottle it themselves. Production is three quarters white. François's aim is to bring out minerality, and new oak is moderate at 20-30%.

Domaine Xavier Monnot

6 Rue Docteur Rolland, 21190
Meursault
+33 03 80 21 29 32
Xavier Monnot
xavier-monnot@orange.fr

16 ha; 120,000 bottles
[map p. 46]

This was Domaine René Monnier until 2005, when René's grandson, Xavier Monnot, renamed it. Previously it was run by René's daughter and her husband, together with Xavier, who took over in 1994, replanted parcels, and renovated the cellar. Vineyards are quite dispersed all over the Côte de Beaune, extending to the Côte Chalonnaise, split equally between red and white.

Domaine Bernard Moreau et Fils

3 Route Chagny, 21190 Chassagne
Montrachet
+33 03 80 21 33 70
Benoit Moreau
domaine.moreau-
bernard@wanadoo.fr

14 ha; 75,000 bottles
[map p. 47]

Auguste Moreau built a cellar at the Champs Gain vineyard in 1809, but the current domain basically dates from its expansion under Marcel Moreau in the 1930s. Bernard Moreau took over in the early 1960s, when he was very young, and gave his name to the domain in 1977. After working in the New World, his sons took over in 1999, with Benoît looking after the vineyards and Alexandre in charge of the cellar. Vineyards are all in Chassagne except for a tiny plot in St. Aubin. The approach to winemaking is traditional, with village wines seeing 25% new oak, premier crus 30-50%, and grand crus (Bâtard and Chevalier Montrachet) receiving 100%. Élevage was lengthened to 18 months in 2004. There's a large plot of red Chassagne Montrachet and little red premier cru; otherwise plantings are white.

Domaine Michel Morey-Coffinet

6 Place Du Grand Four, 21190
Chassagne Montrachet
+33 03 80 21 31 71
Michel Morey
morey.coffinet@orange.fr
www.domainemoreycoffinet.com

The domain was established in the 1970s by Michel Morey and his wife Fabienne with vineyards that came from both sides of the family. Their son, Thibaut, joined the domain in 2000 and is now taking over. (Michel's father's domain, Marc Morey, was run by his sister.) The domain is located in an eighteenth century house with sixteenth century cellars that Michel Morey bought when the domain was created. The estate vineyards are almost all in Chassagne Montrachet, but the range is extended

8.5 ha; 40,000 bottles
[map p. 47]

by a negociant activity under the name of Maison Morey-Coffinet. Whites are three quarters of production and include Bourgogne, village Chassagne, six premier crus, and Bâtard Montrachet, and there are also cuvées from Puligny, Meursault, and Corton Charlemagne. Wine age for only 11 months in barriques in order to retain freshness and be approachable when young.

Domaine Thomas Morey

9 rue Nord, 21190 Chassagne Montrachet
+33 03 80 21 97 47
Thomas Morey
domainethomasmorey@orange.fr
www.thomasmorey-vins.com

13 ha; 60,000 bottles
[map p. 47]

After Bernard Morey retired in 2005, his sons Thomas and Vincent formed their own domains by dividing the vineyards in 2007. Thomas purchased some additional plots, and in 2011 was offered a rental of 3 ha from his neighbor in Chassagne. Altogether he owns 8 ha and rents 5 ha. Alcoholic and malolactic fermentation are rapid, and the wines are aged for only 11 months. Thomas has an unusual policy with regards to sulfur: in order to keep a low dose at bottling, he adds very small doses regularly over the year. White wines are in the majority and include a wide range: Bourgogne, Saint Aubin, Chassagne Montrachet (including several premier crus), Puligny Montrachet, and Bâtard Montrachet.

Domaine Vincent and Sophie Morey

3 hameau de Morgeot, 21190 Chassagne Montrachet
+33 03 80 20 67 86
Vincent Morey
contact@morey-vins.fr
www.morey-vins.com

20 ha; 60,000 bottles
[map p. 47]

Vincent Morey and brother Thomas (see miniprofile) each formed their own domains in 2007 after their father Bernard Morey retired in 2005. Vincent took over Bernard's old premises in the heart of Morgeot and formed a domain with his wife Sophie, who comes from Santenay. Vineyards come from both sides of the family. Vincent and Sophie both had plots in premier cru Les Embrazées, so the combination became their largest holding. There are vineyards also in other premier crus of Chassagne, and in Puligny and Bâtard Montrachet, and of course Santenay. Unusually for a domain in Chassagne, a majority of the vineyards (11 ha) are red, mostly in Santenay. Aging is similar for all cuvées, with 40% new oak for the whites and 50% for the reds.

Domaine Michel Niellon

Le haut des champs, 21190 Chassagne Montrachet
+33 03 80 24 70 17
Michel Coutoux
domainemichelniellon@orange.fr

7.5 ha; 45,000 bottles
[map p. 47]

Three generations are involved at this tiny domain. Michel Niellon began estate-bottling with his father Marcel in the 1960s (when the estate was only 4 ha), since 1991 has been working with his son-in-law, Michel Coutoux, and more recently also with his grandson, Mathieu Bresson. Two thirds of production is white, with a full range from Bourgogne, through Chassagne village and several premier crus, to Chevalier Montrachet. New oak is moderate, varying from 20-30%, but the style is relatively rich.

Domaine Joseph Voillot

Place de l'Église, 21190 Volnay

+33 03 80 21 62 27

Jean Pierre Charlot

joseph.voillot@wanadoo.fr

www.joseph-voillot.com

9 ha; 45,000 bottles [map p. 46]

Split between Volnay and Pommard, the domain has been run since 1995 by Jean-Pierre Charlot, formerly a professor in Beaune, and son-in-law of Joseph Voillot. Production is almost entirely red, much of it from premier crus (four in Volnay and four in Pommard). Holdings are divided into 35 plots, with the largest being 1 ha of Volnay Champans. Most of the vines are old, ranging from 30- to 60-years old. "We work very traditionally, all our vineyards are worked the same way, vinification is the same for all cuvées, we want to show the differences in the vineyards," says cellarmaster Etienne Chaix. "We are interested in freshness and fruit, we don't want to mask them with oak, so we use only 10-15% new oak for the premier crus." The style is traditional in the sense that the wines can be tight and linear when young. Bourgogne Pinot Noir is the lightest, Volnay is a little earthier, and Pommard has more weight and structure. In premier crus, Beaune Aux Coucherais has classic tightness, Volnay Fremiets has more sense of fruits, with some elegance, Champans has more presence with a light sheen on the palate, Pommard Clos Micault actually displays an elegance more resembling Volnay, and Pommard Pèzerolles and Rugiens show more the classic firmness of Pommard and mature in an earthy direction. Two whites from Meursault, lieu-dit Chevalières, and premier cru Les Cras, are upright with increasing sense of salinity.

Côte de Nuits

Domaine Arlaud

41 Rue D'epernay, 21220 Morey St. Denis

+33 03 80 34 32 65

Cyprien Arlaud

contact@domainearlaud.com

www.domainearlaud.com

15 ha; 60,000 bottles
[map p. 106]

Joseph Arlaud founded the domain in 1942 with vineyards from his wife's family, and he and his son Hervé expanded with further purchases. The label shows the historic building in Nuits St. Georges that the domain purchased for its winery in 1966; this is still used for events, but since 2003 production has been at a modern gravity-feed facility in Morey St. Denis. Joseph's grandson, Cyprien Arlaud, has been making the wine since 2004. Vineyards are concentrated in Chambolle Musigny (including three premier crus) and Morey St. Denis (including four premier crus); there are also four grand crus. The domain also makes Gevrey Chambertin and a Bourgogne Aligoté (the only white). Under his own name, Cyprien also has a negociant activity that extends the range to Vosne Romanée (also biodynamic). There's some use of whole clusters for the top wines, and new oak varies from 25-30% for villages and premier crus, more for grand crus.

Domaine Bertagna

Rue Du Vieux Château, 21640 Vougeot

(33) 03 80 62 86 04

Eva Reh-Siddle

contact@domainebertagna.com

www.domainebertagna.com

17 ha; 55,000 bottles
[map p. 106]

The domain was created by Claude Bertagna when he returned from Algeria in 1950. The Gunther-Reh family, of von Kesselstatt in the Mosel in Germany, purchased the state in 1982. Holdings are dominated by Vougeot (6 of the 18 cuvées), including one white cuvée. The only other white is Corton Charlemagne. Altogether the holdings include 12 premier and grand crus. There's also a large vineyard on the Hautes Côtes de Nuits. The flagship wine is the monopole of the Clos de la Perrière premier cru. Use of oak is traditional, with 1-year and 2-year barriques for village wines, 20-30% new for premier crus, and 30-50% for grand crus.

Domaine Louis Boillot et Fils

21220 4 rue du Lavoir, Chambolle Musigny
+33 03 80 62 80 16
Louis Boillot
domaine.louis.boillot@orange.fr

11 ha; 45,000 bottles

Louis Boillot has half the vineyards of his father's domain, Lucien Boillot (now run by his brother Pierre from the original cellars in Gevrey Chambertin). Louis set up his own domain in 2003, and is married to Ghislaine Barthod (see profile); the wines are made in the same cellar. Since 2019, their son Clément Boillet has made the wiens for both estates. (Although all the Boillots are related the Louis Boillot domain in Volnay was completely different, but in any case was renamed from 2009.) Louis's vineyards are mostly in Gevrey Chambertin and Volnay, making him an unusual family estate with holdings on both Côte de Nuits and Côte de Beaune. Grapes are destalked and new wood is usually 20-30%.

Domaine René Bouvier

Chemin De Saule, Brochon, 21220 Gevrey-Chambertin
+33 03 80 52 21 37
Bernard Bouvier
rene-bouvier@wanadoo.fr

17 ha; 100,000 bottles
[map p. 105]

Henri Bouvier founded the estate in 1910, René took over in 1950 and expanded the estate, and Bernard took over in 1992 and expanded further. A new winery on the road north out of Gevrey was built in 2006. Focused on terroir, Bernard aims to produce a cuvée from each plot. The domain is known especially for its Marsannay, where there are four cuvées, both red and white; Bernard is president of the grower's syndicate in Marsannay. Aging is 18 months; new oak is 20-30%, but only premier and grand crus spend the full period in barrique, other cuvées spend the last 6 months in cuve.

Domaine Sylvain Cathiard

24 Rue de la Goillotte, 21700 Vosne Romanée
+33 03 80 62 36 01
Sébastien Cathiard
sylvain.cathiard@orange.fr

4.6 ha [map p. 107]

This small domain has a great reputation with something of a cult following. Grapes were sold to negociants from the 1930s until Sylvain Cathiard took over in 1985; his son Sébastien took over in 2011. Vineyards are mostly in Vosne Romanée; there are 11 plots, with the top being a tiny holding in Romanée St. Vivant. Vines are mostly 40-60-years old. Everything is destemmed; new wood used to be high, up to 100%, but Sébastien has been reducing it.

Domaine Philippe Charlopin-Parizot

18 Route de Dijon, 21220 Gevrey-Chambertin
+33 03 80 58 50 46
Philippe Charlopin
charlopin.philippe21@orange.fr
domaine-charlopin-parizot.com

25 ha; 150,000 bottles
[map p. 105]

Philippe Charlopin purchased his first hectare of vines in 1978 in Gevrey and then continued to build up his domain, now located on the main road to the north out of Gevrey. His son Yann joined in 2004, and in order to make white wines they purchased new plots in Pernand and Corton, and even in Chablis. Most of the wine remains red, with a concentration around Gevrey Chambertin. The seven grand crus include three in Gevrey Chambertin. The wines can be tasted at the wine bar Caveau des Vignerons in Gevrey Chambertin. Grapes are destemmed, and new oak is around a third.

Domaine Bruno Clavelier

6 RN 974, 21700 Vosne Romanée
+33 03 80 61 10 81
Bruno Clavelier
domaine-clavelier@orange.fr
bruno-clavelier.com

6 ha; 30,000 bottles
[map p. 107]

This is an old domain, with many vineyards that were replanted in the 1930s-1940s. Estate bottling started only in 1988, when Bruno took over. There are four village wines from lie-dits in Vosne Romanée, and two premier crus. There are also premier crus in Chambolle Musigny and Gevrey Chambertin, and Corton. The flagship wine is Chambolle Musigny premier cru La Combe d'Orveau, from a plot adjacent to Le Musigny. The only whites are a Bourgogne Aligoté and a Vin de France. Vinification is traditional, with about 30% whole clusters, 20% new oak for village wines, and around a third new oak for premier and grand crus. SO2 is minimized by bottling under inert gas.

Domaine J. Confuron-Cotetidot

10 rue de la Fontaine, 21700 Vosne Romanée
+33 03 80 61 03 39
Jack Confuron-Cotetidot
domaine-confuron-cotetidot@wanadoo.fr

13 ha; 37,000 bottles
[map p. 107]

The domain was founded by Jack Confuron in 1964, and today it is led by his two sons, Jean-Pierre and Yves, who is not only the winemaker here but also at Domaine de Courcel, Château de la Tour (in Vougeot), and Maison Chanson. Holdings are deep all over the Côte de Nuits, with an impressive panoply of premier and grand crus. The Confurons have a long-term interest in culture and selection of Pinot Noir, and the average age of their vines is about 65 years. Harvesting is late, there is no destemming, cuvaison is very long, and new oak varies from 10-20% for village wines, up to 50% for grand crus, with élevage of 22 months. Wines are bottled unfined and unfiltered.

Domaine Drouhin-Laroze

20 Rue Du Gaizot-Bp 3, 21220
Gevrey-Chambertin
+33 03 80 34 31 49
Philippe Drouhin
domaine@drouhin-laroze.com
www.drouhin-laroze.com

12 ha; 60,000 bottles [map p. 105]

Jean-Baptiste Laroze created the domain in 1850, when his granddaughter married Alexandre Drouin the estate was renamed as Drouhin-Laroze, and it is still in the hands of the family, presently Philippe and his children Caroline and Nicolas. The holdings are top heavy with premier and grand crus, four premier crus in Gevrey Chambertin, and six grand crus. The range is extended under the negociant label of Maison Drouhin-Laroze, which adds two premier and two grand crus. and village wines, altogether providing a quarter of production.

Domaine Dupont-Tisserandot

2 Place Marronniers, 21220
Gevrey-Chambertin
+33 04 67 98 27 61
Didier Chevillon
dupont.tisserandot@orange.fr
www.duponttisserandot.com

20 ha; 50,000 bottles
[map p. 105]

The domain has important holdings in Gevrey Chambertin, including grand crus. Marie-Françoise Guillard and Patricia Chevillon took over from their father in 1990: Jean-Louis Guillard has been looking after the vineyards and Didier Chevillon is the winemaker. The domain was an important source of wine for top negociants until Didier took over in 1999. The domain was purchased by Faiveley (see profile) in 2014, who already have significant holdings in Gevrey Chambertin. Dupont-Tisserandot continues to be run independently by the same team, but the style is expected to converge more with Faiveley, especially winemaking is moved to a new facility, possibly in Nuits St. Georges with

Faiveley's. The policy until now has been to destem completely, and to use 1-3-year oak for village wines and 100% new oak for premier and grand crus, with 16-18 months élevage.

Domaine Gilles Duroché

7, Place Du Monument, 21220
Gevrey-Chambertin
+33 03 80 51 82 77
Pierre Duroché
duroche.gilles@wanadoo.fr
domaine-duroche.com

 8.5 ha; 40,000 bottles
[map p. 105]

Philippe Duroché started the domain as such with 3 ha in 1954. His son Gilles sold most of his production to negociants until his son Pierre joined him in 2005. Pierre took over in 2008, and now all production is bottled by the estate. Parcels are in Gevrey and its crus. Vineyards include many old vines and are maintained by selection massale from the domain's own vineyards. After complete destemming, winemaking is artisanal: long élevage (13-15 months) without racking, no fining, and rarely any filtration. The 14 cuvées come from highly fragmented parcels, mostly a quarter to a third hectare each. The red Bourgogne comes from two plots in the vicinity, and the sole white is Bourgogne from an unusual parcel of Chardonnay in Gevrey. The Gevrey Chambertin as such is a blend from several parcels, and there are also several cuvées from lieu-dits with different terroirs. There are three premier crus and four grand crus, including Clos de Bèze, which comes from the oldest vines, planted in 1920. There are two cuvées from Lavaux St. Jacques: the normal cuvée comes from vines around 40 years old, and Lavaut St Jacques Vignes 23 comes from a plot adjacent to Clos St. Jacques where the vines were planted in 1923. Village wines age in 10-20% new oak, premier crus in 30-50%, and grand crus get 50-75% new oak.

Domaine Georges Chicotot

15 Rue Général De Gaulle, 21700
Nuits St. Georges
+33 03 80 61 19 33
Pascale Chicotot
chicotot@aol.com
www.domaine-chicotot.com

7 ha; 25,000 bottles
[map p. 108]

Georges Chicotet is the seventh generation at this family domaine, located on the N74 just south of the town of Nuits St. Georges. The domain had only 5 ha of vineyards in Nuits St. Georges until some additions in Ladoix and Aloxe Corton. Georges, who took over in 1971, was a follower of Guy Accad, a controversial oenologist who believed in extended cold soaks to get more color and tannin in wines. There is no destemming, and cuvaison is long, although new oak is limited to about 10%. Georges's wife Pascale has been the winemaker since 1993; their son Clément is in charge of the vineyards. The top wines are premier crus from Nuits St. Georges, Les Vaucrains and Les Saint Georges. The wines are not filtered or fined at bottling. They are tight when young and need time.

Domaine Heresztyn-Mazzini

27 Rue Richebourg, 21220 Gevrey-
Chambertin
+33 03 80 33 62 71
Florence & Simon Heresztyn-
Mazzini
info@heresztyn-mazzini.com
www.heresztyn-mazzini.com

5.5 ha; 35,000 bottles [map p. 105]

The Heresztyns arrived from Poland in 1932, and after years of working at Domaine Trapet and growing onions on the side, Jan Heresztyn created his own domain in 1959. His granddaughter Florence took over in 2012 together with her husband Simon Mazzini, who also has vineyards in Champagne, and the domain changed its name from Heresztyn. The focus is on Gevrey Chambertin, with a Vieilles Vignes cuvée (the largest production with 500 cases), three lieu-dits, and three premier crus. Florence has introduced the use of whole bunches for fermentation, varying from 50-100%, with new oak ranging from 30-40%.

Domaine Humbert Frères

Rue De Planteligone, 21220
Gevrey-Chambertin
+33 03 80 51 84 23
Frédéric & Emmanuel Humbert
dom.humbert@wanadoo.fr

7 ha; 30,000 bottles
[map p. 105]

Brothers Emmanuel and Frédéric Humbert took over the domain from their parents in 1989. Vineyards in Gevrey Chambertin extend from village wine to four premier crus and Charmes Chambertin, and contain 80-year-old vines planted by their grandfather Fernand Dugat, who had a nursery. (The domain is sometimes known as the third Dugat, after Domaines Dugat and Dugat-Py, also run by grandchildren of Fernand.) There is cold maceration before fermentation, and village wines age in 40% new oak, with 100% new oak for premier and grand crus. The wines are known for their intensity and structure.

Domaine Jean Chauvenet

6 Rue de Gilly, 21700 Nuits St.
Georges
+33 03 80 61 00 72
Christophe Drag
domaine-jean.chauvenet@orange.fr
domainejeanchauvenet.fr

9 ha; 35,000 bottles
[map p. 108]

The Chauvenets are an old winemaking family in Nuits St. Georges, and it was Jean Chauvenet who really created the domain after 1966 when he expanded vineyard holdings and estate bottling. There are village wines from Vosne Romanée and Nuits St. Georges, including two lieu-dits, and seven premier crus. The wines were known as typical examples of Nuits St. Georges, rather solid or even rustic in their youth, but the style lightened after Jean's son-in-law, Christophe Drag, took over in 1999, together with Jean's daughter, Christine. The cellar was renovated in 2016. Grapes are destemmed, then there is cold maceration, and aged with 20-33% new oak, depending on the cuvée.

Domaine Philippe et Vincent Lecheneaut

14 rue-des-Seuillets, 21700 Nuits
St. Georges
+33 03 80 61 05 96
Vincent Lecheneaut
lecheneaut@wanadoo.fr
www.domaine-lecheneaut.fr

10 ha; 55,000 bottles [map p. 108]

The first vineyards were purchased by Fernand Lécheneaut, while he was working at Maison Morin, and he formed the domain when Morin folded in 1980. It really took its present form under his sons, Philippe and Vincent, who took over in 1985, built up the vineyards, and moved to estate bottling. Vineyards are highly fragmented into 70 different plots, and make 18 cuvées. Destemming is common, but some whole clusters are kept, with the proportion increasing in richer vintages. There is a cold soak, fermentation in cement, and then aging in 33-100% new oak.

Domaine Chantal Lescure

34 A Rue Thurot, 21700 Nuits St.
Georges
+33 03 80 61 16 79
François Chavériat
contact@domaine-lescure.com
www.domaine-lescure.com

18.3 ha; 60,000 bottles
[map p. 108]

Chantal Lescure was married to Xavier Machard de Gramont, and they founded a 32 ha estate with vineyards all over the Côte d'Or. After Chantal died in 1996, the estate was split into three: Bertrand Machard de Gramont is a 6 ha estate around Nuits St. Georges; Domaine Machard de Gramont in Premeaux has 20 ha with many of the holdings from the Côte de Beaune; and Chantal Lescure now has 18ha, owned by her sons Aymeric and Thibault, and run by winemaker François Chavériat. Vineyards are split between the Côte de Beaune and Côte de Nuits. New oak is 30-50% for most cuvées, but more for Vosne Romanée and Clos Vougeot.

Domaine Thibault Liger-Belair

32 Rue Thurot, 21700 Nuits St. Georges

+33 03 80 61 51 16

Thibault Liger-Belair

contact@thibaultligerbelair.com

www.thibaultligerbelair.com

🚫 ⚒ 🍇 ☕

8 ha; 40,000 bottles

[map p. 108]

The Liger-Belair family have been making wine in the Côte de Nuits since the eighteenth century, but sold most of the vineyards in the 1930s, when two branches of the family split. In the twenty-first century, they both resurrected domains from their remaining holdings. Comte Liger-Belair established his domain in 2000 in Vosne Romanée (see profile). Thibault Liger-Belair created his domain in Nuits St. Georges with family vineyards that had been rented to other producers; in 2003 he established a negociant activity under the name of Thibault Liger-Belair Successeurs. He also started Domaine des Pierres Roses in Beaujolais in 2009. The domain in Nuits St. Georges has two cuvées of village wine, a premier cru, Vosne Romanée premier cru, and Richebourg and Clos Vougeot. The negociant adds village wines, premier and grand crus from Aloxe-Corton, Chambolle Musigny, and Gevrey Chambertin. Usually each plot is harvested twice: the first crop is fermented as whole clusters, and the second is destemmed. New oak is usually 20-30%, with a maximum of 50%.

Domaine Philippe Livera

7 rue du Château,21220 Gevrey-Chambertin

+33 03 80 34 30 43

Damien Livera

philippe.livera@orange.fr

📅 ⚒ 🍇 ☕

9 ha; 35,000 bottles

[map p. 105]

Also known as the Domaine des Tilleuls, the winery is housed in an old stables. The domain was founded around 1920. Philippe Livera began estate bottling when he took over from his parents in 1986, and his son Damien took charge in 2007. Vineyards extend from the Hautes Côtes de Nuits to Fixin and Gevrey Chambertin, with Chapelle Chambertin at the top (although it makes only 3 barriques). (The domain has half of the Livera inheritance of the grand cru, because some went to the Ponsot domain in a marriage in 1970.) The wine from the home vineyard, as it were, is Clos Village, from the lieu-dit immediately in front of the building. New oak increases from 20% for Hautes Côtes or Fixin, to 30-40% for village wines, and 100% for the grand cru.

Domaine du Château de Marsannay

Route Des Grands Crus, Bp78, 21160 Marsannay-La-Côte

+33 03 80 51 71 11

Catherine Thevenard

chateau.marsannay@kriter.com

www.chateau-marsannay.com

🚶 🏭 🚚 🚜

40 ha; 200,000 bottles

[map p. 105]

Something of a tourist site, the domain is based in a faux château, perhaps really more of a grand manor house, just outside Dijon, which actually was built in the ancient style in 1990 by the Boisseaux family, owners of major negociant Patriarche and the Kriter sparkling wine company. The domain was purchased in 2012, together with the Château de Meursault (see mini-profile) by Olivier Halley, an owner of the Carrefour supermarket chain, who also owns other wineries. The major part of the estate, 28 ha, is in various lieu-dits of Marsannay, but the rest includes some significant premier and grand crus on the Côte de Nuits. Stéphane Follin-Arbelet makes the wines at both the Château de Marsannay and Château de Meursault.

Domaine Alain Michelot

6 Rue Camille Rodier, 21700 Nuits
St. Georges
+33 03 80 61 14 46
Élodie Michelot
domalainmichelot@orange.fr

8 ha; 35,000 bottles [map p. 108]

Founded in 1880, the domain is now its fourth generation, although Alain is handing over to his daughter Élodie and her husband Christophe. Vineyards are in Nuits St. Georges, with seven premier crus, and village and premier cru Morey St. Denis. Clos Vougeot was added in 2010. The domain is known for its powerfully structured wines, although grapes are mostly destemmed and new oak is only 25-30%.

Domaine Mongeard-Mugneret

14 Rue De La Fontaine, 21700
Vosne Romanée
+33 03 80 61 11 95
Vincent Mongeard
domaine@mongeard.com
www.mongeard.com

30 ha; 120,000 bottles
[map p. 107]

The domain goes back to the seventeenth century, and has been known as Mongeard-Mugneret since 1945, following the marriage in the 1920s of Eugène Mongeard and Edmée Mugneret. Their son Jean Mongeard started estate bottling after the domain took its new name. A well known figure in Vosne Romanée, he handed over to his son, Vincent, in 1985. There are important holdings in Nuits St. Georges and Vosne Romanée, including top premier crus, and four grand crus: Echézeaux, Grands Echézeaux, Clos Vougeot and Richebourg. The wines were powerful yet beautifully balanced until the late 1980s, but since then seem to have lost some of their lustre. The domain has gone into oenotourism indirectly by offering packages in connection with a local hotel.

Vignoble Georges Noëllat

1 Rue des Chaumes, 21700 Vosne
Romanée
+33 03 80 61 11 03
Maxime Cheurlin
mc.noellat@free.fr

18 ha
[map p. 107]

Two Noëllat domains, Michel and Georges, are run by grandsons of Ernest Noëllat, the brother of Charles Noëllat, who had a famous domain (incorporated into Domaine Leroy in 1988). Georges Noëllat sold its production after 1990 under a twenty-year contract to Jadot and Drouhin. George's grandson, Maxime Cheurlin, took over in 2010 and resumed estate production from the vineyards in Vosne Romanée and Nuits St. Georges. Maxime is something of a modernist, with destemming, light punch-downs, 30-100% new oak, aging for 14-20 months, and bottling without fining or filtration.

Domaine des Perdrix

Rue des Écoles, 21700 Premeaux-Prissey
+33 03 80 61 26 53
Amaury & Aurore Devillard
contact@domainedesperdrix.com
www.domainedesperdrix.com

15 ha; 70,000 bottles
[map p. 108]

This domain is less well known than it might be, because since its purchase in 1996 by the Devillard family, it has in effect played second fiddle in their holdings to the Château de Chamirey in Mercurey. While Domaine des Perdrix is not open for visits, the wines can be tasted at Château de Chamirey, together with those from other Devillard properties. Holdings for Domaine des Perdrix are concentrated around Nuits St. Georges, with the flagship being the monopole premier cru of Aux Perdrix. The cuvée Les 8 Ouvrées comes from a plot of the oldest vines, planted at very high density in 1922.

Domaine Chantal Rémy

1 place du Monument, 21220
Morey St. Denis
+33 03 80 34 32 59
Chantal Rémy
domaine.chantal.remy@orange.fr
www.domaine-chantal-remy.com

3 ha; 13,000 bottles
[map p. 106]

The Louis Rémy domain was founded in 1820 and is still located in the same building in the center of the village. Louis died in 1982, his wife took over, and then his daughter Chantal returned to take over in 1988. The domain name changed to Chantal Rémy in 1992. When her mother died in 2008, Chantal split the vineyards with her two brothers, so the domain was reduced to only 1.5 ha, although it retained all the grand crus. Chantal's son Florian has been making the wine since 2013; the style has become fresher. The flagship wine is a monopole, Clos des Rosiers, just behind the village, and adjacent to both Clos des Lambrays and Clos de Tart. This was once classified as premier cru, but it became a rose garden, before being replanted with vines. There are some negociant wines under the label Héritiers Louis Rémy.

Domaine Philippe Rossignol

59 Avenue de la Gare, 21220
Gevrey-Chambertin
+33 03 80 51 81 17
Philippe Rossignol
sceaphilipperossignol@hotmail.fr

6 ha; 20,000 bottles
[map p. 105]

Philippe Rossignol took over the family vineyards in 1975, and his son Sylvain joined the domain in 2005. His brother-in-law is Joseph Roty (see mini-profile). The focus is on Gevrey Chambertin, with a Fixin from a small plot of old vines called en Tabellion near the premier crus. New oak is a third for the village Gevrey, and increases for the premier crus; Estournelles St. Jacques is the top wine.

Domaine Joseph Roty

24 rue du Mal de Lattre de Tas-
signy, 21220 Gevrey-Chambertin
+33 03 80 34 38 97
Françoise Roty
domainejosephroty@orange.fr

15 ha; 50,000 bottles
[map p. 105]

Joseph Roty had a reputation for being reticent if not inaccessible, refusing to discuss his winemaking techniques. The family has been in Gevrey since the eighteenth century, and Joseph created the domain with family vineyards in the 1960s. Many of the plots have old vines, with an average age over 60 years; the oldest plot goes into the Charmes Chambertin Très Vieilles Vignes, from the first planting after phylloxera, in 1881. Since Joseph's death in 2008, his sons Philippe and Pierre-Jean have been running the domain. Philippe made some Marsannay under his own name as well as the wines from Gevrey, but died prematurely in 2015. Pierre-Jean, who had been looking after the vineyards, now makes the wine as well. The style is powerful, structured, and rich.

Domaine Emmanuel Rouget

18 Route Gilly Les Citeaux, 21640 Flagey Échézeaux
+33 03 80 62 86 61
Emmanuel Rouget
domaine.clf@wanadoo.fr

7 ha

Emmanuel Rouget is Henri Jayer's nephew, and started working with his uncle in 1976. Henri handed his domain over to him as he retired gradually between 1996 and 2001. The domain includes the plot of Cros Parantoux in Vosne Romanée that was Henri Jayer's most famous cuvée. Emmanuel started bottling wines under his own name from various family vineyards in 1985, and included some from the Jayer vineyards after 1996 although Henri Jayer continued to bottle some wine until 2001, but since then all production has been labeled as Emmanuel Rouget. Winemaking follows Henri's precepts, with complete destemming, pre-fermentation cold maceration, up to 100% new oak, all aimed at bringing out fruit.

Domaine Anne et Hervé Sigaut

12 rue-des-Champs, 21220 Chambolle Musigny
+33 03 80 62 80 28
Anne Sigaut
herve.sigaut@wanadoo.fr
www.domaine-sigaut.com

7.2 ha; 30,000 bottles [map p. 106]

This small family domain is totally focused on Chambolle Musigny, with village wine (coming from ten plots), lieu-dit Les Bussières (a plot of 50-year old vines) and four premier crus. The only exception is a small plot of Morey St. Denis premier cru. Anne and Hervé took over from Maurice Sigaut in 1990. The cellar was renovated in 2004. The domain is not officially organic, but Hervé follows the lunar calendar for winemaking. There's cold maceration before fermentation, and aging in around a third new oak. The style showcases the elegance of Chambolle Musigny, and Les Bussières is a top example at village level.

Domaine Taupenot-Merme

33 Route Des Grands Crus, 21220 Morey St. Denis
+33 03 80 34 35 24
Romain Taupenot
domaine.taupenot-merme@wanadoo.fr

13 ha [map p. 106]

The domain has vineyards from two sides of the family. the Taupenot vineyards are in Saint Romain and Auxey-Duresses; the Merme vineyards run from Nuits St. Georges to Gevrey Chambertin, and originated when the Maume Morizot estate was divided. One part became Perrot-Minot (see profile); another part, immediately across the street, became Taupenot-Merme. Romain Taupenot has been in charge since 1998. The holdings on the Côte de Nuits are impressive, but somehow the estate does not quite seem to fulfill their potential. The attitude here is somewhat commercial.

Domaine du Château de la Tour

Clos de Vougeot, 21640 Vougeot
(33) 03 80 62 86 13
Claire Naigeon
contact@chateaudelatour.com

6 ha; 26,000 bottles
[map p. 106]

The domain owns the largest single holding in Clos Vougeot and has the distinction of being the only producer allowed to make its wines within the clos. It has been owned by the same family since M. Beaudet purchased it in 1899. François Labet, who is the son of M. Beaudet's granddaughter, also runs his father's family estate, Pierre Labet, in Beaune. Although there is only the one holding in Clos Vougeot, there are usually two cuvées: Clos Vougeot *tout court*, and a Vieilles Vignes from a 1 ha plot near the center of the clos, planted in 1910. Sometimes there is also a Cuvée Hommage Jean Morin from this plot.

Index of Estates by Rating

Index of Organic and Biodynamic Estates

Domaine Guy Amiot et Fils
Domaine Amiot-Servelle
Domaine du Marquis d'Angerville
Domaine Arlaud
Domaine de l'Arlot
Domaine de Bellene
Domaine Bertagna
Domaine Bonneau du Martray
Domaine René Bouvier
Domaine Michel Bouzereau et Fils
Domaine Henri et Gilles Buisson
Domaine Buisson-Charles
Domaine Chandon de Briailles
Domaine Jean Chartron
Domaine Louis Chenu et Filles
Domaine Bruno Clavelier
Domaine Comte Armand
Domaine J. Confuron-Cotetidot
Domaine de Courcel
Domaine Vincent Dancer
Maison Joseph Drouhin
Domaine David Duband
Domaine Bernard Dugat-Py
Domaine Dujac
Domaine d'Eugénie
Domaine Jean Fournier
Domaine Jean-Noël Gagnard
Maison Alex Gambal
Domaine Génot Boulanger
Domaine Georges Chicotot
Domaine Henri Gouges
Domaine Jean Grivot
Domaine Antonin Guyon

Domaine Heresztyn-Mazzini
Domaine Antoine Jobard
Domaine Rémi Jobard
Domaine Michel Lafarge
Domaine Comtes Lafon
Domaine François Lamarche
Domaine Hubert Lamy
Domaine Leflaive
Domaine Lejeune
Maison Benjamin Leroux
Domaine Leroy
Domaine Chantal Lescure
Domaine Thibault Liger-Belair
Domaine du Comte Liger-Belair
Domaine Michel Magnien
Domaine Pierre Matrot
Domaine François Mikulski
Domaine Hubert de Montille
Domaine Pierre Morey
Domaine Thomas Morey
Domaine de La Pousse d'Or
Domaine Jacques Prieur
Domaine de La Romanée-Conti
Domaine Rossignol-Trapet
Domaine Guy Roulot
Domaine Étienne Sauzet
Domaine du Clos de Tart
Domaine Taupenot-Merme
Domaine du Château de la Tour
Domaine Trapet Père et Fils
Domaine Cécile Tremblay
Domaine de La Vougeraie

Index of Estates by Appellation

Domaine du Château de Meursault
Domaine François Mikulski
Domaine Xavier Monnot
Domaine Pierre Morey
Domaine Jacques Prieur
Domaine Guy Roulot
Morey St. Denis
Domaine Arlaud
Domaine Dujac
Domaine Robert Groffier Père Et Fils
Domaine des Lambrays
Domaine Michel Magnien
Domaine Henri Perrot-Minot
Domaine Ponsot
Domaine Chantal Rémy
Domaine du Clos de Tart
Domaine Taupenot-Merme
Domaine Cécile Tremblay
Nuits St. Georges
Domaine de l'Arlot
Domaine David Duband
Domaine Faiveley
Domaine Georges Chicotot
Domaine Henri Gouges
Domaine Jean Chauvenet
Maison Dominique Laurent
Domaine Philippe et Vincent Lecheneaut
Domaine Chantal Lescure
Domaine Thibault Liger-Belair
Maison Marchand-Tawse
Domaine Alain Michelot
Domaine des Perdrix
Domaine Daniel Rion et Fils
Domaine de La Vougeraie
Pernand Vergelesses
Domaine Bonneau du Martray
Domaine Rapet Père et Fils
Pommard
Domaine Jean-Marc Boillot
Domaine Comte Armand
Domaine de Courcel
Domaine Michel Gaunoux
Domaine Aleth Girardin
Domaine Lejeune
Puligny Montrachet
Domaine Henri Boillot
Domaine François Carillon
Domaine Jacques Carillon

Domaine Jean Chartron
Maison Chartron et Trébuchet
Domaine Benoît Ente
Domaine Leflaive
Maison Olivier Leflaive Frères
Domaine Paul Pernot
Domaine Étienne Sauzet
Saint-Aubin
Domaine Marc Colin et Fils
Domaine Hubert Lamy
Saint-Romain
Domaine Henri et Gilles Buisson
Domaine Alain Gras
Santenay
Domaine Anne-Marie et Jean-Marc Vincent
Savigny-lès-Beaune
Domaine Simon Bize
Domaine Chandon de Briailles
Domaine Louis Chenu et Filles
Domaine Antonin Guyon
Volnay
Domaine du Marquis d'Angerville
Domaine Jean-Marc Bouley
Domaine Yvon Clerget
Domaine Michel Lafarge
Domaine Hubert de Montille
Domaine de La Pousse d'Or
Domaine Joseph Voillot
Vosne Romanée
Domaine Arnoux-Lachaux
Domaine Sylvain Cathiard
Domaine Bruno Clavelier
Domaine J. Confuron-Cotetidot
Domaine d'Eugénie
Domaine Jean Grivot
Domaine Anne Gros
Domaine François Lamarche
Domaine Leroy
Domaine du Comte Liger-Belair
Domaine Méo-Camuzet
Domaine Mongeard-Mugneret
Domaine Georges Mugneret-Gibourg
Vignoble Georges Noëllat
Domaine de La Romanée-Conti
Vougeot
Domaine Bertagna
Domaine du Château de la Tour

Index of Estates by Name

Printed in Great Britain
by Amazon

33835783R00113